OXFORD EARLY CHRISTIAN TEXTS

General Editor
HENRY CHADWICK

—————

AUGUSTINE

De bono coniugali
De sancta uirginitate

The Oxford Early Christian Texts series provides reliable working Greek and Latin texts, with English translations and brief commentaries, of important writers of the Patristic period.

AUGUSTINE

De bono coniugali
De sancta uirginitate

EDITED AND TRANSLATED BY
P. G. WALSH

CLARENDON PRESS · OXFORD

2001

OXFORD
UNIVERSITY PRESS

Great Clarendon Street, Oxford OX2 6DP

Oxford University Press is a department of the University of Oxford.
It furthers the University's objective of excellence in research, scholarship,
and education by publishing worldwide in

Oxford New York

Athens Auckland Bangkok Bogotá Buenos Aires Cape Town
Chennai Dar es Salaam Delhi Florence Hong Kong Istanbul Karachi
Kolkata Kuala Lumpur Madrid Melbourne Mexico City Mumbai
Nairobi Paris São Paulo Singapore Taipei Tokyo Toronto Warsaw

with associated companies in Berlin Ibadan

Oxford is a registered trade mark of Oxford University Press
in the UK and in certain other countries

Published in the United States
by Oxford University Press, Inc., New York

British Library Cataloguing in Publication Data
Data available

Library of Congress Cataloging in Publication Data
Data applied for

ISBN 0-19-826995-1

1 3 5 7 9 10 8 6 4 2

Typeset in Baskerville by Jayvee
Trivandrum, India
Printed in Great Britain
on acid-free paper by
Biddles Ltd.,
Guildford and King's Lynn

FOREWORD

The Christian era in which Augustine lived was happily free from the prudery reflected in Cicero's *De officiis* (1. 127): 'All persons of sound mind avoid references to the parts of the body which we use from necessity . . . it is indecent to speak of them.' In these treatises the sexual aspects of marriage are discussed without embarrassment in a manner which is conventional in our own age. In the nineteenth century, however, Christian sensibilities were deeply disturbed by such frank discussion. Witness the Introduction to the translation of *De bono coniugali* in *The Library of the Fathers* (1847): 'The Editors are of course aware of the danger there is in reading a treatise like the following in a spirit of idle curiosity, and they beg any reader who has not well assured himself that his aim is right and holy to abstain from perusing it.'

Similar misgivings are expressed by Harnack and other Church historians earlier in this century. It is doubtless for this reason that these treatises have until recently been so little translated or read. They have of course been the bedrock of Catholic moral theology from the Council of Trent ('It is better to remain in virginity or celibacy than to be bound by marriage') to the encyclicals of Pius XII (*Casti Connubii*) and Paul VI (*Humanae Vitae*), and they remain closely relevant to the current controversies in the areas of marriage, celibacy, and consecrated virginity; *De bono coniugali* is twice quoted in Vatican II's document, *Gaudium et Spes*, 48, 50.

I wish to thank the learned advisers to the Press for many helpful suggestions made at the outset of this enterprise, and in particular Professor Henry Chadwick, editor of this series, for his friendly support and advice.

P.G.W.

CONTENTS

INTRODUCTION

The Good of Marriage and *On Holy Virginity* are closely interconnected. They were composed in sequence, and the implicit theme in both is the interrelation between them as differing modes of Christian life. As Augustine states in the *Retractationes*: 'After I composed *The Good of Marriage*, it was anticipated that I would write *On Holy Virginity*, and I did not postpone it.'[1] The probable date of composition as indicated by the order of books mentioned in the *Retractationes* is AD 401. He had recently embarked upon renewed study of the Book of Genesis in *De Genesi ad litteram*, but he laid this aside for what he regarded as a more urgent pastoral undertaking. A year or so earlier, a *libellus* composed by Petilian, the Donatist bishop of Constantine, had been put into his hands with an urgent entreaty for a Catholic response; in the second of the three books of his *Contra litteras Petiliani*, reference is made to Pope Anastasius as still alive; he died in April 402. Though the date of 401 for our two treatises is not absolutely secure and has been challenged, it remains the most probable option.[2]

Augustine's Personal Experience, AD 372–400

Augustine brought a wealth of personal experience to bear on the issues of marital life and continence; the *Confessions* as autobiography interweaves the theme of moral conversion with that of intellectual development. At the age of seventeen he already lived with a

---

[1] See Appendix 1 (*ad fin.*).

[2] In his *Retractationes*, Augustine assembles the writings of this period as follows: 2. 21 *De opere monachorum*, composed 'cum apud Carthaginem monasteria esse coepissent' (first mention of them is at the Council of Carthage, AD 397, so *c*.400). 2. 22 *De bono coniugali*; 2. 23 *De sancta uirginitate*; 2. 24 *De Genesi ad litteram* 'per idem tempus'. 2. 25 *Contra litteras Petiliani* 'antequam finirem libros *de Genesi ad litteram*'. At 2. 51. 118 he writes 'hodie Anastasius sedet' so this was composed before Pope Anastasius' death in April 402. Hence the suggested date for our two treatises of 401. For the suggestion of an earlier date *c*.397, see Appendix 1 n. 2.

concubine, a relationship which continued in total fidelity from 372 to 385, and which resulted in the birth of one child, a son Adeodatus, in 373. As a woman of low social standing from Carthage, she could never have aspired to marriage with a man who at that time had high political ambitions; she was sent back to Africa in 385, and Augustine's mother Monnica arranged a suitable match for him with a girl as yet too young for marriage. Meanwhile Augustine (in his own words 'not a lover of marriage, but a slave to lust') procured a second concubine.[3]

Inevitably this sexual history presupposes a knowledge of marital intimacies and crises—techniques of contraception if not abortion, discomforts of pregnancy, temptations to infidelity, stresses of parenthood. At the same time his association with the Manichees, who tolerated but discouraged such sexual activities by their *auditores*, and his clear preference for intellectual friendships with male friends, suggest that his lustful propensities imposed a burden rather than encouraged regular indulgence. The *Confessions* 'reflects a sense of sharp contrast between his sexual needs and his longing for clear, unproblematic relationships'. The dramatic climax to the *Confessions*—the vision of Lady Continence and the children's game inspiring him to 'take up and read' Paul's exhortation to renounce the lusts of the flesh—reflects a clear sense of relief and release.[4]

Following this conversion in the summer of 386 and his baptism at Milan at Easter 387, Augustine returned to Africa in 388, eventually settling with a circle of friends on his family estate at Thagaste to continue the quasi-monastic mode of life which after his conversion they had embraced at Cassiciacum. But as eminent intellectuals in an African Church challenged on every side by Donatists, Manichees, and pagans, they could not remain in obscure retirement for long; for Augustine the death of his son Adeodatus at the early age of seventeen may have been an additional incentive to move on to Hippo in 391, with the intention of establishing a monastery there and perhaps also to challenge the Donatist dominance in the town. The bishop Valerius, an immigrant Greek in sore

[3] See *Conf.* 6. 11. 19, 6. 13. 23, 6. 15. 25.
[4] For Augustine's knowledge of techniques of contraception, see n. 24 on *De bono coniugali*; B. D. Shaw, 'The Family in Late Antiquity: The Experience of Augustine', *Past and Present* 115 (1987), 3–51, esp. 45 f. The citation is from Peter Brown, *The Body and Society* (New York, 1988), ch. 19 the whole of which ('Augustine, Sexuality, and Society') is an important contribution. For the climax to the *Confessions*, see 8. 11. 27, 29.

need of such authoritative support for the welfare of his diocese, not only fostered his monastic aspirations but also intrigued to have him acclaimed first a priest in 391, and then as coadjutor bishop in 395. It was shortly after this in 397 that he began to write the *Confessions*, which is not merely 'a masterpiece of strictly intellectual autobiography', but also an oblique appeal to contemporary Christians of literary bent to embrace a life of continence. It is likely that he had completed his personal testament in the first nine books shortly before composing his works on marriage and virginity.[5]

The Numidians among whom Augustine had returned to live as bishop until his death in 430 were traditionally notorious for sexual licence. For Livy, they were 'more eager for sex than all barbarians' (ante omnes barbaros effusi in uenerem), and according to Salvianus, a younger contemporary of Augustine, Christianity had not improved their ways; 'There is not an African', he writes, 'who is not a slave to lewdness.' There is doubtless an element of exaggeration in such claims, but Augustine understood all too well the tendency of male members of his flock towards promiscuity. His listeners wearied as in his sermons he constantly harped on the theme of adultery. 'I know that there is many a man who rages against me inwardly when his wife reproaches him with his infidelity, and who then thinks "That man must have been here again", or "My wife has been in church again" . . . Come, come, the men would say. God cares nothing for the sins of the flesh.' Augustine especially condemned the exploitation of household slaves as concubines, and he urges wives to stand on their Christian rights. 'I want the wife to be a jealous wife . . . In all other things be subject to your husbands, but in this defend your cause.' Such sermons as these cast a flood of light on Augustine's insistence in *The Good of Marriage* on lifelong fidelity.[6]

Augustine's concern as bishop for the ordered marital life of his flock was complemented by his advancement of the monastic life; he argued that the number of Christians was now so great, and the fecundity of the nations so widespread, that an adequate future

[5] For the purpose of his visit to Hippo, to found a monastery there, see Sermon 355. 2; forced ordination as priest and bishop, Possidius, *Vita* 4. 2; *Ep.* 26. 3. For the citation of the nature of the *Confessions*, P. Brown, *Augustine of Hippo* (London, 1967), 167.
[6] The Numidians' love-life, Livy 29. 23. 4; Salvianus, *De gubernatione dei*, 7. 16. 65. For the citations of *Serm.* 9. 3f. and 14, 224. 3, 392. 4f., see the informative and entertaining account of F. Van der Meer, *Augustine the Bishop* (London, 1961), 180ff.

progeny was assured. In Milan he had witnessed Ambrose's encouragement of a celibate life for the clergy, and in the course of his
return to Africa he had spent several months in Rome, where he
witnessed an increasing number of women opting for a life of virginity or chaste widowhood. One of his urgent priorities on his
enthronement as bishop was the establishment of monastic communities for men, and from them several of his close associates were
appointed to bishoprics or responsible priesthoods, and spread the
monastic movement further. It is no coincidence that *De sancta
uirginitate* followed closely after *De opere monachorum*, a work undertaken at the behest of Aurelius, bishop of Carthage. So far as consecrated virgins were concerned, it is clear that Augustine promoted
for them a life of poverty in community rather than the widespread
practice at Milan and Rome of the less exacting life in private residences; and again, he rejected the practice not uncommon elsewhere of consecrated virgins residing in the houses of clerics.[7]

Marriage and Sexual Renunciation in the Graeco-Roman Tradition[8]

The practice of ritual virginity had little appeal in the traditional
Roman culture. Recent studies confirm the claim of Ambrose that
the six Vestal virgins at Rome were not necessarily virgins (they may
earlier have been wives), that they retired after thirty years rather
than pledged lifelong commitment, and that the duties were undertaken more from family ambition than from any conviction of the
ritual purity of the virgin state. The Christian emphasis on the
importance of consecrated virginity therefore introduced a new
and dynamic element into religious practices in the Western world.[9]

Roman marriage was essentially a family concern. Though the
consent of bride and groom was required by Roman law, the pater-
familias arranged the match, and his consent was necessary. The
bride could legally be as young as twelve, and in senatorial families

---

[7] For the confidence in an adequate future progeny in the Church, see *De bono coniugali*
[IX] 9. For Augustine's monastic intimates turned bishops, see Brown, *Augustine of Hippo*,
143 f. Augustine's preference for virgins' life in community, *De sancta uirginitate* [XLV] 46.

[8] This topic has attracted an enormous bibliography in recent years. See especially
S. Treggiari, *Roman Marriage* (Oxford, 1991); S. Dixon, *The Roman Family* (Baltimore and Lon-
don, 1992); Gillian Clark, *Women in Late Antiquity* (Oxford, 1993); E. A. Clark, *Women in the
Early Church* (Wilmington, Del., 1983), all with earlier bibliographies.

[9] Treggiari, *Roman Marriage*, 138; Mary Beard, 'The Sexual Status of Vestal Virgins', *JRS*
70 (1980), 13 ff., and 'Re-reading (Vestal) Virginity', in R. Hawley and B. Levick (eds.), *Women
in Antiquity* (London, 1995), ch. 11. For Ambrose's observations, see n. 41 to *De bono coniugali*.

girls were frequently married by their early or middle teens to men considerably older, in order to cement close-knit relations between the families of the dominant class. Brides in the lower strata of society may have married a little later. The disparity in ages between wife and husband accentuated the dependence of the one upon the other; in Augustine's words, 'one governing and the other obeying', though by Cicero's time there were celebrated examples of emancipated wives. Extramarital relations by wives were scandalous, whereas such activities by men were widely tolerated except by philosophers of the Stoic persuasion. Though in earlier times the availability of divorce was one-sided, by Cicero's time women when marrying often refrained from passing into the *manus* of their husbands, so that with the consent of their fathers they could divorce and remarry virtually at will. But with the advent of the Christian era, Constantine sought to restrict the easy access to divorce not only by women, but also by men.[10]

In general, however, the scope for a fulfilled life for women was largely restricted to the raising of families under the control of the head of the household. The advent of Christianity introduced opportunities for highly educated women to adopt a more independent role by undertaking a life of consecrated virginity. 'Women of the patristic era who renounced traditional sexual and domestic roles did indeed have new worlds open to them, worlds of scholarship and contemplation, pilgrimage and charitable endeavour.' Inspired by the women who had followed Christ and were companions of Paul, who headed early Christian communities and became intrepid martyrs by the baptism of blood, high-born ladies at Rome demonstrated their Christian allegiance by forsaking marriage for a life of scriptural study and charitable endeavour. Some of those who gathered round Jerome were widows like Marcella, Melania the elder, Paula and her daughter Blesilla; others were virgins like Eustochium, the daughter of Paula and the recipient of Jerome's celebrated Letter 22, and Marcellina, sister of Ambrose.[11]

[10] For the age of Roman girls at marriage, see K. Hopkins, 'The Age of Roman Girls at Marriage', *Population Studies* 18 (1965), 309 ff.; B. D. Shaw, 'The Age of Roman Girls at Marriage: Some Reconsiderations', *JRS* 77 (1987), 30 ff. For men, R. P. Saller, 'Men's Age at Marriage and its Consequences in the Roman Family', *CP* 82 (1987), 21 ff. For Constantine's legislation, see n. 23 to *De bono coniugali*.

[11] The initial citation is from E. A. Clark, *Women in the Early Church*, 16. See also J. W. Drijvers, 'Virginity and Asceticism in Late Roman Western Elites', in J. Blok and P. Mason (eds.), *Sexual Asymmetry* (Amsterdam, 1987), 241 ff.

In the course of the fourth century this cult of consecrated virginity became widespread. In Italy alone convents were established at Verona, Bologna, and Milan as well as Rome. John Chrysostom (*Hom. 66 on Matt. 3*) claims that in Antioch there were 3,000 virgins and chaste widows under the guidance of the Church, a number claimed likewise for Rome by Gregory the Great two centuries later (*Ep.* 7. 26). It is pertinent to probe the range of motives which inspired this movement towards virginity and away from marriage. Though Basil (*Ep.* 199. 18) wisely counsels postponement of such a decision until the age of sixteen or seventeen, some girls may have opted for virginity to shy away from prearranged marriages at an immature age; others may have been induced into it by the arguments of clerics such as Augustine advances in his *De sancta uirginitate* [X] 10; others still will have been attracted by the enhanced social status. It is surely no coincidence that Augustine devotes the second half of *De sancta uirginitate* to the importance of humility, and in a sermon he berates virgins who regard themselves as superior to their parents (*Serm.* 354. 8). He makes it clear that there were women in some African convents who were unsuitable on more serious grounds.[12]

Scriptural Authority and Patristic Views on Marriage and Virginity

In his two treatises on marriage and virginity, Augustine sought above all to be faithful to scriptural injunctions. The first Letter of Peter (3: 1–7) admonishes wives to accept the authority of husbands as slaves accept the word of their masters, and by the purity of their lives to win over spouses who as yet were pagans. It counsels against bodily adornment, and recommends imitation of Sara's submission to Abraham in the Old Testament. Husbands in turn are counselled to honour their wives 'as the weaker sex . . . and heirs of the gracious gift of life'. Paul in Colossians 3: 18f., 1 Tim. 2: 9–15 ('I permit no woman to teach or to have authority over a man'), and Tit. 2: 4f. echoes these recommendations repeatedly. At Eph. 5: 22ff. a similar relationship between husband and wife is prescribed,

[12] I take the citations from John Chrysostom and Basil from Gillian Clark, *Women in Late Antiquity*, 50ff., and that from Gregory the Great from Drijvers, 'Virginity and Asceticism'. For the suggestion that choosing virginity was in protest against male domination, see I. M. Lewis, *Ecstatic Religion* (Harmondsworth, 1975), 40ff. For unsuitable virgins in convents, *De bono coniugali* [XII] 14, [XXIII] 30.

and here alone Paul makes the celebrated comparison with that
between Christ and his Church ('This is a great mystery, and I am
applying it to Christ and his Church'), a concept adapted from Jewish thought, the nuptials between Jahweh and Israel (Hosea 3: 1 ff.)[13]

The passage of Paul which dominates *De bono coniugali* is 1 Cor.
7: 3 ff.: 'The husband should give to his wife her conjugal rights, and
likewise the wife to her husband. For the wife does not have authority over her own body, but the husband does; likewise the husband
does not have authority over his own body, but the wife does. Do not
deprive one another except perhaps by agreement at a set time to
devote yourselves to prayer: and then come together again, so that
Satan may not tempt you because of your lack of self-control. This
I say by way of concession (κατὰ συγγνώμην), not of command. I wish
that all were as I myself am. But each has a different gift from God,
one having one kind, and another a different kind. To the unmarried and the widows, I say that it is well for them to remain unmarried as I am. But if they are not practising self-control, they should
marry, for it is better to marry than to be aflame with passion. To the
married I give this command—not I but the Lord—that the wife
should not separate from her husband, but if she does separate, let
her remain unmarried or else be reconciled to her husband, and
that the husband should not divorce his wife.'

It is notable that Paul does not allow Matthew's one justification
for putting away a wife (19: 9), and Augustine cites the combined
authority of Mark, Luke, and Paul against Matthew. Second,
whereas the Vulgate renders the Greek κατὰ συγγνώμην as *secundum
indulgentiam*, Augustine's rendering, *secundum ueniam*, is interpreted as
meaning that sexual intercourse for pleasure rather than for procreation is a venial sin; Stoic influences may be at work in this misinterpretation of Paul's text, a reading which was destined to have a
long history in the moral theology of the Middle Ages.[14]

In the same passage (1 Cor. 7.25 ff.), Paul addresses virgins as well
as married women, and accordingly provides the scriptural basis for
his instruction in *De sancta uirginitate*:

Now concerning virgins, I have no command of the Lord, but I give my opinion as
one who by the Lord's mercy is trustworthy. I think that in view of the impending

[13] See J. H. Crehan, *Catholic Dictionary of Theology*, 3. 240 ff.
[14] For Augustine's rejection of Matthew by counter-citations from the other scriptural
authorities, see n. 16 to *De bono coniugali*. For his misinterpretation of Paul, see n. 28 to *De bono
coniugali*.

crisis (διὰ τὴν ἐνεστῶσαν ἀνάγκην) it is as well for you to remain as you are. Are you bound to a wife? Do not seek to be free. Are you free from a wife? Do not seek a wife. But if you marry, you do not sin, and if a virgin marries, she does not sin. Yet those who marry will experience distress in this life, and I would spare you that . . . The married man is anxious about the affairs of the world, how to please his wife . . . The unmarried woman and virgin are anxious about the affairs of the Lord, so that they may be holy in body and spirit, but the married woman is anxious about the affairs of the world, how to please her husband . . . He who marries his fiancee does well, and he who refrains from marriage will do better. A wife is bound as long as her husband lives. But if the husband dies, she is free to marry anyone she wishes, only in the Lord. But in my judgement she is more blessed if she remains as she is.

The Greek phrase διὰ τὴν ἐνεστῶσαν ἀνάγκην is rendered in the Vulgate as 'propter instantem necessitatem'; Paul is referring to the imminence of the Second Coming. Augustine's text has 'propter praesentem necessitatem', and he interprets the phrase as referring to the practical problems posed by serving a married partner rather than being free to serve the Lord. It is a moot problem whether he inherited this reading from his biblical source, or whether it is his own revision because by his day the Parousia had become a more distant prospect.

Many of the Greek Fathers offered widely-ranging interpretations of the scriptural exhortations on marriage and virginity, but Augustine at this stage of his life did not read Greek fluently, so such influence as they exercised upon him came obliquely through the mediation of others.[15] More relevant to his treatises are the earlier African apologists Tertullian and Cyprian, and above all his mentor at Milan Ambrose.

Though Tertullian with his rigorous asceticism strongly promotes virginity and suggests that marriage is for those who cannot otherwise resist temptation, and indeed after turning to Montanism condemns it still more savagely as human weakness, he is none the less concerned to defend the institution against the heresy of Marcion: 'For we know and pursue and promote sanctity without condemning marriage.' In his *De monogamia*, he stresses that marriage is necessary for the propagation of the human race. Again, in the treatise addressed to his wife he eulogizes the institution of marriage. His description of virginity vis-à-vis marriage 'non ut malo

[15] See Brown, *Augustine of Hippo*, 271, 412.

bonum, sed ut bono melius' finds an echo in Augustine's discussion. Cyprian too left his mark on Augustine's treatment; in his *De habitu uirginum* he stresses that the Lord does not enjoin but encourages virginity, and he suggests that the 'many mansions' in heaven of which Jesus speaks indicate that virgins will obtain greater honour after death than those who are married.[16]

Ambrose is by far the most potent influence on Augustine's attitudes to marriage and virginity. Though like most of his Christian predecessors he stresses that consecrated virginity is superior to the married state ('Marriage is honourable, but celibacy is more honourable. That which is good need not be avoided, but that which is better should be chosen'), he is emphatic that marriage is not to be despised ('I encourage marriage, and condemn those who discourage it . . . The one who condemns marriage condemns children . . . and human society.'). God is the guardian of marriage: 'If anyone dishonours the couch of another, he sins against God and thereby forfeits his fellowship in the heavenly mystery (*sacramenti*).' But in the ideal Christian marriage which he approves, the partners are to observe ascetic behaviour; a husband must not play adulterer to his own wife. This appears in the injunction to the Christians of Vercelli, which draws 'the future contours of the Catholicism of the Latin West'.[17]

Undoubtedly, however, Ambrose places greater emphasis on virginity, as the various titles of his works composed between AD 377 and 385 (*De uirginibus, De uirginitate, De institutione uirginis, Exhortatio uirginis*) indicate. Of these works, the first of the three books of *De uirginibus* has a particularly close bearing on Augustine's two treatises; the echoes are too frequent to be coincidental. The most striking feature of Ambrose's discussions is the glorification of Mary as perfect virgin and perfect mother; we find here the most comprehensive teaching of Marian theology up to his day, and Augustine's extended account in *De sancta uirginitate* echoes Ambrose at many points.[18]

---

[16] See Tertullian, *Adv. Marc.* 1. 29, *Ad uxorem* 2. 9 (The Latin citation is from the first of these); Cyprian, *De habitu uirginum* 33, is echoed at *De sancta uirginitate* [XXVI] 26.

[17] For the citations, see *De uirginibus* 1. 33. 4; *De Abraham* 1. 7; *Ep.* 2. 8. The final quotation is from Brown, *The Body and Society*, ch. 17.

[18] The most useful account of this aspect of Ambrose's teaching is in B. Ramsey, *Ambrose* (London, 1997), 50 ff., 71 ff. See also Brown, *The Body and Society*; F. Homes Dudden, *The Life and Times of St Ambrose* (Oxford, 1935), esp. ch. 6; A. Paredi, *Saint Ambrose, His Life and Times*, tr. M. J. Costelloe (Notre Dame Press, 1964), ch. 15. For Augustine's discussion, see *De sancta uirginitate* [II] 2 ff.

Augustine and Manichaeism

The Good of Marriage was directed in part against the Manichees, who denied the validity of that title. Earlier in his life Augustine had been an outer adherent (*auditor*) of the sect for about a decade between 374 and his arrival in Milan, but once reconverted to Christianity he launched a series of attacks on the beliefs to which he had earlier subscribed. In composing the two treatises on marriage and virginity he is thus able to draw not only on his recollections of living as a Manichee, but also on his *De Genesi contra Manichaeos* (*c*.389), *De moribus Manichaeorum* (388–9), *Contra Fortunatum* (392), *Contra epistolam (Manichaei) quam uocant fundamenti* (397), and *Contra Faustum* (*c*.400).[19]

The fundamental belief of the Manichees was that there are two eternal first principles, God and Satan, holding dominion over the worlds of light and darkness. Satan had invaded and appropriated a part of the kingdom of light, and had established in it Adam and Eve whom he had endowed with diabolical powers. The marriage which they established is therefore a monstrous mélange of light and darkness. The sensuality which draws men and women together is a weapon forged by Satan to overcome the power of good. God did not establish marriage; the account in *Genesis* is a fiction. In the dualism which emerges, the soul is from God and the body from Satan. All believers must accordingly renounce the flesh and preserve their virginity. Only the Elect or inner circle, however, were bound by such renunciation, which demanded strict control over mouth, hand, and genitals; the Auditors for their part during the period of their purification were permitted relations with women. But they were not to father children, for procreation is the work of the devil. It is a pardonable fault to seek sexual relations provided that sensual pleasure is the sole aim; thus it is preferable to exploit a concubine rather than to take a wife. Augustine's earlier career, the birth of Adeodatus apart, thus conformed with the spirit of the sect.

The Manichees were savage critics of the Old Testament. They were contemptuous of the God who presided over it as being subject

---

[19] For a clear popular account of Manichaeism, see J. J. O'Meara, *The Young Augustine* (London, 1954), ch. 4; see also G. Bonner, *St Augustine of Hippo* (2nd edn. Norwich, 1986), ch. 4; Brown, *Augustine of Hippo*, ch. 5. The most learned account is that of H. C. Puech, *Le Manichéisme: son fondateur, sa doctrine* (Paris, 1949).

to fear, envy, and anger. Of particular concern to Augustine was the scorn which they poured on the Patriarchs for their sexual procliv- ities; in opposition to their claims he presents them and their wives as models of sexual restraint who contracted marriage solely to bear the children who would ensure the coming of Christ and the birth of the Church—a singularly unpersuasive thesis, but one which Augus- tine with his belief in the inerrancy of the scriptures clearly held.

Though Diocletian's edict of AD 297 had ordered the burning of Manichees and their books, the injunction had little effect on the sect's progress in Africa up to the time when Augustine became bishop. He was especially anxious that former friends who had remained Manichees should see the light, and that impressionable youths of intellectual bent such as he himself had been a quarter of a century before should not be attracted to it. Hence even after AD 401 he continued to criticize the tenets of the deviant sect.[20]

Augustine, Jovinian, and Jerome [21]

The greater threat, however, to the vision of marriage and virginity which Augustine had inherited from Ambrose came from a diamet- rically opposite quarter. About 390–2 a monk named Jovinian at Rome propounded the thesis that virginity was no more meritori- ous in the Christian life than marriage. In support of this argument he adduced the sanctity of the Old Testament Patriarchs and their wives. Jovinian advanced these claims:

1. There is no distinction between the married, the widowed, and the unmarried so far as spiritual perfection is concerned.
2. Once Christians are baptized, they cannot again fall under the dominion of the devil. If they sin, they can repent.
3. Mortification of the flesh does not advance Christian perfec- tion more than indulgence showing gratitude to God.
4. At the Final Judgement, there will be no differentiation between the rewards.
5. Mary conceived Jesus virginally, but lost her virginity in child-bearing.[22]

---

[20] See *Contra Felicem* (AD 404), *Contra Secundinum* (AD 405).
[21] For what follows, see especially J. N. D. Kelly, *Jerome* (London, 1975), 180 ff.; G. Com- bès, Oeuvres de Saint Augustin, 2 (Paris, 1948), 623 ff.
[22] The first four of these theses are adduced in Jerome's rebuttal; the fifth is cited by Ambrose, *Ep.* 42. 4 ff., and by Augustine, *De nuptiis et concupiscentia* 2. 15.

The document of Jovinian was condemned (*conscriptio temeraria*) at a Roman synod summoned by Pope Siricius, and he was excommunicated. When he retired to Milan, the synod under Ambrose confirmed the Roman decrees (*conscriptio horrifica*). But Jovinian's stance had won considerable sympathy at Rome, as a result of which nuns were abandoning the life of virginity, and clerics were paying less regard to the developing cult of celibacy. In consequence a group of prominent Christians in the capital wrote to Jerome as a leading apologist for the faith, begging him to respond; this was the occasion of his pamphlet *Against Jovinian* (AD 393–4) composed in two books, in the first of which he dismisses Jovinian's first thesis, making the case for the superiority of virginity over marriage ('Nuptiae terram replent, uirginitas Paradisum')[23] on the authority of the Old and New Testaments, and painting a lurid picture of the difficulties of married life. The second book was devoted to rebutting the following three theses; it appears that he had no knowledge of Jovinian's observations on Mary's virginity, or he chose to ignore them.

Jerome's friends at Rome were appalled at the tone and negative assessment of marriage as a Christian mode of life, and though Jerome's subsequent letter to Pammachius sought to limit the damage by denying that he had condemned marriage, the work was disastrously counter-productive. Augustine's later reflections in the *Retractationes* indicate that the drift from religious life continued for years after the pamphlet appeared. Though he was anxious to emphasize that Jovinian and his followers were the main target in his analyses of marriage and virginity,[24] he sought also to dispel the resentment among the married laity caused by Jerome's *uituperatio nuptiarum* in his disastrous foray into the controversy.[25]

The Good of Marriage

Augustine begins his treatise by considering the institution of marriage from combined philosophical and scriptural viewpoints to argue that marriage is a natural basis of society established for companionship and the furtherance of the human race. After his brief excursus into the Book of Genesis, he reverts to this initial generalization by arguing that procreation and fellowship are the reasons

---

[23] *Adu. Jouin.* 1. 16.   [24] Cf. *De nuptiis et concupiscentia* 23; *De haeresibus* 82.
[25] Jerome's follow-up letter, *Ep.* 52. For the evidence of the *Retractationes*, see Appendix 1.

why marriage is a good; faithful companionship alone suffices if a couple cannot beget a child. Though at first sight his speculation about whether Adam and Eve could have had children before the Fall seems an irrelevance, in fact he is raising the question to point to procreation as the first of God's purposes in establishing the married state in Paradise. Though he here reaches no definite conclusion, he speculates that the bodies of our first parents were mortal, and that they therefore could have begotten children, a view which he later adopts in his mature thought, when he argues that such sexual activity could have been controlled by reason rather than by lust.[26]

The companionship which ensures that marriage is a good must be lifelong [IV]; Augustine now turns to the importance of fidelity, which demands that sexual relations be confined to married partners alone. He goes so far as to argue that unmarried partners, provided that their cohabitation is lifelong and does not exclude the possibility of children, can be living out a true marriage. He contrasts relationships of temporary convenience, which constitute adultery or fornication, with marriages which though exploited for lust rather than procreation embody the good of fidelity. In this sense marriage acts as a vital safeguard against illicit sex; he repeatedly stresses that lustful behaviour within marriage is 'pardonable', implicitly rejecting the insulting claim made by Jerome and others that a husband or wife can be an adulterer in marriage, by laying greater stress on fidelity as the mark of Christian commitment in marriage [VII].

Augustine now turns to a comparison between marriage on the one hand and widowhood and virginity on the other. He stresses by apposite examples that an activity can be good even if others are better. Some goods are to be sought not for themselves but for other purposes; so sex within marriage has procreation as its object, and it is sinful if it is not sought for this purpose. If the end sought proves to be unnecessary, it is better to forgo it; this is the case with marriage. For the Patriarchs and their wives sexual intercourse was necessary to create the community which would welcome Christ's coming, but such a plentiful community now exists, so that only the incontinent should marry. In so doing, they do not sin; marriage

---

[26] See n. 6 to *De bono coniugali*.

makes their lustful behaviour pardonable, especially since it obviates the thrust towards extramarital sex.

Procreation and fidelity therefore make a marriage good [XI], and the partners in it can be holy even if one is an unbeliever. Such holiness, however, is dependent on observing scriptural standards of decorum, and is accordingly comparatively rare. Whereas the Patriarchs behaved punctiliously in marriage, and would have opted for continence if that had been required of them, few of Augustine's married contemporaries could make the same boast. Even so, their lustful practices in marriage are preferable to exploiting concubines for the purpose of procreation.

Augustine here makes a distinction between Christian and secular marriage [XV]. Christian marriage embodies a *sacramentum*, an oath of lifelong allegiance to a single partner which holds good even if the partners are sterile. Whereas in the Old Testament the need for children justified polygamy if the first wife consented, that situation no longer applies. Sexual intercourse is vital to a nation, but it must be indulged in a disciplined and lawful way, as it was in the era of the Patriarchs. Augustine here depicts marriage as the middle of three rungs of a ladder, to which the Fathers descended from their higher perch, whereas his contemporaries ascend to it from their lustful rung below. The men of old sought new life in the spirit, not in the flesh like the people of his day. Though polygamy was permitted for the purpose of more procreation in the Old Testament, polyandry, being opposed to the fertility ordained by nature, was not. Augustine now investigates the symbolic significance of *sacramentum* as applied to marriage. It points to the unity which will prevail in the future Jerusalem. He uses the analogy of the debarment from ordination of a candidate who has been married more than once; the bishop with a single wife signifies the unity of the one Church with her husband Christ, and the same is true of each and every marriage.

In his anxiety to counter the derisive condemnation of the Manichees [XIX], Augustine again turns to the Patriarchs to argue that they indulged in sex for procreation, not with the natural and laudable aim of perpetuating their families, but to populate Israel with the stock from which Christ would emerge. They thus nurtured offspring in the spirit rather than the flesh. The Manichees claimed that the ceremonies of purification described in *Leviticus* indicate that the Israelites considered intercourse as unclean;

Augustine offers another possible explanation for those regulations. But above all it is the continence of the Fathers which he seeks to contrast with that practised in his own society. He argues that continence, like other virtues, lies in the mind. The person who best uses earthly goods is he who can also refrain from using them. Christ is the supreme example of this, for unlike John the Baptist he did not fast continually [XXI]. The Fathers of old behaved similarly in their sexual activity. Abraham admittedly fathered offspring; his continence lay in his mental make-up. In the Christian era, however, he who possesses continence must practise it. Here Augustine confronts Jovinian and his followers who enquire of the celibate whether he is better than Abraham who was married. The celibate is to answer no, but is to add that in the modern age celibacy is to be preferred to marriage, whereas in Abraham's time the opposite was the case. The debate should centre not on personalities, but on the issues, for individuals possess varying merits, and are not comparable by the criterion of a particular good. Augustine instances the good of obedience vis-à vis continence, the one a divine command and the other a counsel; the disobedient virgin ranks below the obedient spouse. Here he attacks the anti-social conduct of some virgins, a sure indication of an insufficiently discriminating process of acceptance for community life. In addressing youthful male recruits to the monasteries, he implores them to realize that their virginity does not allow them to rise superior to the Patriarchs whose marriages were motivated by obedience.

Augustine now [XXIV] summarizes the main lines of his teaching. Procreation and fidelity are essential features of all marriages; the *sacramentum* is the third requirement for Christian marriage. He develops the significance of *sacramentum* by comparing it with the ordination of priests, in which a character is stamped upon the candidate and can never be effaced. The three essentials for a Christian marriage are underscored by Pauline citations. Finally, in reverting yet again to the Patriarchs, he specifically cites the Manichees as opponents in maintaining that for the Fathers obedience ranked higher than continence. As for the continent men and women of his own day, they are assured of a greater reward in heaven, but are adjured to ponder and practise the virtue of humility.

A review of the main lines of *De bono coniugali* indicates Augustine's firm adherence to the scriptural precepts as he interprets them, and

above all to the doctrines of St Paul. By citation of them he presents
a positive view of marriage as a corrective to the negative vision of
Jerome. Marriage is emphatically a good, embodying as it does the
three goods of *proles, fides, sacramentum*. This trinity becomes the
staple description of marriage; Augustine echoes and clarifies them
in other works, notably in *De Genesi ad litteram*:

> The good of marriage is threefold: *fides, proles, sacramentum*. Fidelity ensures that no
> sexual intercourse takes place with another outside the bond of marriage. The off-
> spring is to be lovingly welcomed, affectionately nurtured, religiously reared. The
> *sacramentum* lays down that the marriage is not split asunder, and that a husband or
> wife rejected by the partner should not be joined to another, even for the sake of
> offspring.[27]

Interestingly, in this account the order of the three varies from that
in *De bono coniugali*, where *proles* takes precedence over *fides*. The two
works were being composed about the same time, and there is a
certain ambivalence in Augustine's notion of the relative importance of *proles* and *fides*. He makes it clear that procreation is the purpose for which God established the sexual act, but throughout
De bono coniugali he insists that sexual intercourse indulged by couples
committed to lifelong *fides* without that intention is pardonable,
especially as it lessens the danger of adultery or fornication.

Holy Virginity

The introductory chapter bridges the two treatises by repeating the
closing observations of *De bono coniugali*: virgins of both sexes are not
to regard themselves as superior to the married fathers and mothers
of the Old Testament, whose offspring and marriages were vital for
the future Christian dispensation. Their virginity merits praise, but
they must be on their guard against pride. This is to be Augustine's
twofold theme in the treatise, virginity in itself and the humility
necessary in virgins.

The discussion of virginity in itself is divided into three parts.
First [II–VI], Christ and Mary are adduced as types of fecund virginity; second and at greatest length [VII–XXI], virginity is praised as
surpassing conjugal fidelity; and third [XXII–XXX], the rewards in

---

[27] *De Genesi ad litteram* 9. 7; cf. *De peccato originali* 39: 'generandi ordinatio, fides pudicitiae,
conubii sacramentum.'

heaven for the various modes of Christian life are discussed. The influence of Ambrose is marked at various points of this section.

The Church, the bride of Christ, imitates Mary in her virginity [II]; both combine virginity with fecundity. The Church is holiest in those members who are virgin in both body and spirit. Christ attests by his own words that the spiritual relationship with him is more important than any connection by blood.

Mary had already vowed her virginity to God before the Annunciation [IV], intending by so doing to serve as an example to virgins even before she knew that she was to be the mother of Christ. Like her, the Church is Christ's mother, for in the spiritual sense she brings to birth the members of Christ; in that sense, too, every devoted soul is his mother, for they bring forth into the Church the children who are to be his members. Mary alone is both mother and virgin physically; she is also Christ's daughter spiritually. Christ was to be born of a virgin to indicate that his members were to be born spiritually of the virgin Church. Both virgins and the married are Christ's mother spiritually, but physically the married are mothers of Adam, so that they hasten to bring their offspring to be baptized.

Augustine now [VII] embarks on his comparison between virginity and marriage. He stresses that even if married women have sexual intercourse solely to bear children, their offspring are not Christians until mother Church gives birth to them, though they co-operate with the Church in that process. So such physical fecundity bears no comparison with the virginity which is wholly consecrated to God. Thus the continence of virginity maintained for the Creator is to be accorded greater honour than marital chastity. So today all who can should opt for a life of virginity, for unlike the era of the Old Testament the present age has abundance of Christians. If numerical growth were regarded as equally important as virginity, it would be more feasible to purchase pagan slaves to turn into Christians! Augustine makes this ironical observation [X] to demonstrate the falsity of the hypothesis. Similarly, the argument that married people rank as high as virgins because they bring to birth other virgins is dismissed, for virgins are one thing and consecrated virgins another. Virgins in the market for a husband, seeking to impress a range of possible suitors, are in a pitiable plight; by contrast the consecrated virgin seeks only Christ, to conceive him spiritually and to remain a virgin for him physically. The consecrated

virgin is the offspring not of any natural mother, but of the Church; only a sacred virgin can give birth to sacred virgins.

Marriage is a good [XIII] because of its threefold attributes of *proles, fides, sacramentum,* but these are human goods, whereas consecrated virginity rises above them to angelic heights, ensuring for virgins greater distinction in heaven. Those who argue that the value of virginity lies in a cosier life on earth free of domestic worries are mistaken; they misinterpret Paul's meaning. When he speaks of 'the present necessity', his point is that because married people are preoccupied more by worldly than by heavenly concerns, they will attain a lesser distinction in heaven.[28]

Augustine next [XV] interprets the implications of Paul's advice to marry or not to marry at 1 Cor. 7, distinguishing between divine command and counsel. The Lord's command is that neither wife nor husband should renounce the other; Paul's counsel to the unmarried is not to seek a partner. In embracing marriage you choose the lesser good but do nothing wrong, but the trials of marriage are a further reason to choose virginity, unless you lack self-control. The Manichees are wrong to interpret Paul's 'They will have tribulation of the flesh, but I would spare you that' as an injunction against marriage, as the rest of Paul's chapter clearly shows; their technique of selective interpretation undermines the authority of scripture.

Those who embrace consecrated virginity [XVIII] should rank their calling above that of marriage, but without disparaging the married state: 'opt for the greater gift in such a way as not to condemn the lesser.' Here Augustine rounds on Manichees and Jovinian alike, the first for condemning marriage and the second for equating its merit with that of virginity. He counsels the middle way of pronouncing marriage as a good, but a lesser good. So Paul's 'I would spare you that' does not threaten married people like Susanna with eternal punishment [XX]. Augustine argues passionately that the Manichees' assault on marriage, and their claim that married people will be condemned at the Judgement-seat, is a monstrous perversion of the message of scripture. Augustine defends this seemingly irrelevant apologia for marriage by stressing that the merit of virginity is the greater for such comparison. If virgins take due note of scripture's approval of marriage, they will embrace their

---

[28] For the misinterpretation of Paul's phrase, see above, p. xvi.

own calling more eagerly because it is pronounced the better: the Pauline teaching bears this out.

He now [XXII] turns to the final topic of this second heading of virginity considered in itself, the question of rewards in heaven. He first underlines the point made earlier, that consecrated virginity seeks not comfort in this life but greater glory in the next. After quoting Matthew on eunuchs who have castrated themselves for the kingdom of heaven, he goes back to Isaiah's discussion of eunuchs to argue that the Old Testament prophet too is referring to consecrated virgins: the promise of a place of renown in God's house refers not to earthly distinction, but to glory in heaven. Jovinian had argued that virgins and married would receive the same reward in heaven, citing the parable of the labourers in the vineyard; Augustine offers a refinement on the interpretation of that passage.

The treatise now [XXVII] takes on a highly lyrical tone, invoking the mystical vision of the *Apocalypse* to describe the heavenly joys which consecrated virgins alone will enjoy in heaven. When they are bidden to follow the Lamb, 'follow' means imitate; as virgins they are to imitate the virgin Christ. The eight Beatitudes are the apposite means of imitation for virgins and non-virgins alike; non-virgins who cannot follow the Lamb on the virgins' path will participate in their joy.

Augustine next [XXX] addresses those whose vocation is as yet undecided, urging them to embrace virginity, which transcends the good of marriage. Here he embarks on his third and final theme, the humility which is vital for this manner of life. Pride and its daughter envy are the foes of charity. He states at the outset that he will make a pioneering study of humility gathered from scriptural passages. The centurion, the Canaanite woman, the tax-collector are adduced as models, this last in contrast to the Pharisee who disparages the sinner if only in thought; and again, the child whom Jesus sets before his disciples, and by contrast the sons of Zebedee who seek to be exalted. Christ himself, in washing the feet of his disciples immediately before his death, offers the most inspiring example of all.

The exhortation is brought closer to home [XXXIII] by citing Paul's animadversions on women who are busybodies, on widows who seek second husbands, and on virgins too fond of bodily adornment. These Augustine regards as yet too immature to embrace humility; he turns instead to virgins free of such defects, for whom self-satisfaction is a hazard.

The treatise now [XXXV] concentrates on Christ as the noblest exemplar of humility, focusing especially on his words 'For I am meek and humble of heart'. The models of humility already quoted, the tax-collector and the centurion, and also Zacchaeus and Mary Magdalen, must look to him to learn humility. Christ is implored to turn his gaze on consecrated boys and girls, and impress them with the message that he is meek and humble of heart. The model of humility for the consecrated virgin is not the tax-collector, nor the repentant sinner, but Jesus himself; the root of his humility lies in his charity, which is not envious nor proud. Telling contrasts are made between the tax-collector, unwilling to raise his eyes to heaven, and Christ who came down from heaven for us, between Mary Magdalen seeking forgiveness by washing Jesus' feet and Christ imparting forgiveness as he washed the feet of his disciples. The virgin must beware of playing the Pharisee and boasting to God of her merits. She must have fear—not fear of earthly hazards but fear of the Lord, the fear of perfect love, not the fear of eternal damnation.

The holy Spirit finds rest in the humble who tremble at God's words [XXXIX]. The warnings of scripture and the hazards of human existence both enjoin humility. Those members of religious communities who fall from grace are a warning against pride; those who remain faithful owe their fidelity to divine favour. Since 'he to whom little is forgiven loves but little', they are to count as forgiven the sins which the Lord has enabled them to avoid.

The first reason for being humble [XLI] is because consecrated virginity is a gift from God. Virgins must pray with the Psalmist that they will execute God's commands, and if they fail they must pray for the gift of repentance. Continence is itself a gift from God, as is the wisdom to realise that being a divine gift it should instil humility in us.

Second [XLIII], in acknowledging that virginity is divinely bestowed, the virgin must beware of pride in despising others, as the Pharisee despised the tax-collector. She should not hesitate to rank virginity above the married state, but she must not claim that as an individual she is better than one who is married; their relative merits can be tested only at a time of trial. Martyrdom offers the prospect of such a trial. Augustine now [XLV] reviews the rewards anticipated for martyrs, virgins, chaste widows, and married persons as interpreted from the parable of the Sower. The triple division between fruits a hundredfold, sixtyfold, thirtyfold is

insufficiently flexible to match the wide range of recipients. Certainly no one will rank virginity as high as martyrdom.

So the virgin can rightly claim that virginity ranks above marriage [XLVII], but not that as an individual she rises above a married person. Such a comparison at a time of trial could indicate that the married person would be more intrepid in the face of torture.

Virgins are to be on their guard against sinning [XLVIII]. When Christ bids us pray for forgiveness of our debts, he reminds us that none should boast of being sinless. The apostle John urges us to confess our faults, but we must not do so with the intention of returning to them. Those whose faults are trivial must beware in case pride makes them more grievous. Sceptical reference is made here to the Pelagian belief that some individuals may live wholly blameless lives.

Augustine now [LI] embarks on the final section of his mini-treatise on humility. He first underlines the importance of the virtue for the virgins who aspire to perfection; he next suggests practical ways in which it can be practised; and above all he dwells on its advantages. Such humility brings a transformation in behaviour. Freedom from marriage-bonds enables virgins to meditate on Christ's humility, and to avoid the jealousies endemic in human marriages.

The treatise ends [LVI] on a highly rhetorical note with reference to 'The Song of the Three Holy Children'. They are an exemplar of that combination of holiness and humility to which consecrated virgins should aspire. As the children did not burn in the furnace, so virgins will not burn with lust for sexual intercourse.

Augustine summarizes the theme of *De sancta uirginitate*, and its connection with *De bono coniugali*, in his *Retractationes*.[29] Though emphatic in refuting condemnation of the married state by the Manichees and by Jerome, he makes clear to his readers his conviction that consecrated virginity is the higher calling. At this time in AD 401 when he was enthusiastically establishing separate monastic communities for men and for women, his treatise is an impassioned recommendation of such a life of continence, together with a cautionary warning not to embrace it for the wrong reasons (it is evident that unsuitable entrants were already disturbing the harmony

---

[29] See Appendix 1.

of some of these communities). Hence the twofold theme of the excellence of virginity and its rewards on the one hand, and the importance of Christlike humility on the other.

In later years Augustine laid increased emphasis on the ascetic ideal, which was fuelled by his obsessive conviction that concupiscence made chastity in marriage difficult of attainment. This left him open to the charge by Julian of Eclanum and other Pelagians that he was still a Manichee. In fact, however, his fundamental attitude never diverged: marriage was a good, but consecrated virginity was better.[30]

*

Augustine's Bible[31]

As is pointed out in Appendix 2. Augustine's citations of the Latin of the Old and New Testaments frequently differ from the Latin Vulgate. In his day several Latin versions of the Bible were circulating in Africa, and he collected and consulted a number of these. But the version which he recommends above all others is the *Itala*, 'as it keeps more closely to the words without sacrificing clarity of expression'.[32] *Itala* is the name which Augustine uses for the Old Latin (pre-Vulgate) version current in Italy in his day; its name distinguishes it from the African versions from which it may have been derived. It is probable that Augustine became familiar with it during his time in Milan, when he heard Ambrose discourse on the allegorical sense of the Old Testament.[33]

In recommending the *Itala*, Augustine adds that in study of the Old Testament, Greek manuscripts of the Septuagint should be consulted to remedy defective readings, since the Septuagint was composed by its seventy scholars under the reliable guidance of the holy Spirit. It is doubtful, however, if he himself was able to follow this practice as early as AD 401, for his competence in Greek is a later

---

[30] See esp. *Opus imperfectum contra Iulianum, Praef.*: 'I wrote this book (sc. *De nuptiis et concupiscentia*) because I knew that the report had reached him that the Pelagians say that we condemn marriage. In this book, using my strongest arguments, I distinguished the good of marriage from the evil of carnal concupiscence, which conjugal modesty uses well.' For general reviews of Augustine's thought on this subject after AD 401, see Brown, *The Body* ch. 19; E. Clark, *St Augustine on Marriage and Sexuality* (Washington, DC, 1996).

[31] See G. Bonner in *The Cambridge History of the Bible*, i (Cambridge, 1970), 544 ff.

[32] *De doctrina Christiana* 2. 53, as rendered by R. P. H. Green, *Oxford Early Christian Texts* (1995).

[33] F. C. Burkitt, 'St Augustine's Bible and the Itala', *JTS* 11 (1910), 258 ff., 447 ff.

development. The recommendation to consult the Septuagint appears in *De doctrina Christiana*, which though begun perhaps as early as AD 395, was not completed until more than thirty years later.[34]

Augustine made use also of Jerome's translations. On two occasions in *De doctrina Christiana* he refers approvingly to Jerome's rendering from the Hebrew of the Prophets,[35] but as this translation from the Hebrew was not completed until AD 405–6,[36] he cannot have utilized it for our two treatises. So far as Jerome's work on the New Testament is concerned, his translation of the Four Gospels was completed as early as 384, so that Augustine was able to exploit it from about 400 onwards.[37] But it has become increasingly clear that the Vulgate version of the other books of the New Testament was not the work of Jerome, and that he had abandoned the idea of publishing a revised version of them.[38] In these treatises there are clear divergences between Augustine's text of the Pauline and other epistles and the Vulgate, and it seems clear that he resorted to the *Itala* for his citations of these books,[39] as for the books of the Old Testament. The minor variations between Augustine's citations of the Gospels and the Vulgate will be attributable to the familiarity with which he cites from memory (whether from the Itala or the Vulgate) or slightly paraphrases well-known passages.

Text and English Translations

The text in this volume is based on the impressive edition of J. Zycha in the CSEL series.[40] He collated twenty manuscripts ranging from the sixth to the twelfth century, and divided them into three families:

1. *C* (Parisinus 13367) 6th cent.; *B* (Bernensis 152), 11th cent.
2. *P* (Palatinus 210), 7th cent., and manuscripts descended from *P* dating from the 9th–12th cents.

---

[34] See Green, *De doctrina Christiana*, pp. xi ff. It is uncertain when the passage was written between these two dates. For Augustine's later proficiency in Greek, see Brown, *Augustine of Hippo*.

[35] 4. 48 and 116; cf. *Civ. Dei* 18. 43.   [36] Kelly, *Jerome*, 161.

[37] C. H. Milne, *A Reconstruction of the Old Latin Text or Texts used by Saint Augustine* (Cambridge, 1926), pp. xi ff., cited by Bonner, *Cambridge History of The Bible*, i. 545.

[38] See Kelly, *Jerome*, 88.   [39] See nn. 12, 47 to *De bono coniugali*.

[40] CSEL 41 (Vienna, 1900), 187–231, 235–302.

3. *K* (Coloniensis 76), 8th cent., and manuscripts descended from *K*, mostly from the 11th and 12th cent.

In Zycha's judgement, '*C* is far superior in value to the rest . . . *P* rightly claims second place after *C*, and is nearer to the first than to the third . . . Of the third family *K* excels the rest . . . For the establishment of the text, *CP* offers enough at all points.'

The other modern edition of the two treatises appears in the series Oeuvres de saint Augustin; *De bono coniugali* in vol. 2 (ed. G. Combès, Paris, 1948), 32–99, and *De sancta uirginitate* in vol. 3 (ed. J. Saint-Martin, Paris, 1949), 105–227. These editions offer good translations and useful annotations, but the texts, reproduced (not always accurately) from Migne (*PL* 40), are not wholly reliable.

On the few occasions when I venture to differ from a reading in Zycha's text (See Appendix 3) I have considered it sufficient to cite the readings of *CBPK* and of the *PL* text as cited by Combès and Saint-Martin.

As I indicate in the Foreword, modern translations of these works are few. C. L. Cornish provides an accurate but laboured version in The Library of the Fathers; *Seventeen Short Treatises of St Augustine* (Oxford, 1847). There are translations of *De bono coniugali* (by Wilcox) and *De sancta uirginitate* (by McQuade) in vol. 27 of the series The Fathers of the Church (Washington, DC, 1955).

SELECT BIBLIOGRAPHY

Arjava, Antti, *Women and Law in Late Antiquity* (Oxford, 1996).

Beard, M., 'The Sexual Status of Vestal Virgins', *JRS* 70 (1980), 12 ff.

—— 'Re-reading (Vestal) Virginity', in R. Hawley and B. Levick (eds), *Women in Antiquity* (London, 1995), ch. 11.

Berrouard, M.-F., 'De bono coniugali' in *Augustin-Lexikon*, i (Basel, 1986–94), 658 ff.

Bonner, G., *St Augustine of Hippo* (2nd edn. Norwich, 1986).

—— 'Libido and Concupiscentia in St Augustine', *Studia Patristica* 6 (Berlin, 1962), 303 ff.

—— 'Augustine as Biblical Scholar', in P. R. Ackroyd and C. F. Evans (eds.), *The Cambridge History of the Bible*, i (Cambridge, 1970), 541 ff.

Brown, Peter, *Augustine of Hippo* (London, 1967).

—— *The Body and Society: Man, Woman and Sexual Renunciation in Early Christianity* (New York, 1988).

Cameron, A., 'Neither Male nor Female', *GR* 27 (1980), 60 ff.

Clark, E. (ed.), *St Augustine on Marriage and Sexuality* (Washington, DC, 1996).

—— *Women in the Early Church* (Wilmington, Del., 1983).

Clark, G., *Women in Late Antiquity: Pagan and Christian Lifestyles* (Oxford, 1993).

Crouzel, H., *Mariage et Divorce, Célibat et caractère sacerdotaux dans l'église ancienne* (Turin, 1982).

Dixon, S., *The Roman Family* (Baltimore and London, 1992).

Drijvers, J. W., 'Virginity and Asceticism in Late Roman Western Elites', in J. Blok and P. Mason (eds.), *Sexual Assymetry* (Amsterdam, 1987), 241 ff.

Gardner, Jane, *Women in Roman Law and Society* (London, 1986).

Godefroy, L., 'Le mariage dans les Pères', *DTC* 9.2 (Paris, 1927), 2127 ff.

Green, R. P. H. (ed.), *Augustine, De doctrina Christiana* (Oxford, 1995).

Grubbs, J. E., *Law and Family in Late Antiquity: Constantine's Legislation on Marriage* (Oxford, 1995).

Homes Dudden, F., *Saint Ambrose, his Life and Times* (Oxford, 1935).

Hopkins, M. K., 'The Age of Roman Girls at Marriage', *Population Studies* 18 (1965), 309 ff.

Hunter, D. G., *Marriage in the Early Church* (Minneapolis, 1992).

Kelly, J. N. D., *Jerome* (London, 1975).

Leclercq, J., *Marriage and the Family*, tr. T. R. Hanley (New York, 1941).

Markus, R. A., *The End of Ancient Christianity* (Cambridge, 1990).

Marrou, H., and La Bonnardière, A. M., *S. Augustin et l'augustinisme* (Paris, 1955).

Noonan, John T., Jr., *Contraception* (2nd edn. Cambridge, Mass., 1986).

O'Donnell, J. J., *Augustine, Confessions*, 3 vols. (Oxford, 1992).

Pereira, H., *La Doctrine du mariage selon saint Augustin* (Paris, 1930).

Puech, H. C., *Le Manichéisme, son fondateur, sa doctrine* (Paris, 1949).

Ramsey, A., *Ambrose* (London, 1997).

Rist, J. M., *Augustine: Ancient Thought Baptized* (Cambridge, 1994).

Saller, R. P., 'Man's Age at Marriage and its Consequences in the Roman Family', *CP* 82 (1987), 21 ff.

Shaw, B. D., 'The Age of Roman Girls at Marriage: some Reconsiderations', *JRS* 77 (1987), 30 ff.

Schmitt, K., *Le Mariage Chrétien dans l'oeuvre de S. Augustin* (Paris, 1983).

Treggiari, S., *Roman Marriage* (Oxford, 1991).

Van der Meer, F., *Augustine the Bishop* (London, 1961), esp. 160 ff.

Viden G., 'The Twofold View of Women: Gender Construction in Early Christianity', in L. L. Loven and A. Strömberg (eds.), *Aspects of Women in Antiquity* (Jonserad, 1998).

ABBREVIATIONS

DE BONO CONIUGALI

THE GOOD OF MARRIAGE

[I]   1. Quoniam unusquisque homo humani generis pars est, et sociale quiddam est humana natura¹ magnumque habet et naturale bonum, uim quoque amicitiae, ob hoc ex uno deus uoluit omnes homines condere, ut in sua societate non sola similitudine generis sed etiam cognationis uinculo tenerentur. Prima itaque naturalis humanae societatis copula uir et uxor est. Quos nec ipsos singulos condidit deus et tamquam alienigenas iunxit, sed alteram creauit ex altero, signans etiam uim coniunctionis in latere, unde illa detracta formata est.² Lateribus enim sibi iunguntur, qui pariter ambulant et pariter quo ambulant intuentur. Consequens et conexio societatis in filiis, qui unus honestus fructus est non coniunctionis maris et feminae, sed concubitus. Poterat enim esse in utroque sexu etiam sine tali commixtione alterius regentis, alterius obsequentis amicalis quaedam et germana coniunctio.³

[II]   2. Nec nunc opus est ut scrutemur et in ea quaestione definitam sententiam proferamus, unde primorum hominum proles posset exsistere, quos benedixerat deus dicens *Crescite et multiplicamini, et implete terram*,⁴ si non peccassent, cum mortis condicionem corpora eorum peccando meruerint, nec esse concubitus nisi mortalium corporum possit.⁵ Plures enim de hac re sententiae diuersaeque exstiterunt, et si examinandum sit ueritati diuinarum scripturarum quaenam earum potissimum congruat, prolixae disputationis negotium est.⁶

Siue ergo sine coeundi complexu alio aliquo modo, si non peccassent, habituri essent filios ex munere omnipotentissimi creatoris, qui potuit etiam ipsos sine parentibus condere, qui potuit carnem

¹ In this exordium on marriage as the base of community, Augustine echoes the doctrine of Classical philosophers (notably Aristotle, *Politics* 1252ᵇ, and especially Cicero, *De officiis* 1. 50 ff.), and superimposes upon it the biblical account of the creation of man and woman in *Genesis*.

² Cf. Gen. 2. 21 f.

³ 'A true union of friendship' is a striking innovation in the concept of ancient marriage, for in Plato's *Lysis*, in the two books on friendship in Aristotle's *Nicomachean Ethics*, and in Cicero's *De amicitia*, friendship is envisaged wholly in terms of the relationship between men, considered on a higher plane than that between man and wife. But 'with the one governing and the other obeying' echoes Aristotle, *Politics* 1254ᵇ: 'The male is by nature superior, and the female inferior; the one rules and the other is ruled.' The same formula appears in the philosopher Callicratidas; see Treggiari, *Roman Marriage*, 195 f. Augustine seems here concerned to endow Christian marriage with a dignity higher than the institution had enjoyed earlier, whereas in other treatises he reverts to more traditional Graeco-Roman attitudes; see Rist, *Augustine*, 212.

⁴ Gen. 1: 28. This extended discussion of how Adam and Eve could have obeyed the injunction 'Increase and multiply' in the age of innocence before the Fall seems at first sight

1. Every individual belongs to the human race, and by virtue of his [I] humanity he is a social being.[1] In addition, he possesses the great and natural blessing of a capacity for friendship. It was with these purposes that God decided to create all humanity from one man, so that all would be kept in community with each other not only by similarity of species but also by the bond of kinship. Hence the first natural link in human society is that between man and wife. Even these God did not create as separate individuals and then unite them as strangers by birth, but he fashioned the wife from the husband, and signalled the strength of their union by the flank from which she was drawn and formed;[2] for those who walk together, and together observe the direction which they are taking, are joined side by side in unity. The next link in the chain of community is children, the sole worthy outcome not of the union between male and female, but of sexual intercourse; for even without such sexual association there could exist a true union of friendship between the two sexes, with the one governing and the other obeying.[3]

2. It is not necessary at this time to search out and to deliver a [II] definitive judgement on how the offspring of the first human beings could have come into existence if they had not sinned (for God had blessed them, and told them to 'increase and multiply, and fill the earth').[4] It was only then that their bodies by sinning deserved to undergo the fate of death, and sexual intercourse can take place only between mortal bodies.[5] There have been several different theories on this matter, and if we had to investigate which of them most closely accords with the truth of the divine scriptures, it would involve lengthy discussion.[6]

One possibility is that if they had not sinned they would have had children in some way other than sexual intercourse through the gift of the almighty Creator, for he was able to create Adam and

a curious divergence from the main theme of the treatise. Its insertion may be attributable to the fact that Augustine in 401 was beginning work on his *De Genesi ad litteram*, which was to preoccupy him for the next thirteen years. The emerging view that the sexual act when directed towards procreation is good in itself, directed against those who regarded it as evil, lends it relevance in the context of marriage here. See Markus, *The End of Ancient Christianity*, 57f.

[5] Augustine does not raise the question why immortal bodies should not have sexual intercourse because he bows to the authority of scripture; cf. Matt. 22: 30.

[6] Augustine reverts to the question in *The City of God* 14. 23ff., to argue that if there had been no Fall, sexual intercourse would have been controlled by the will rather than motivated by lust.

Christi in utero uirginali formare et, ut iam ipsis infidelibus loquar,
qui potuit apibus prolem sine concubitu dare;[7] siue ibi multa mys-
tice ac figurate dicta sint, aliterque sit intellegendum quod scriptum
est, *Implete terram et dominamini eius*,[8] id est, ut plenitudine et perfec-
tione uitae ac potestatis id fieret, ut ipsum quoque incrementum et
multiplicatio, qua dictum est *Crescite et multiplicamini*, prouectu mentis et copia uirtutis intellegatur, sicut in psalmo positum est *Multi-
plicabis me in anima mea in uirtutem*,[9] nec data sit homini prolis ista
successio nisi posteaquam causa peccati futura erat in morte deces-
sio; siue corpus non spiritale illis hominibus, sed primo animale factum erat,[10] ut oboedientiae merito postea fieret spiritale ad
immortalitatem capessendam non post mortem, quae *inuidia diaboli
intrauit in orbem terrarum*[11] et facta est poena peccati, sed per illam
commutationem quam significat apostolus ubi ait *Deinde nos uiuentes
qui reliqui sumus simul cum illis rapiemur in nubibus in obuiam Christo in
aera*,[12] ut illa corpora primi coniugii et mortalia fuisse intellegamus
prima conformatione et tamen non moritura nisi peccassent, sicut
minatus erat deus[13] (tamquam si uulnus minaretur quia uulnerabile
corpus erat, quod tamen non accidisset nisi fieret quod ille uetuis-
set), ita ergo possent etiam per concubitum talium corporum gen-
erationes subsistere, quae usque ad certum modum haberent
incrementum nec uergerent tamen in senium, aut usque in senium
nec tamen in mortem donec illa benedictionis multiplicatione terra
impleretur. Si enim uestibus Israhelitarum praestitit deus per annos
quadraginta sine ullo detrimento proprium statum,[14] quanto magis
praestaret corporibus oboedientium praecepto suo felicissimum
quoddam temperamentum[15] certi status, donec in melius conuert-
erentur non morte hominis, qua corpus ab anima deseritur, sed
beata commutatione a mortalitate ad immortalitatem, ab animali
ad spiritalem qualitatem!

---

[7] It was commonly believed in antiquity that bees did not copulate; their fertilization in
flight was discovered only in 1791 by F. Huber. Augustine doubtless recalls Virgil, *Georgics* 4.
197ff. For a modern account of the bees' behaviour, see M. Davies and J. Kathirithamby,
Greek Insects (1986), 47–83. Augustine may be following Ambrose, *De uirginibus* I. 8. 40f.

[8] Gen. 1: 28. He takes this view earlier in *De Genesi contra Manichaeos* 1.19.

[9] Ps. 137 (138): 3. Augustine's text differs from the Vulgate.

[10] The distinction is explained in *The City of God* 13. 23: 'spiritual' bodies have the substance
of flesh, but do not experience corruption or even weariness; they require no material nour-
ishment, and they are immortal.

[11] Cf. Wisd. 2. 24.   [12] 1 Thess. 4: 17.   [13] Cf. Gen. 2: 17.

[14] Cf. Deut. 29: 5.

Eve themselves without the aid of parents, He was able to fashion Christ in the flesh in a virgin's womb, and—I cite this example for the unbelievers—He was able to furnish bees with offspring without sexual intercourse.[7] A second possibility is that in scripture many statements are mystical and metaphorical, and so we must interpret in a different sense the words 'Fill the earth, and subdue it'.[8] This explanation would suggest that the words were to be fulfilled by fullness and perfection of life and power, so that the growth and numerical increase referred to in the words 'Increase and multiply' are to be understood as achieved by the development of mind and abundance of virtue. As the psalm has it, 'Thou shalt multiply me in my soul by abundant virtue.'[9] On this supposition, the offspring which succeeded Adam were granted him only after his relapse into sin made his future death a certainty. A third possibility is that the bodies of our first parents were initially not spiritual but animal creations,[10] to enable them to become spiritual later through the merit of obedience. They would thus have attained immortality not after death, which entered the world through the devil's malice[11] and became punishment for sin, but through that transformation to which the Apostle points when he says: 'Then we who are alive, who are left, shall be caught up together with them in the clouds to meet Christ in the air.'[12] On this assumption we are to understand that in the first marriage, the bodies when first fashioned were mortal, yet were not doomed to die unless they sinned. This was the point of God's threat;[13] it was as though he threatened to inflict a wound on a body vulnerable to it, but one which would not have been inflicted if the forbidden act had not been committed. So generations of such bodies could likewise have originated through sexual intercourse. They could have matured to a certain stage without declining into old age, or they could have advanced into old age without dying, until the earth could be filled by the multiplying granted by God's blessing. If God allowed the garments of the Israelites to remain undamaged for forty years,[14] how much more could he have allowed the bodies of those who obeyed his law that most blessed halfway house[15] of a settled status until they were changed for the better—changed not by that human death in which the body is forsaken by the soul, but by a blessed transformation from mortality to immortality, from animal to spiritual nature!

[15] *temperamentum* is the technical word for 'mixture' in medicine. It is used here to indicate the combination of the animal body in the present and the spiritual body in the future.

[III]   Harum sententiarum quae uera sit, uel si alia uel aliae possunt adhuc ex illis uerbis exculpi, quaerere ac disserere longum est.

3. Illud nunc dicimus, secundum istam condicionem nascendi et moriendi quam nouimus et in qua creati sumus, aliquid boni esse coniugium masculi et feminae; cuius confederationem ita diuina scriptura commendat ut nec dimissae a uiro nubere liceat alteri quamdiu uir eius uiuit, nec dimisso ab uxore liceat alteram ducere, nisi mortua fuerit quae recessit.[16] Bonum ergo coniugii, quod etiam dominus in euangelio confirmauit, non solum quia prohibuit dimittere uxorem nisi ex causa fornicationis, sed etiam quia uenit inuitatus ad nuptias,[17] cur sit bonum merito quaeritur. Quod mihi non uidetur propter solam filiorum procreationem, sed propter ipsam etiam naturalem in diuerso sexu societatem;[18] alioquin non iam diceretur coniugium in senibus, praesertim si uel amisissent filios uel minime genuissent. Nunc uero in bono licet annoso coniugio, etsi emarcuit ardor aetatis inter masculum et feminam, uiget tamen ordo caritatis inter maritum et uxorem, qui quanto meliores sunt tanto maturius a commixtione carnis suae pari consensu se continere coeperunt, non ut necessitatis esset postea non posse quod uellent, sed ut laudis esset primum noluisse quod possent. Si ergo seruatur fides honoris et obsequiorum inuicem debitorum ab alterutro sexu, etiamsi languescentibus et prope cadauerinis utrisque membris, animorum tamen rite coniugatorum tanto sincerior quanto probatior, et tanto securior quanto placidior castitas perseuerat. Habent etiam id bonum coniugia, quod carnalis uel iuuenalis incontinentia, etiamsi uitiosa est, ad propagandae prolis redigitur honestatem, ut ex malo libidinis aliquid boni faciat copulatio coniugalis,[19] deinde quia reprimitur et quodam modo

---

[16] Cf. Matt. 19: 9. Augustine here omits mention of Matthew's proviso 'except for unchastity', but he includes it two sentences later. In his *De adulterinis coniugiis* (AD 419–20), in response to Pollentius' defence of Matthew that adultery provides justification for putting away a wife, Augustine argues that the combined evidence of Mark 10: 11 f., Luke 16: 18, and 1 Cor. 7: 39, in which no such exception is made, overrides the testimony of Matthew.

[17] Cf. John 2: 2, the account of the marriage-feast at Cana. The Fathers lay great weight on Jesus' presence and his first miracle performed there as evidence of his approval of marriage; see the texts assembled by L. Godefroy in *DTC* 9.2, 2045–72. Augustine, *In Ioann.* 9. 2 (*PL* 35. 1459) writes: 'The Lord attended the wedding so that the chastity of marriage should be strengthened, and the sacrament of marriage demonstrated.'

[18] In this important passage, Augustine anticipates insights into the theology of marriage more popularly ascribed to documents of Vatican II; see *The Church in the Modern World*, 48, where Christian marriage is described as 'mutual self-bestowal'. Augustine's phrase, 'ordo caritatis inter maritum et uxorem', is especially notable in this regard.

It would involve long investigation and discussion to establish [III] which of these suggestions is true, or whether one or more different explanations can even now be derived from those words of scripture.

3. What we now assert is that in our present situation of birth and death, which we experience and in which we were created, marriage between male and female is something good. Divine scripture recommends this compact, on condition that a woman cast out by her husband is not permitted to marry another for as long as her husband is alive, and a husband rejected by his wife cannot take another unless the one who has left him dies.[16]

The question why the good of marriage is a good deserves investigation. The Lord himself ratified this in the gospel, not merely by forbidding a man to dismiss his wife except for fornication, but also by his presence at a marriage when invited to it.[17] The explanation why marriage is a good lies, I think, not merely in the procreation of children, but also in the natural compact itself between the sexes.[18] If this were not the case, we would not now speak of marriage between the elderly, especially if they had lost their children, or had not had any at all. But as things stand, in a good marriage between elderly partners, though the youthful passion between male and female has withered, the ordered love between husband and wife remains strong. The better the couple are, the earlier they have begun by mutual consent to abstain from sexual intercourse—not because it had become physically impossible for them to carry out their wishes, but so that they could merit praise by prior refusal to do what they were capable of doing. If, then, an honourable fidelity is maintained by both sexes and replaces the compliance owed to each other, even if the physical powers of both are failing and virtually dead, the chastity of souls truly united continues the purer the more it has proved itself, and the safer as it is more serene.

Marriages promote this further good: carnal or youthful incontinence, which is admittedly a defect, is applied to the honourable task of begetting children, and so intercourse within marriage engenders something good from the evil of lust.[19] Moreover, the

---

[19] *Libido*, the conventional Classical word for lust, and *concupiscentia*, its equivalent in Christian Latin, are virtually interchangeable when applied to sexual activity by Augustine. They denote the passionate and uncontrolled element in sexuality, excusable when directed towards procreation (see *De nuptiis et concupiscentia* 1. 15–17, AD 419–21), a human weakness rather than a sin (Ibid. 1. 23. 25). In his later debate with Julian of Eclanum, Augustine suggests that lust arose when owing to the Fall Adam lost control over his body. See Gerald Bonner, '*Libido* and *concupiscentia* in St Augustine', *Studia Patristica* 6 (Berlin, 1962), 303–14.

uerecundius aestuat concupiscentia carnis, quam temperat
parentalis affectus. Intercedit enim quaedam grauitas feruidae
uoluptati,* cum in eo quod sibi uir et mulier adhaerescunt, pater et
mater esse meditantur.

[IV]   4. Huc accedit quia in eo ipso, quod sibi inuicem coniuges debitum soluunt, etiamsi id aliquanto intemperantius et incontinentius
expetant, fidem tamen sibi pariter debent. Cui fidei tantum iuris
tribuit apostolus ut eam potestatem appellaret dicens: *Mulier non
habet potestatem corporis sui, sed uir; similiter autem et uir non habet potestatem
corporis suit, sed mulier.*[20] Huius autem fidei uiolatio dicitur adulterium, cum uel propriae libidinis instinctu uel alienae consensu
cum altero uel altera contra pactum coniugale concumbitur. Atque
ita frangitur fides quae in rebus etiam corporeis et abiectis magnum
animi bonum est; et ideo eam saluti quoque corporali, qua etiam
uita ista continetur, certum est debere praeponi.[21] Etsi enim exigua
palea prae multo auro paene res nulla est, fides tamen cum in negotio paleae sicut in auri sincera seruatur, non ideo minor est quia in
re minore seruatur.

Cum uero ad peccatum admittendum adhibetur fides, mirum si
fides appellanda est; uerumtamen qualiscumque sit, si et contra
ipsam fit, peius fit, nisi cum propterea deseritur ut ad ueram fidem
ac legitimam redeatur, id est ut peccatum emendetur uoluntatis
prauitate correcta. Tamquam si quisque, cum hominem solus
expoliare non possit, inueniat socium iniquitatis et cum eo
paciscatur ut simul id faciant spoliumque partiantur, quo facinore
commisso totum solus auferat. Dolet quidem ille et fidem sibi
seruatam non esse conqueritur; uerum in ipsa sua querela
cogitare debet potius in bona uita ipsi humanae societati fuisse

---

[20] 1 Cor. 7: 4. The Latin translation of the Greek οὐκ ἐξουσιάζει, 'non habet potestatem',
introduces a tension between the biblical teaching and a wife's status in Roman law, if on
marriage she had passed into the *manus* of her husband. This is presumably why Augustine
lays such stress on the word 'power'. Paul's insistence on the rights of one partner against the
other appears at first sight to collide with recent legislation in England; the rights of a wife
over her own body are established by the fact that a husband can be charged with rape if he
forces his wife into sexual intercourse against her will. In view of what follows, however, Paul
may have meant that such power extends merely to prohibition of sexual intercourse outside
marriage, and to total refusal to exercise it within marriage.

[21] The curious allusion to 'bodily health', made in the context of condemnation of adultery, may refer to the necessity to practise sexual restraint in the absence of a spouse (as in a
modern context, when husbands in Rome or Paris pack off their wives and families on
holiday, and themselves remain at work), even if this endangers physical or mental well-

lustful tendencies of the flesh are kept in subjection, and their hot passion becomes more seemly, for parental love constrains it. This is because a sense of responsibility obtrudes into the heat of pleasure, for as they cleave together as man and wife, they reflect on their roles as father and mother.

4. A further point. In the very act in which married partners pay [IV] the debt they owe to each other, even if they demand this too passionately and too lustfully, they owe equal fidelity to each other. Such legitimacy is accorded to this fidelity by the Apostle that he called it a 'power', when he said: 'A wife does not have power over her own body, but her husband has; likewise a husband does not have power over his body; his wife has.'[20] Betrayal of this fidelity is called adultery, when through the prompting of one's own lust, or through acceding to the lust of another, sexual intercourse takes place with another man or woman contrary to the marriage-pact. In this way that fidelity is shattered which even in material and sordid things is a great good of the spirit. So this fidelity must certainly be ranked even higher than the bodily health on which our very life depends.[21] A wisp of chaff is as nothing compared with abundant gold, but if fidelity is maintained uncorrupted in dealings in chaff as in gold, it is of no less account for being observed in something less valuable.

When fidelity is maintained in a sinful act, it would be odd to have to call it fidelity; yet whatever its nature, any act which flies in its face becomes worse, unless it is abandoned to resume a true and lawful fidelity, in other words to remedy the sin by correcting the wickedness of the will. Take the example of a person who being unable to rob another unaided, seeks out an accomplice in wickedness, and bargains with him to do the deed together, and to share the spoils. Then, once the crime has been committed, he bears off all the loot himself. His partner is aggrieved, and complains that faith has not been kept with him. But in making that very complaint, if he feels it quite unjust that faith has not been kept in that sinful alliance, he should reflect that he himself ought rather to have kept faith with the community of

being. The fidelity on which Augustine lays such stress is, on the evidence especially of funeral inscriptions, one of the greatly admired qualities in the Roman wife; see Treggiari, *Roman Marriage*, 237f. For Augustine's further emphasis on *fides*, see [XXIX] 32 below.

---

* uoluptati *P*: uoluptatis *CK, Zycha*

seruandam[22] ne praeda iniqua ex homine fieret, si sentit quam inique sibi in peccati societate seruata non fuerit.

Ille quippe utrubique perfidus profecto sceleratior iudicandus est. At si id quod male fecerant ei displicuisset et propterea cum participe facinoris praedam diuidere noluisset, ut homini cui ablata fuerat redderetur, eum perfidum nec perfidus diceret. Ita mulier, si fide coniugali uiolata fidem seruet adultero, utique mala est; sed si nec adultero, peior est. Porro si eam flagitii paeniteat et ad castitatem rediens coniugalem pacta ac placita adulterina rescindat, miror si eam fidei uiolatricem uel ipse adulter putabit.

[v]   5. Solet etiam quaeri cum masculus et femina, nec ille maritus nec illa uxor alterius, sibimet non filiorum procreandorum sed propter incontinentiam solius concubitus causa copulantur ea fide media, ut nec ille cum altera nec illa cum altero id faciat, utrum nuptiae sint uocandae.[23] Et potest quidem fortasse non absurde hoc appellari conubium, si usque ad mortem alicuius eorum id inter eos placuerit, et prolis generationem, quamuis non ea causa coniuncti sint, non tamen uitauerint ut uel nolint sibi nasci filios uel etiam opere aliquo malo agant ne nascantur.[24] Ceterum si uel utrumque uel unum horum desit, non inuenio quemadmodum has nuptias appellare possimus.

Etenim si aliquam sibi uir ad tempus adhibuerit donec aliam dignam uel honoribus uel facultatibus suis inueniat quam comparem ducat, ipse animo adulter est, nec cum illa quam cupit inuenire sed

---

[22]   The analogy of the two thieves robbing an innocent man initially squares with an adulterous pair who wrong a husband, but not with the later episode when the one double-crosses the other (unless the adulteress is subsequently unfaithful to her lover as well). Augustine's pronouncement that the duped accomplice instead of smarting under injustice 'ought rather to have kept faith with the community of mankind' reflects the Stoic attitude outlined in Cicero, *De officiis* 3. 19 ff., where the rule of conduct prescribed is that our fellowship with the community of mankind forbids us to exploit any individual for our own profit—a principle which, claims Cicero, is at the root of all law, national and international.

[23]   This question of what constitutes a marriage (with its distinctly modern overtones) is weighed by Augustine against the contemporary secular practice. The definition of marriage by Modestinus (*Digest* 23. 2. 1: 'The union of male and female in lifelong association, the sharing of prerogatives divine and human') was honoured more in the breach than in the observance. Constantine introduced more stringent conditions for divorce and remarriage: a wife could divorce her husband only if he were a murderer, poisoner, or tomb-violator, and a husband could divorce his wife only for adultery, poisoning, and procuring (*Codex Theodosianus* 3. 16. 1; T. D. Barnes, *Constantine and Eusebius* (Cambridge, Mass., 1961), 52). This discouraged entry into formal unions. The demands made upon Christians were more rigorous than those imposed by Roman law (see J. E. Grubbs, *Law and Family in Late Antiquity: Constantine's Legislation on Marriage*, Oxford, 1995). Augustine specifies here not only lifelong commitment, but also the stipulation that they do not avoid having children.

mankind[22] by living a good life; he would thus have prevented the ill-gotten booty from being taken from that person.

True, the first man who was doubly faithless is to be adjudged the greater wrongdoer. But if the other had dissented from their evil deed, and on that account had refused to share the booty with his partner in crime to enable it to be restored to the man from whom it was taken, even a faithless person would not call him faithless. It is the same with a woman if she has been unfaithful in her marriage, but keeps faith with her adulterer. She is certainly wicked, but if she does not keep faith with her adulterer either, she is worse. Moreover, should she repent of her evil deed, resume the chaste life of her marriage, and renounce her adulterous compact and designs, I should be surprised if even the adulterer himself would believe that she had broken faith.

5. A further question often raised is when a man and a woman, [v] neither of them married to anyone, have sex with each other not to have children, but merely to indulge in intercourse because they cannot control their lust. But they show fidelity to each other in that the man does not have sex with another woman, nor the woman with another man. The question is whether this should be called a marriage.[23] Doubtless without absurdity it can indeed be labelled a marriage, provided that they agree to maintain the relationship until one of them dies; provided, too, that they do not avoid having children, even if they did not cohabit for this purpose, and provided that they do not ensure that none are born either through reluctance to have children born to them or through taking some evil means to frustrate such births.[24] But if one or both of these necessary conditions are lacking, I do not see how we can call this a marriage.

Indeed, if a man takes on some woman for the moment, until he can find some other worthy of his status or his wealth whom he can marry as his equal, he is an adulterer at heart, not with the one whom he is keen to search out, but with the one with whom he has sexual intercourse without the intention of partnership in

---

[24] Augustine seems to be making a distinction between contraception and abortion here. He may have had personal experience of techniques of contraception, since from fifteen years of his association with his first concubine (*Conf.* 4. 2. 2, 6. 15. 25) he had only one surviving child; see B. Shaw, *Past and Present* 115 (1987), 45. He reveals acquaintance with the rhythm method (and rejects it) in *De moribus ecclesiae catholicae et de moribus Manichaeorum* 2. 18. 65 (AD 388). *Coitus interruptus*, favoured by the Manichees, is also condemned (*Contra Faustum* 22. 38, AD 397–8). So far as abortion is concerned, it had been condemned at the Council of Elvira (canon 61, c. AD 306), and Augustine like Ambrose (*Hexam.* 5. 58) stigmatizes it as murder (*De nuptiis et concupiscentia* 1. 13. 15; 1. 15. 17). See Rist, *Augustine*, 246 ff.; J. T. Noonan, *Contraception* (2nd edn. Cambridge, Mass., 1986), ch. 4; E. A. Clark, *Women in the Early Church*, 55 ff.

cum ista cum qua sic cubat ut cum ea non habeat maritale consor-
tium.[25] Vnde et ipsa hoc sciens ac uolens impudice utique miscetur
ei cum quo non habet foedus uxorium. Verumtamen si ei tori fidem
seruet et, cum ille uxorem duxerit, nubere ipsa non cogitet atque a
tali prorsus opere continere se praeparet, adulteram quidem fortassis facile appellare non audeam; non peccare tamen quis dixerit,
cum eam uiro, cuius uxor non est, misceri sciat?

Iam uero si ex illo concubitu, quantum ad ipsam attinet, nonnisi
filios uelit et quidquid ultra causam procreandi patitur inuita
patiatur, multis quidem ista matronis anteponenda est quae,
tametsi non sunt adulterae, uiros tamen suos plerumque etiam continere cupientes ad reddendum carnale debitum cogunt, non
desiderio prolis sed ardore concupiscentiae ipso suo iure intemperanter utentes. In quarum tamen nuptiis bonum est hoc ipsum, quod
nuptae sunt. Ad hoc enim nuptae sunt, ut illa concupiscentia
redacta ad legitimum uinculum non deformis et dissoluta fluitaret,
habens de se ipsa irrefrenabilem carnis infirmitatem, de nuptiis
autem indissolubilem fidei societatem, de se ipsa progressum
immoderate coeundi, de nuptiis modum caste procreandi. Etsi
enim turpe est libidinose uti uelle* marito, honestum est tamen
nolle misceri nisi marito, et non parere nisi de marito.[26]

[VI]   Sunt item uiri usque adeo incontinentes ut coniugibus nec
grauidis parcant. Quidquid ergo inter se coniugati immodestum
inuerecundum sordidum gerunt, uitium est hominum non culpa
nuptiarum.[27]

6. Iam in ipsa quoque immoderatiore exactione debiti carnalis,
quam eis non secundum imperium praecipit† sed secundum
ueniam concedit apostolus, ut etiam praeter causam procreandi
sibi misceantur,[28] etsi eos praui mores ad talem concubitum impel-
lunt, nuptiae tamen ab adulterio seu fornicatione defendunt.

[25] This was Augustine's own experience as described at *Conf.* 6. 5. 25: 'The woman with
whom I habitually slept was torn away from my side because she was a hindrance to my marriage. She had returned to Africa vowing that she would never go with another man.' (Chadwick's *World Classics* translation; see also his Introduction, pp. xvi f.) Hence he would not
perhaps 'readily call her an adulterer'.

[26] Augustine again underlines fidelity as a central feature of the good of marriage; see [IV]
4 above.

[27] Since Augustine (with Stoic moralists) argues that sexual intercourse is solely for the
purpose of procreation, his logic demands that it should not be exercised in pregnancy.

[28] 1 Cor. 7: 6. The statement of Paul (τοῦτο δὲ λέγω κατὰ συγγνώμην, οὐ κατ' ἐπιταγήν) was
interpreted by rigorist Christians as meaning that indulging in sex for purposes other than

THE GOOD OF MARRIAGE

marriage.[25] So too if the woman knows and approves the situation, she is clearly in an immoral relationship with the man with whom she does not have the compact of a wife. However, should she maintain sexual fidelity with him, and after he takes a wife she gives no thought to marriage herself and steels herself to refrain utterly from such sexual intercourse, I should not perhaps readily presume to call her an adulterer. But would anyone claim that she does not sin when he knows that she is having intercourse with one not her husband?

But if for her part all that she seeks from that intercourse is children, and she undergoes unwillingly such sexual activity as is not aimed at procreation, she is to be ranked higher than many matrons. True, they are not adulterers, but often they compel their husbands to pay the debt of the flesh when men are eager to show restraint. They do this not because they want children, but to exploit their rights in the heat of lust without self-control. Yet their marriages do embrace a good, which is precisely the fact that they are married, for the purpose of their marrying was to confine such lust within lawful bonds so that it did not play fast and loose in a degrading and degenerate way. Such lust in itself involves weakness of the flesh which is out of control, but within marriage it promotes alliance in fidelity which cannot be dissolved. In itself it leads to uncontrolled coupling, but in marriage is the means of chaste procreation. Though it is shameful lustfully to exploit a husband, it is none the less honourable to reject intercourse with anyone except a husband, and to bear children only to a husband.[26]

A further point. Some men are so lacking in self-control that they [vi] do not spare their wives even in pregnancy. So if married couples perform between them any immodest, shameful, or degrading acts, these are to be accounted human failings rather than blamed on marriage.[27]

6. Even when such physical debts are demanded intemperately (which the Apostle permits in married couples as pardonable, allowing them to indulge in sex beyond the purpose of procreation, rather than laying down the law as command),[28] and though debased habits impel partners to such intercourse, marriage is none the less a safeguard against adultery or fornication. Nor is marriage

procreation was a venial sin. Augustine accepts this strained interpretation, but lays stress on the positive value of sexual intercourse within marriage as maintaining marital fidelity.

---

* uelle *B, Combès*: uel *CPK, Zycha*
† praecipit *K, Combès*: praecepit *CP, Zycha*

Neque enim illud propter nuptias admittitur, sed propter nuptias ignoscitur. Debent ergo sibi coniugati non solum ipsius sexus sui commiscendi fidem liberorum procreandorum causa, quae prima est humani generis in ista mortalitate societas, uerum etiam infirmitatis inuicem excipiendae ad illicitos concubitus euitandos mutuam quodam modo seruitutem ut, etsi alteri eorum perpetua continentia placeat, nisi ex alterius consensu non possit; et ad hoc enim *uxor non habet potestatem corporis sui, sed uir; similiter et uir non habet potestatem corporis sui, sed mulier,*[29] ut et quod non filiorum procreandorum, sed infirmitatis et incontinentiae causa expetit uel ille de matrimonio uel illa de marito, non sibi alterutrum negent, ne per hoc incidant in damnabiles corruptelas, temptante Satana, propter incontinentiam uel amborum uel cuiusquam eorum.

Coniugalis enim concubitus generandi gratia non habet culpam; concupiscentiae uero satiandae, sed tamen cum coniuge, propter tori fidem uenialem habet culpam; adulterium uero siue fornicatio letalem habet culpam. Ac per hoc melior est quidem ab omni concubitu continentia quam uel ipse matrimonialis concubitus qui fit causa gignendi.[30]

[VII]   Sed quia illa continentia meriti amplioris est, reddere uero debitum coniugale nullius est criminis, exigere autem ultra generandi necessitatem culpae uenialis, fornicari porro uel moechari puniendi criminis, cauere debet caritas coniugalis ne, dum sibi quaerit unde amplius honoretur, coniugi faciat unde damnetur. *Qui* enim *dimittit uxorem suam excepta causa fornicationis, facit eam moechari.*[31] Vsque adeo foedus illud initum nuptiale cuiusdam sacramenti res est, ut nec ipsa separatione inritum fiat, quandoquidem uiuente uiro et a quo relicta est moechatur si alteri nupserit, et ille huius mali causa est qui reliquit.

7. Miror autem, si quemadmodum licet dimittere adulteram uxorem, ita licet ea dimissa alteram ducere. Facit enim de hac re sancta scriptura difficilem nodum, dicente apostolo ex praecepto domini mulierem a uiro non debere discedere; quodsi discesserit, manere innuptam aut uiro suo reconciliari,[32] cum recedere utique et manere innupta nisi ab adultero uiro non debeat, ne recedendo ab eo qui adulter non est faciat eum moechari. Reconciliari autem uiro uel tolerando, si se ipsa continere non potest, uel correcto for-

---

[29] 1 Cor. 7: 4.   [30] This is Augustine's interpretation of 1 Cor. 7: 7.
[31] Matt. 5: 32.   [32] 1 Cor. 7: 10 f.

the cause of such behaviour, but marriage makes it pardonable. So married couples owe fidelity to each other not merely in performance of the sexual act to bring forth children—and this is the primary compact between the human species in this mortal life of ours—but also in ministering, so to say, to each other, to shoulder each other's weakness, enabling each other to avoid illicit sexual intercourse. Thus even if one of the couple would prefer permanent continence, this can be exercised only with the consent of the other; for in this respect too 'the wife has not dominion over her body; the husband has; likewise the man has not dominion over his body; his wife has'.[29] So when a husband seeks from his marriage, or a wife from her husband, the means not of begetting children but of coping with weakness and lack of self-control, they should not in either case deny this to each other, for the danger is that at Satan's prompting they may as a result stoop to depravities which bring damnation through a lack of control on the part of one or both of them.

Intercourse in marriage, then, when undertaken to beget children, carries no blame. When indulged to satisfy lust, so long as it is with a married partner, it bears only venial blame because it preserves fidelity to the marriage-bed. Adultery or fornication, however, is mortally sinful. In this sphere, abstention from all sexual intercourse is better even than intercourse in marriage undertaken to beget children.[30]

Such abstention, then, gains greater merit; it is no sin to meet the [VII] obligation owed to a spouse; but to demand that debt beyond the requirement to beget children is a venial sin. Beyond that, fornication and adultery are serious sins deserving of punishment. Therefore a loving partner in marriage should beware that in pursuit of greater personal merit he is not the cause of the damnation of a spouse. 'For the man who puts away his wife, except for fornication, causes her to commit adultery.'[31] The sealing of the marriage compact is so clearly governed by a kind of sacrament that it is not made void even by the act of separation; for if a wife marries another while her husband is still alive, she commits adultery even if he has abandoned her, and he is the cause of this evil for having left her.

7. I wonder, however, since it is lawful to renounce an adulterous wife, whether it is permitted to marry another after renouncing her. Holy scripture poses a difficult problem here. The Apostle states that according to the Lord's command a woman must not leave her husband, but if she does so, she must remain unmarried, or be reconciled to her husband.[32] But surely unless her husband is an

sitan iuste potest. Quomodo autem uiro possit esse licentia ducen-
dae alterius si adulteram reliquit, cum mulieri non sit nubendi alteri
si adulterum reliquerit, non uideo.[33]

Quae si ita sunt, tantum ualet illud sociale uinculum coniugum
ut, cum causa procreandi colligetur, nec ipsa causa procreandi solu-
atur. Possit enim homo dimittere sterilem uxorem et ducere de qua
filios habeat, et tamen non licet, et nostris quidem iam temporibus
ac more Romano nec superducere ut amplius habeat quam unam
uiuam;[34] et utique relicta adultera uel relicto adultero possent
plures nasci homines, si uel illa alteri nuberet uel ille alteram duceret. Quod tamen si non licet, sicut diuina regula praescribere uidetur, quem non faciat intentum, quid sibi uelit tanta firmitas uinculi
coniugalis?

Quod nequaquam puto tantum ualere potuisse, nisi alicuius rei
maioris [ex]* hac infirma mortalitate hominum quoddam sacramentum adhiberetur, quod deserentibus hominibus atque id dissoluere cupientibus inconcussum illis maneret ad poenam,
siquidem interueniente diuortio non aboletur illa confoederatio
nuptialis, ita ut sibi coniuges sint etiam separati, cum illis autem
adulterium committant, quibus fuerint etiam post suum repudium
copulati, uel illa uiro uel ille mulieri. Nec tamen nisi in ciuitate dei
nostri, *in monte sancto eius*, talis est causa cum uxore.[35]

[VIII]   Ceterum aliter se habere iura gentilium quis ignorat, ubi inter-
posito repudio sine reatu aliquo ultionis humanae et illa cui uoluerit
nubit, et ille quam uoluerit ducit? Cui consuetudini simile aliquid
propter Israhelitarum duritiam uidetur permisisse Moyses de
libello repudii. Qua in re exprobratio quam approbatio diuortii
magis apparet.[36]

---

[33] Throughout this treatise, Augustine is concerned to stress that the playing-field, so to
speak, in extra-marital sex is equal for both wife and husband. At *Ep.* 259. 3, for example, he
urges a man whose wife had left him to abandon his irregular behaviour.

[34] Bigamous marriage (if this is Augustine's meaning here) had in fact always been forbidden at Rome; see Jane F. Gardner, *Women in Roman Law and Society* (Beckenham, 1986), 91 ff.

[35] Ps. 47 (48): 2. Here Augustine introduces the theme of *sacramentum*, which is central to
his teaching on Christian marriage. The Latin word ('that which makes sacred') was used to
specify an oath taken over a contract, or a military oath of allegiance. The word was subsequently used in the Latin bible to translate Eph. 5: 32 in its reference to marriage: 'This is a
great μυστήριον ('mystery', 'secret revealed by God'), and I apply it to Christ and the Church.'
In the Greek Fathers μυστήριον is used to mean a visible sign of invisible grace; Augustine uses
sacramentum both in the general sense of a token of divine reality (to specify such things as the
Creed, the Lord's Prayer, and the practice of exorcism), and in the more technically sacramental sense with reference to baptism and the eucharist (*De doctrina Christiana* 3. 31). See
J. N. D. Kelly, *Early Christian Doctrines* (London, 1960), 193 ff., 422 ff.

adulterer she should not leave him and remain unmarried, in case by quitting one who was not an adulterer she causes him to commit adultery. However, on the supposition that she herself cannot live a life of continence, she can perhaps be appropriately reconciled to her husband, either by bearing with him or if he changes his ways. But how a man can possibly be free to marry another after leaving a wife who is an adulteress, when a woman does not have such freedom to marry another after she has parted from an adulterer, I do not see.[33]

Since this is the case, the bond of fellowship between spouses is so strong that though the purpose of their attachment is for begetting children, the marriage is not dissolved even in order to beget them. A man could put away a barren wife and marry one by whom to have children, but that is not permitted; indeed, nowadays the Roman norm prescribes that a man cannot marry again and have more than one wife living.[34] Admittedly if an adulterous wife or husband were abandoned and one or other of them married another, more persons would be born; yet if, as the divine law seems to lay down, this is not permitted, who would not become alive to the significance of so strong a marriage-bond?

My belief is that the bond would certainly not have been so strong had not some sacred symbol of something more profound than this feeble mortality of ours become attached to it, and when people abandoned it and were keen to dissolve it, it remained unshaken to punish them; for the marriage-alliance is not rescinded by the divorce which comes between them, and so they remain wedded to each other even when separated; and they commit adultery with those to whom they are attached even after their divorce, whether the wife associates with a man, or the husband with a woman. However, it is only 'in the city of our God, upon his holy mountain' that this situation with a wife applies.[35]

But who is unaware that the laws of the pagans rule otherwise,   [VIII] for when divorce separates them, both wife and husband marry whom each wants without any guilt subject to human punishment? Something similar to this practice seems to have been allowed by Moses pertaining to notice of dismissal, because of the Israelites' hardness of heart. But in that instance censure rather than approval of divorce is manifest.[36]

---

[36] Deut. 24: 1 makes it clear that at that date a man could put away his wife without compelling reason. At Matt. 19: 3 ff., Mark 10: 2 ff., Jesus criticizes this permissiveness, ascribing it to the Israelites' hardness of heart.

---

* ex *seclusi*

8. *Honorabiles* ergo *nuptiae in omnibus et torus immaculatus.*[37] Quod non sic dicimus bonum ut in fornicationis comparatione sit bonum; alioquin duo mala erunt quorum alterum peius. Aut bonum erit et fornicatio, quia est peius adulterium (peius est enim alienum matrimonium uiolare quam meretrici adhaerere), et bonum adulterium quia est peior incestus (peius est enim cum matre quam cum aliena uxore concumbere), et donec ad ea perueniatur quae, sicut ait apostolus, *turpe est etiam dicere,*[38] omnia bona erunt in comparatione peiorum.

Hoc autem falsum esse quis dubitet? Non ergo duo mala sunt conubium et fornicatio, quorum alterum peius, sed duo bona sunt, conubium et continentia, quorum alterum est melius; sicut ista temporalis sanitas et imbecillitas non sunt duo mala, quorum alterum peius, sed ista sanitas et immortalitas duo bona sunt, quorum alterum melius. Item scientia et uanitas non duo mala sunt, quorum uanitas peius, sed scientia et caritas duo bona sunt, quorum caritas melius. Namque *scientia destruetur*, ait apostolus, et tamen huic tempori necessaria est; *caritas* autem *nunquam cadet.*[39] Sic et mortalis ista generatio, propter quam fiunt nuptiae, destruetur; ab omni autem concubitu immunitas et hic angelica meditatio est et permanet in aeternum. Sicut autem ieiuniis sacrilegorum meliora sunt prandia iustorum, ita nuptiae fidelium uirginitati anteponuntur impiarum. Verumtamen neque ibi prandium ieiunio sed iustitia sacrilegio, neque hic nuptiae uirginitati sed fides impietati praefertur. Ad hoc enim iusti, cum opus est, prandent, ut tamquam boni domini quod iustum et aequum est seruis corporibus praebeant; ad hoc autem sacrilegi ieiunant, ut daemonibus seruiant.[40] Sic ad hoc nubunt fideles ut maritis pudice copulentur; ad hoc autem sunt uirgines impiae, ut a uero deo fornicentur.[41]

Sicut ergo bonum erat quod Martha faciebat occupata circa

---

[37] Hebr. 13: 4.

[38] Eph. 5: 12, presumably referring to homosexual practices as at Rom. 1: 24-7.

[39] 1 Cor. 13: 8.

[40] Before initiation into Graeco-Roman mystery religions, candidates were required to abstain for ten days from meat and sex; see Livy 39. 9. 4 (the Bacchanalia); Propertius 2. 33A. 1 f., 2. 28. 1 f.; Apuleius. *Met.* 11. 23 (meat and wine), 11. 28, 11. 30.

[41] Augustine refers here to the Vestal Virgins at Rome. There is controversy about their virginal status. It appears that they lived celibate lives for a fixed period, but they could perhaps have been wives earlier, and they could retire after thirty years. Indeed, lifelong celibacy seems without precedent in Roman society; see Mary Beard, 'The Sexual Status of Vestal Virgins',

8. So 'let marriage be honoured among all, and the marriage-bed be undefiled'.[37] We do not declare it a good by calling it a good by comparison with fornication; otherwise there will be two evils, of which the second is the worse. Or fornication will also be a good, because adultery is worse—for it is worse to damage another's marriage than to consort with a prostitute. And adultery will be a good because incest is worse—for it is worse to have intercourse with your mother than with someone else's wife. We may finally reach the point which in the Apostle's words 'is disgraceful even to mention'.[38] Everything will be good by comparison with what is worse.

But who can doubt that this is false? So marriage and fornication are not two evils, of which the second is the worse; rather, marriage and continence are two goods, of which the second is the better. Take this analogy: health and sickness in this passing world are not two evils, of which the second is the worse, but our health in the here and now and immortality are two goods, of which the second is the better. Or again, knowledge and falsity are not two evils of which falsity is the worse, but knowledge and charity are two goods, of which charity is the better. For 'knowledge will be eliminated', says the Apostle, though it is essential for this time on earth, but 'charity will never die'.[39] In the same way the begetting of mortals, which is the purpose of marriage, will be eliminated, whereas freedom from sexual intercourse, the life of contemplation fit for angels in this world, extends into eternity. But just as meals taken by the just are better than fastings undertaken by the profane, so marriage between the faithful ranks above the virginity of the godless. However, in the first case feasting is not preferred to fasting, but justice to impiety, and in the second, marriage is not ranked above virginity, but faith before godlessness. For the reason why the just take food when they need it is so that as good masters they may give what is just and right to their slaves, that is to their bodies, whereas the profane fast in order to serve demons.[40] In the same way faithful wives marry to have chaste intercourse with their husbands, whereas the godless remain virgins to be unfaithful to the true God.[41]

So just as Martha's activity was good when she busied herself with serving the saints, but her sister Mary's was better in 'sitting at the Lord's feet listening to his words', we likewise praise the good

<hr />

JRS (1980), 12–27, and 'Re-reading (Vestal) Virginity', in R. Hawley and B. Levick (eds.), *Women in Antiquity* (London, 1995), ch. 11. Ambrose claims that being constrained to live celibate lives for only a fixed period, they could not be reckoned true virgins; see *De uirginitate* 13, *De virginibus* 1. 15, *Ep.* 18. 11 f.; F. Homes Dudden, *St Ambrose, His Life and Times* (Oxford, 1935), 147.

ministerium sanctorum, sed melius quod Maria soror eius *sedens ad pedes domini et audiens uerbum eius*; ita bonum Susannae in coniugali castitate laudamus, sed tamen ei bonum uiduae Annae⁴² ac multo magis Mariae uirginis anteponimus. Bonum erat quod faciebant quae de substantia sua Christo ac discipulis eius necessaria ministrabant; sed melius qui omnem suam substantiam dimiserunt ut expeditiores eundem dominum sequerentur.

In his autem binis bonis, eius quae isti siue quae Martha et Maria faciebant, fieri non posset quod melius est nisi altero praetermisso aut relicto. Vnde intellegendum est non ideo malum putandum esse nuptias quia, nisi ab eis abstineatur, non potest haberi uidualis castitas aut uirginalis integritas, neque enim ideo malum erat quod Martha faciebat quia, nisi inde abstineret, soror eius non faceret quod melius erat; aut ideo malum est suscipere iustum aut prophetam in domum suam, quia nec domum habere debet, ut quod melius est faciat, qui uult ad perfectionem Christum sequi.

[IX]   9. Sane uidendum est alia bona nobis deum dare, quae propter se ipsa expetenda sunt, sicut est sapientia salus amicitia, alia quae propter aliquid sunt necessaria, sicut doctrina cibus potus somnus coniugium concubitus; horum enim quaedam necessaria sunt propter sapientiam sicut doctrina, quaedam propter salutem sicut cibus et potus et somnus, quaedam propter amicitiam sicut nuptiae uel concubitus; hinc enim subsistit propagatio generis humani, in quo societas amicalis magnum bonum est.⁴³ His itaque bonis, quae propter aliud necessaria sunt, qui non ad hoc utitur propter quod instituta sunt, peccat alias uenialiter, alias damnabiliter. Quisquis uero eis propter hoc utitur, propter quod data sunt, bene facit. Cui ergo non sunt necessaria, si non eis utitur, melius facit. Proinde ista bona cum opus habemus bene uolumus; sed melius ea nolumus quam uolumus, quia tunc melius nos habemus cum ea necessaria non habemus. Ac per hoc bonum est nubere, quia bonum est filios procreare, matrem familias esse; sed melius est non nubere, quia melius est ad ipsam humanam societatem hoc opere non egere. Ita enim iam sese habet humanum genus, ut aliis qui se non continent non solum per nuptias occupatis sed multis etiam per inlicitos concubitus luxuriantibus, bono creatore de malis eorum faciente quod

⁴² Luke 10: 39 f., Dan. 13 ff., Luke 2: 36 ff.   ⁴³ See n. 3 above.

that Susanna did in remaining chaste in her marriage, but we rank higher than this the good of the widow Anna,[42] and much more that of the virgin Mary. In providing from their own store necessities for Christ and his disciples, they did what was good, but the action of those who abandoned all their possessions to be less encumbered in following the same Lord was better.

But in both these forms of good, that of the men who abandoned their possessions and that of Martha and Mary, the better course could not have been followed without passing over or renouncing the alternative. Hence we must realize that marriage is not to be considered an evil merely because a widow's chastity or a maiden's virginity cannot be attained unless marriage is renounced. The reason, then, why Martha's conduct was not evil was not because, had she refrained from doing what she did, her sister would not have done the better thing; nor is it evil to welcome a just man or a prophet into one's house merely because one who wishes to follow Christ perfectly ought not in seeking to do the better thing even to own a house.

9. We must surely realize that God bestows on us some goods [IX] worth seeking for their own sake, such as wisdom, health, friendship; and others which are necessary for some other purpose, such as learning, food, drink, sleep, marriage, and sexual intercourse. Of this second category, some are necessary to attain wisdom, like learning; some for the sake of health, like food, drink, and sleep; some for friendship, like marriage and sexual intercourse (for the propagation of the human race depends on this last, and the alliance of friendship within it is a great good).[43] It follows that when a person does not employ these goods for that other necessary purpose for which they were established, he sins in some cases venially and in others mortally; whereas the person who directs them for the purpose for which they were given acts well. In the event that a person does not need them, he does better not to use them. So according as we have need of these goods, we do well to desire them, but we do better not to want them rather than to want them, for we are better off when we do not find them necessary. In this sense it is good to marry, for it is good to have children and to become the mother of a household; but it is better not to take a husband, for it is better not to have need of marital relations in the interests of human society itself. For the present state of the human race is such that not only are there some not practising continence who are joined in marriage, but there are many indulging themselves in illicit

bonum est, non desit numerositas prolis et abundantia successionis, unde sanctae amicitiae conquirantur.

Ex quo colligitur primis temporibus generis humani maxime propter dei populum propagandum, per quem et prophetaretur et nasceretur princeps et saluator omnium populorum, uti debuisse sanctos isto, non propter se expetendo sed propter aliud necessario, bono nuptiarum; nunc uero, cum ad ineundam sanctam et sinceram societatem undique ex omnibus gentibus copia spiritalis cognationis exuberet, etiam propter solos filios conubia copulare cupientes, ut ampliore continentiae bono potius utantur, admonendi sunt.[44]

[x]   10. Sed noui quid* murmurent: 'Quid si' inquiunt 'omnes homines uelint ab omni concubitu continere, unde subsisteret genus humanum?' Vtinam omnes hoc uellent, dumtaxat in caritate *de corde puro et conscientia bona et fide non ficta*![45] Multo citius dei ciuitas compleretur et adceleraretur terminus saeculi. Quid enim aliud hortari apparet apostolum ubi ait, cum inde loqueretur *Vellem omnes esse sicut me ipsum*?[46] Aut illo loco: *Hoc autem dico, fratres: tempus breue est; reliquum est ut et hi qui habent uxores tamquam non habentes sint; et qui flent tamquam non flentes; et qui gaudent tamquam non gaudentes; et qui emunt tamquam non ementes; et qui utuntur hoc mundo tamquam non utantur; praeterit enim figura huius mundi. Volo uos sine sollicitudine esse.* Deinde subiungit: *Qui sine uxore est, cogitat ea quae sunt domini, quomodo placeat domino. Qui autem matrimonio iunctus est, cogitat quae sunt mundi, quomodo placeat uxori. Et diuisa est mulier innupta et uirgo; quae innupta est sollicita est ea quae sunt domini, ut sit sancta et corpore et spiritu; quae autem nupta est sollicita est quae sunt mundi, quomodo placeat uiro.*[47] Vnde mihi uidetur hoc tempore solos eos qui se non continent coniugari oportere, secundum illam eiusdem apostoli sententiam: *Quodsi se non continent, nubant; melius est enim nubere quam uri.*[48]

---

[44]   The spirit of optimism at the growth of the Christian Church at this period (*c*.400) is pronounced here. There is a conviction that God 'has subjugated the Roman empire to the worship of his name' (*De consensu euangelistarum* 1. 14. 21); 'The whole world has become a choir praising Christ' (*Enarr. in Ps.* 149. 7). I take these citations from R. A. Markus, *Saeculum: History and Society in the Theology of St Augustine* (Cambridge, 1970), 30; Markus adds that this identification of the Roman order with the Christian in Augustine's mind proves illusory in little more than a decade. As a recommendation that more persons should embrace a life of continence, the argument turns out to be particularly frail.

[45]   I Tim. 1: 5.   [46]   1 Cor. 7: 7.

[47]   1 Cor. 7: 29–34. The phrase 'Et diuisa est mulier innupta et uirgo; quae innupta est . . .' varies from the Vulgate; the same version appears at *De sancta uirginitate* 22 below.

[48]   1 Cor. 7: 9.

intercourse. The good Creator brings good out of these evils, so that crowds of children are not lacking, and large numbers to follow us, from whom blessed friendships can be sought out.

We infer from this that in the early days of the human race it was the duty of the saints to exploit the good of marriage to multiply the people of God, so that through them the Prince and Saviour of all peoples would be predicted in prophecy and then born. It was not to be sought for its own sake, but was necessary for that other purpose. But now, since there is a teeming abundance of spiritual kindred from all nations on every side to enter upon our holy and pure fellowship, even those zealous to be joined in marriage solely to beget children should be urged to embrace the more honourable good of continence instead.[44]

10. But I know what people are murmuring: 'Suppose', they [x] remark, 'that everyone sought to abstain from all intercourse? How would the human race survive?' I only wish that this was everyone's concern so long as it was uttered in charity 'from a pure heart, a good conscience, and faith unfeigned';[45] then the city of God would be filled much more speedily, and the end of the world would be hastened. For what else is the Apostle clearly urging when he says, speaking on this issue: 'Would that all were as I myself am?'[46] Or in that same passage: 'But, brethren, I say this: the time is short; what remains is that those who have wives should behave as if they had none; that those who weep, as though not weeping; and those who rejoice, as though not rejoicing; and those who buy, as though not buying; and those who deal with the world, as though they do not. For the shape of this world is passing away. I want you to be free of anxiety.' Then he adds: 'He who is without a wife gives thought to the things of the Lord, how to please the Lord. But he who is joined in marriage gives thought to worldly things, how to please his wife. The unmarried woman as virgin is set apart; if she is unmarried, she is preoccupied with the things of the Lord, so as to be holy in body and spirit, whereas the married woman is preoccupied with the things of the world, how to please her husband.'[47] So it seems to me that at this time only those who cannot practise continence should marry, in accordance with the dictum of the same Apostle: 'If they do not possess self-control, let them marry, for it is better to marry than to burn.'[48]

* quid *codd., Zycha*: qui *Combès*

11. Nec ipsis tamen peccatum sunt nuptiae quae, si in comparatione fornicationis eligerentur, minus peccatum essent quam fornicatio, sed tamen peccatum essent. Nunc autem quid dicturi sumus aduersus euidentissimam uocem apostoli dicentis: *Quod uult, faciat; non peccat, nubat,** et *Si acceperis uxorem, non peccasti, et si nupserit uirgo, non peccat?*[49] Hinc certe iam dubitare fas non est nuptias non esse peccatum. Non itaque nuptias secundum ueniam concedit apostolus (nam quis ambigat absurdissime dici non eos peccasse, quibus uenia datur?) sed illum concubitum secundum ueniam concedit qui fit per incontinentiam, non sola causa procreandi et aliquando nulla causa procreandi, quem nuptiae non fieri cogunt, sed ignosci impetrant; si tamen non ita sit nimius ut impediat quae seposita esse debent tempora orandi, nec immutetur in eum usum qui est contra naturam, de quo apostolus tacere non potuit, cum de corruptelis nimis[†] immundorum et impiorum hominum loqueretur.[50]

Concubitus enim necessaria causa generandi inculpabilis, et solus ipse nuptialis est. Ille autem qui ultra istam necessitatem progreditur, iam non rationi sed libidini obsequitur. Et hunc tamen non exigere sed reddere coniugi, ne fornicando damnabiliter peccet, ad personam pertinet coniugalem. Si autem ambo tali concupiscentiae subiguntur, rem faciunt non plane nuptiarum. Verumtamen si magis in sua coniunctione diligunt quod honestum quam quod inhonestum est, id est quod nuptiarum quam id quod non est nuptiarum, hoc eis auctore apostolo secundum ueniam conceditur. Cuius delicti non habent hortatrices nuptias sed deprecatrices, si dei misericordiam non a se auertant, uel non abstinendo quibusdam diebus ut orationibus uacent, et per hanc abstinentiam sicut per ieiunia commendent preces suas, uel immutando naturalem usum in eum usum qui est contra naturam, quod damnabilius fit in coniuge.

[XI] 12. Nam cum ille naturalis usus, quando prolabitur ultra pacta nuptialia, id est ultra propagandi necessitatem, uenialis sit in uxore, in meretrice damnabilis, iste qui est contra naturam execrabiliter fit in meretrice, sed execrabilius in uxore. Tantum ualet ordinatio creatoris et ordo creaturae ut in rebus ad utendum concessis, etiam

---

[49] 1 Cor. 7: 36, 28.   [50] Rom. 1: 26f.

* nubat *CPK, Zycha*: si nubat *cett., Combès*
† nimis *CK, Zycha*: nimiis *cett., Combès*

11. However, for these persons marriage is no sin. If it were chosen in preference to fornication, it would be the lesser sin of the two, but none the less a sin. But as things stand, what riposte can we make to those clearest of pronouncements of the Apostle: 'Let her do what she will; she does not sin. Let her marry.' And 'If you take a wife, you have not sinned, and if a virgin marries, she does not sin.'[49] This makes it clear now that it is impious to doubt that marriage is no sin. So the Apostle does not permit marriage as something pardonable (for who could doubt the utter absurdity of claiming that persons granted pardon have not sinned?). Rather, what he permits as pardonable is sexual intercourse indulged through incontinence, without the sole purpose of begetting a child and sometimes without any intention of having one. Marriage does not force this to happen, but it obtains pardon for it, so long as it is not so excessive that it occupies times to be set aside for prayer, or degenerates into unnatural practices; the Apostle could not remain silent about these when he spoke of the corrupt behaviour of unclean and impious men.[50]

The fact is that intercourse necessary for begetting children carries no blame, and it alone is proper to marriage. But the intercourse which goes beyond this necessity is no longer subject to reason, but to lust. However, intrinsic to the character of marriage is the refusal to demand it oneself, but also a willingness to grant it to one's spouse, so that he may not sin mortally through fornication. But if both partners are slaves to such lustfulness, their behaviour is clearly alien to marriage. However, if in their intercourse they love what is honourable more than what is not, in other words what is proper to marriage more than what is not, the Apostle's authority concedes that their behaviour is pardonable. But their marriage excuses rather than encourages this fault—excuses it so long as they do not brush aside God's mercy from them, either by failing to abstain from sex on certain days so as to be free for prayer, and to use such abstinence as a mode of fasting to win approval for their prayers, or by having recourse not to natural practices but to unnatural ones, which are more mortally sinful in a partner in marriage.

12. Whereas the natural exercise of sex in its stealthy progression beyond the marriage-compact, that is, beyond the requirement to beget children, is pardonable in a wife but mortally sinful in a prostitute, the unnatural use of it is abominable in a prostitute, but more abominable still in a wife. The Creator's ordinance and the creature's ordered observance are so binding that it is far more [XI]

cum modus exceditur, longe sit tolerabilius quam in ea quae concessa non sunt uel unus uel rarus excessus. Et ideo in re concessa
immoderatio coniugis, ne in rem non concessam libido prorumpat,
toleranda est. Hinc est etiam quod longe minus peccat quamlibet
assiduus ad uxorem quam uel rarissimus ad fornicationem. Cum
uero uir membro mulieris non ad hoc concesso uti uoluerit, turpior
est uxor si in se quam si in alia fieri permiserit.[51]

Decus ergo coniugale est castitas procreandi et reddendi carnalis
debiti fides; hoc est opus nuptiarum, hoc ab omni crimine defendit
apostolus dicendo: *Et si acceperis uxorem, non peccasti; et si nupserit uirgo,
non peccat*; et *Quod uult faciat; non peccat, nubat.*[52] Exigendi autem
debiti ab alterutro sexu immoderatior progressio propter illa quae
supra dixit coniugibus secundum ueniam conceditur.

13. Quod ergo ait *Quae innupta est, cogitat ea quae sunt domini, ut sit
sancta et corpore et spiritu*,[53] non sic accipiendum est ut putemus non
esse sanctam corpore christianam coniugem castam. Omnibus
quippe fidelibus dictum est: *Nescitis quia corpora uestra templum in uobis
est spiritus sancti quem habetis a deo?*[54] Sancta sunt ergo etiam corpora
coniugatorum fidem sibi et domino seruantium, cui sanctitati
cuiuslibet eorum nec infidelem coniugem obsistere, sed potius sanctitatem uxoris prodesse infideli uiro, aut sanctitatem uiri prodesse
infideli uxori idem apostolus testis est dicens: *Sanctificatus est enim uir
infidelis in uxore, et sanctificata est mulier infidelis in fratre.*[55] Proinde illud
dictum est secundum ampliorem sanctitatem innuptarum quam
nuptarum, cui merces etiam debetur amplior secundum quod isto
bono illud est melius, quia et hoc solum cogitat, quomodo placeat
domino. Neque enim femina fidelis seruans pudicitiam coniugalem
non cogitat quomodo placeat domino, sed utique minus, quia cogitat etiam quae sunt mundi, quomodo placeat uiro. Hoc enim de
illis dicere uoluit, quod possunt habere quodam modo de necessitate conubii ut cogitent quae sunt mundi, quomodo placeant uiris
suis.[56]

---

[51] Augustine presumably has in mind anal and oral sex.   [52] 1 Cor. 7: 28, 36.
[53] 1 Cor. 7: 34.   [54] 1 Cor. 6: 19.
[55] 1 Cor. 7: 14. The phrase 'mulier infidelis in fratre' (differing from the Vulgate's 'mulier
infidelis per uirum fidelem') appears again at *De coniugiis adulterinis* 1. (13) 14, glossed by 'hoc
est, in Christiano'.
[56] 1 Cor. 7: 34.

acceptable even to overstep the limit in what it is permitted to use than to transgress once or occasionally in what is not. So a spouse's lack of self-control in what is permitted is to be tolerated so that lust may not force its way into what is not permitted. So it is also the case that a man sins far less by making any number of approaches to his wife than by even the most occasional recourse to fornication. But when a man seeks to exploit a woman's sexual parts beyond what is granted in this way, a wife behaves more basely if she allows herself rather than another to be used in this way.[51]

Therefore the glory of marriage consists in chaste procreation and fidelity in granting the debts of the flesh. This is the function of marriage, and this is what the Apostle defends from every accusation when he says: 'And if you take a wife, you have not sinned; and if a virgin marries, she does not sin', and 'Let her do what she wishes; she does not sin, let her marry.'[52] But if the partner of either sex makes too importunate advances in demanding the marriage-debt, this is permitted to married couples as pardonable, for the reasons which he gave earlier.

13. So when he says: 'The woman who is unmarried thinks of the things of the Lord, that she may be holy in both body and spirit',[53] this must not be interpreted to make us believe that a chaste Christian wife is not holy in body; for the following words were addressed to all the faithful: 'Do you not know that your bodies are the temple within you of the holy Spirit, whom you have from God?'[54] So the bodies of married couples who preserve fidelity to each other and to the Lord are also holy. That this holiness in one or other of them is not hindered even by an unbelieving partner, but rather that the holiness of a wife is beneficial to an unbelieving husband, or the holiness of a husband is beneficial to an unbelieving wife, is also attested by the Apostle in these words: 'For the unbelieving husband is sanctified in the wife, and the unbelieving woman is sanctified in her brother.'[55] So those earlier words were said with regard to the greater sanctity of the unmarried over married women, and a greater reward is due to the sanctity of the first, in that the second is good but the first is better, for the unmarried woman thinks only of how to please the Lord. Not that the faithful woman who preserves conjugal chastity has no thought of how to please the Lord, but clearly she gives less thought to it because she also ponders earthly things, how to please her husband; for Paul was concerned to say of them that they can in a sense regard it as a necessary feature of marriage to ponder how they are to please their husbands.[56]

[XII]   14. Quod utrum de omnibus nuptis dixerit, an de talibus quales
ita multae sunt ut paene omnes putari possint, non immerito dubi-
tatur. Neque enim et illud quod de innuptis ait, *Quae innupta est, cogi-*
tat ea quae sunt domini, ut sit sancta et corpore et spiritu, ad omnes innuptas
pertinet, cum sint quaedam uiduae mortuae quae in deliciis uiuunt.[57] Verumtamen quod attinet ad quamdam distinctionem et
quasi proprietatem innuptarum atque nuptarum, sicut nimium
detestanda est quae continens a nuptiis, id est a re concessa, non
continet a deliciis uel luxuriae uel superbiae uel curiositatis et uer-
bositatis, ita rara nupta est quae in ipso quoque obsequio coniugali
non cogitat nisi quomodo placeat deo, *ornando se non intortis crinibus*
aut auro et margaritis et ueste pretiosa, sed quod decet mulieres promittentes
pietatem per bonam conuersationem.[58]

Talia quippe coniugia Petrus quoque apostolus praecipiendo
describit. *Similiter* inquit *mulieres obaudientes maritis suis, ut et si qui non*
credunt uerbo per mulieris conuersationem sine loquela lucrifieri possint, uidentes
timorem et castam conuersationem uestram; ut sint non quae a foris ornantur
capillorum incrispationibus aut circumdatae auro aut ueste decora, sed ille
absconditus cordis uestri homo in illa perpetuitate quieti et modesti spiritus, qui
et apud dominum locuples est. Nam sic quaedam sanctae mulieres, quae in
dominum sperabant, ornabant se, obsequentes uiris suis, quomodo Sara
obaudiebat Abrahae dominum illum uocans, cuius factae estis filiae benefacientes
et non timentes ullum uanum timorem. Viri simili ratione concordes et caste
uiuentes cum uxoribus uestris et tamquam uasi infirmiori et subiecto tribuite hon-
orem quasi coheredibus gratiae, et uidete ne impediantur orationes uestrae.[59]
Itane uero coniugia talia non cogitant *ea quae sunt domini, quomodo*
placeant domino? Sed perrara sunt (quis negat?) et in ipsa raritate
paene omnes qui tales sunt non ut tales essent coniuncti sunt, sed
iam coniuncti tales facti sunt.[60]

[XIII]   15. Qui enim nostri temporis homines christiani, nuptialium
uinculo liberi ualentes ab omni concubitu se continere, cum iam
tempus esse perspicerent, sicut scriptum est, *non amplectendi, sed*

---

[57] Echoing 1 Tim. 5.5–6.
[58] 1 Tim. 2: 9 f. The catalogue of women's misdemeanours is traditional, descended from
Juvenal 6 and other antifeminist diatribes. But see n. 105 below.
[59] 1 Pet. 3: 1–7.
[60] Augustine rather crudely seeks to dissuade his readers from embarking on marriage as
a Christian vocation, while at the same time conceding that there were impressive examples
of married couples living Christian lives.

14. Whether his comments refer to all married women, or merely [XII]
to those whose numbers are so great that they can be regarded as virtually all of them, is subject to reasonable doubt. Likewise his statement about the unmarried, 'The woman that is unmarried ponders
the things of the Lord, that she may be holy in both body and spirit',
does not apply to all the unmarried, for there are certain widows
whose lives of luxury make them spiritually dead.[57] However, in
addressing the difference, so to say, between the unmarried and the
married, and what we may call the peculiar character of each, we
observe that just as we must greatly abhor the woman who abstains
from the licit status of marriage but not from the degenerate pleasures of extravagance, or arrogance, or curiosity and gossip, so too
the married woman is a rare species who in addition to the obedience
of married life thinks only of how to please God, 'adorning herself
not with braided hair, gold, pearls, and expensive clothes, but with
good works as is proper for women who profess devotion to God'.[58]

Such marriages as these the apostle Peter also describes when
offering this advice: 'In like manner wives should be obedient to
their husbands, so that even if some husbands do not believe in the
word, they may without discussion profit from association with a
wife when they observe your reverence and chaste behaviour. Do
not be like the women who when outdoors are adorned with hair
curled or with trappings of gold or fine clothes. Rather, let your
adornment be the hidden self within your hearts in the constancy of
a quiet and modest spirit, which is true wealth in the sight of the
Lord. For this was how certain holy women who hoped in the Lord
adorned themselves in obedience to their husbands, as Sara obeyed
Abraham, calling him lord. You have become her daughters when
you do good, and entertain no empty fear. You husbands likewise,
living harmoniously and chastely with your wives, you must both
show honour as to weaker vessels subject to you, since they are your
coheirs in grace, and ensure that your prayers are not hindered.'[59]
So do not such marriages as these 'ponder the things of the Lord,
how they are to please the Lord?' But they are few and far between
(who denies it?), and of these few virtually all did not join in marriage to become like that, but were already married when they
became such.[60]

15. For what Christian men of our day who are free of the mar- [XIII]
riage-bond and are able to discipline themselves from all carnal
intercourse, being aware in scripture's words that now is the time

abstinendi ab amplexu,[61] non potius eligerent uel uirginalem uel uidualem continentiam conseruare quam tribulationem carnis, sine
qua coniugia esse non possunt (ut alia taceantur a quibus parcit
apostolus)[62] nullo iam cogente humanae societatis officio sustinere?
Sed cum dominante concupiscentia fuerint copulati, si eam postea
uicerint, quia non ita licet dissoluere coniugium sicut licebat non
conligare, fiunt tales quales profitetur forma nuptiarum; ita ut uel
pari consensu ascendant celsiorem sanctitatis[63] gradum aut, si non
ambo sunt tales, erit qui talis est non exactor sed redditor debiti,
seruans in omnibus castam religiosamque concordiam.

Illis uero temporibus cum adhuc propheticis sacramentis salutis
nostrae mysterium uelabatur, etiam qui ante nuptias tales erant[64]
officio propagandi nuptias copulabant, non uicti libidine sed ducti
pietate; quibus si optio talis daretur, qualis reuelato nouo testamento data est, dicente domino *Qui potest capere, capiat*,[65] non eos
dubitat etiam cum gaudio suscepturos fuisse, qui diligenter intentus
legit quomodo coniugibus utebantur, cum et plures habere uni uiro
licebat, quas castius habebat quam nunc unam quilibet istorum
quibus uidemus quid secundum ueniam concedat apostolus.
Habebant enim eas in opere generandi, *non in morbo desiderii, sicut
gentes quae ignorant deum*.[66] Quod tam magnum est ut multi hodie
facilius se tota uita ab omni concubitu abstineant quam modum
teneant non coeundi nisi prolis causa, si matrimonio copulentur.
Nempe multos habemus fratres et socios caelestis hereditatis
utriusque sexus continentes, siue expertos nuptias siue ab omni tali
commixtione integros; nempe innumerabiles sunt.[67] Quem tandem
audiuimus inter familiaria colloquia siue eorum qui coniugati sunt

---

[61] Eccle. 3: 5.

[62] Cf. 1 Cor. 7: 28. Ambrose's disquisition on the trials of married life (*De uirginibus* I.
6. 25 ff.), and Jerome's celebrated diatribe on the discomforts of marriage (*Against Helvidius* 20)
are doubtless in Augustine's mind.

[63] Augustine thinks of such married couples as Paulinus of Nola and Therasia, who had
recently (AD 395) arrived at Nola to live a monastic life as brother and sister.

[64] That is, favouring a life of sexual abstinence.

[65] Matt. 19: 12, with reference to those who embrace celibacy.

[66] 1 Thess. 4: 5, Here and later in the treatise, Augustine idealizes the sexual behaviour of
the patriarchs and their wives, partly to counter the arguments of Jovinian and partly to
defend them against the taunts of the Manichaeans; see Introd., p. xix.

[67] This is an indication that already by 401 Augustine had established thriving monastic
communities of both sexes in his diocese of Hippo. The first notice of monastic life in Africa
is given by the Council of Carthage in 397. One monastery for men was built on ground
bequeathed by Augustine's predecessor as bishop, Valerius (*Serm.* 355. 2). Augustine set up
another in his own house, and two more near Hippo (Serm 356. 10, 15). *Ep.* 210 ('To Felicitas,

'not for embracing, but for abstaining from embraces',[61] would not choose rather to maintain the continence of the virgin or the widow than to endure that tribulation of the flesh from which no marriages can be exempt (to say nothing of other pains which the Apostle refrains from mentioning),[62] now that no obligation to the human community compels it? But once the lusting of the flesh comes over them and they marry, suppose they subsequently control that urge; since they have not the option of dissolving the marriage as they had the option of not marrying, they become what the status of marriage proclaims them to be. Thus they either by mutual agreement attain a higher level of holiness,[63] or if both are not of this persuasion, the one who is will not demand the debt of marriage, but will grant it, preserving throughout a chaste and devoted harmony with the other.

But in the days of old when the mystery of our salvation was as yet cloaked in the sacred signs of prophecy, even those who were of that mind before marrying[64] contracted a marriage for the obligation of begetting children. They were not overcome by lust but were constrained by devotion. If offered the choice such as was given in the revelation of the New Testament by the Lord's words 'Let anyone accept this who can',[65] they would have embraced it with joy; no one, if he reads with careful attention how they treated their wives at the time when a husband could have several, doubts this, for the husband had more chaste relations with them than any of our contemporaries treats his one wife nowadays, as we observe the concession which the Apostle makes to them by way of pardoning them. For those men of old married wives for the task of begetting children, and 'not in the disease of lust, like the Gentiles who do not know God'.[66] This issue looms so large that many today observe life-long abstinence from all sexual intercourse more readily than restrict themselves to sexual intercourse solely for begetting children, should they be joined in marriage. Indeed, we have many brethren and associates of both sexes sharing our inheritance of heaven who observe continence. They have either had a taste of marriage or no experience of any such intercourse; their number indeed is beyond counting.[67] Yet in friendly conversation with

brother Rusticus, and the Sisters') and *Ep.* 211 (the famous source of Augustine's monastic Rule) provide detail of the conventual life of women. When he died in 430, Augustine left 'a sufficient body of clergy and monasteries of men and women' (Possidius, *Vita* 31). See J. H. Baxter, *St Augustine, Select Letters* (Loeb edn., London, 1930), 368 n., 374 n.

siue qui fuerunt, indicantem nobis nunquam se coniugi esse com-
mixtum nisi sperando conceptum? Quod ergo praecipiunt coniugatis apostoli, hoc est nuptiarum; quod autem uenialiter concedunt
aut quod impedit orationes, non cogunt nuptiae sed ferunt.

[XIV]   16. Itaque si forte (quod utrum fieri possit ignoro, magisque fieri
non posse existimo) sed tamen, si forte ad tempus adhibita concu-
bina filios solos ex eadem commixtione quaesiuerit, nec sic ista
coniunctio uel earum nuptiis praeponenda est quae ueniale illud
operantur. Quid enim sit nuptiarum considerandum est, non quid
sit nubentium et immoderatius nuptiis utentium. Neque enim si
agris inique ac perperam inuasis ita quisque utatur ut ex eorum
fructibus largas elemosynas faciat, ideo rapinam iustificat; neque si
alius ruri paterno uel iuste quaesito auarus incumbat, ideo cul-
panda est iuris ciuilis regula, qua possessor legitimus factus est. Nec
tyrannicae factionis peruersitas laudabilis erit, si regia clementia
tyrannus subditos tractet; nec uituperabilis ordo regiae potestatis, si
rex crudelitate tyrannica saeuiat. Aliud est namque iniusta potestate iuste uelle uti, et aliud est iusta potestate iniuste uti. Ita nec con-
cubinae ad tempus adhibitae, si filiorum causa concumbant,
iustum faciunt concubinatum suum, nec coniugatae, si cum maritis
lasciuiant, nuptiali ordini crimen imponunt.[68]

[XV]   17. Posse sane fieri nuptias ex male coniunctis honesto postea
placito consequente manifestum est. Semel autem initum conubium* in ciuitate dei nostri, ubi etiam ex prima duorum hominum
copula quoddam sacramentum nuptiae gerunt, nullo modo potest
nisi alicuius eorum morte dissolui. Manet enim uinculum nuptiarum etiamsi proles, cuius causa initum est, manifesta sterilitate
non subsequatur, ita ut iam scientibus coniugibus non se filios
habituros separare se tamen uel ipsa causa filiorum atque aliis copulare non liceat. Quod si fecerint, cum eis quibus se copulauerint
adulterium committunt; ipsi autem coniuges manent.[69]

[68] Throughout this paragraph, Augustine is concerned to distinguish between the good of
marriage as institution (even when exploited for ends other than procreation) and the evil of
concubinage (even when practised solely for procreation). The analogy of the illegal and the
rightful owners of estates is well conceived. But the contrast between king and tyrant seems
hardly relevant to the age of Augustine; he may have recalled Cicero's contrast (*Republic*
2. 12–51) between the benevolent monarchy of Rome's earlier kings and the tyranny of Tar-
quinius Superbus.
[69] Thus the *sacramentum*, which in its traditional sense at Rome was an oath of allegiance,
binds the couple in lifelong union and marital fidelity.

---

     * conubium *cett.*, *Zycha*: concubitum *C*

people now or previously married, have we heard any one of them telling us that they have never had intercourse with their partner except in the hope of conceiving a child? So what the apostles recommend to married people is of the essence of marriage; but what they allow as pardonable, or what hinders their prayers, is not enforced but tolerated by the married state.

16. Therefore (I do not know if this can happen, and I rather [XIV] think that it cannot), still, if a man takes a concubine for the time being and indulges in intercourse solely to beget children, such a relationship even as this is not to be preferred to marriages with wives who practise the intercourse which gains pardon. For we must focus on the nature of marriage, not on the character of women who marry and exploit marriage too licentiously. Suppose one of us has unjustly and culpably taken over an estate, and from the harvest there donates substantial alms; he cannot thereby justify the seizure. Or supposing that another man in miserly fashion sits tight on an estate inherited or justly obtained; the process of civil law by which he became the lawful owner is not to be blamed on that account. Again, the criminal behaviour of a tyrant's clique will not merit praise if the tyrant treats his subjects with the clemency shown by a king, nor is the status of kingly power blameworthy if a king rages with the cruelty of a tyrant. For it is one thing to seek to use unlawful power justly, and another to use lawful power unjustly. It is the same with the temporary possession of concubines: even if they have intercourse to produce children, it does not make their concubinage lawful. On the other hand, even if wives play the wanton with their husbands, that does not put a stigma on the status of marriage.[68]

17. Clearly a couple in an illicit relationship can be married if an honourable decision is taken later. But in the city of our God, once [XV] a marriage has been contracted, it can in no way be dissolved except by the death of one of them, because from the initial union of the two persons the marriage bears a sacramental character. For the bond of marriage remains even if the offspring for which the marriage was contracted is not forthcoming because of evident sterility. In consequence, even though the partners now realize that they will not have children, it is not permitted to separate and to have intercourse with others, even to have children. Should they do so, they commit adultery with those with whom they have sex, while they themselves remain man and wife.[69]

Plane uxoris uoluntate adhibere aliam, unde communes filii nascantur unius commixtione ac semine, alterius autem iure ac potestate, apud antiquos patres fas erat; utrum et nunc fas sit non temere dixerim. Non est enim propagandi necessitas quae tunc fuit, quando et parientibus coniugibus alias propter copiosiorem poster- itatem superducere licebat, quod nunc certe non licet. Nam tantum adfert oportunitatis ad aliquid iuste agendum seu non agendum temporum secreta distinctio ut nunc melius faciat qui nec unam duxerit, nisi se continere non possit. Tunc autem etiam plures inculpabiter ducebant et qui se multo facilius continere possent, nisi aliud pietas illo tempore postularet.

Sicut enim sapiens et iustus, qui iam concupiscit *dissolui et esse cum Christo*,[70] et hoc magis optimo delectatur, non iam hic uiuendi cupiditate sed consulendi officio sumit alimentum ut maneat in carne, quod necessarium est propter alios, sic misceri feminis iure nuptiarum officiosum fuit tunc sanctis uiris, non libidinosum.

[XVI]   18. Quod enim est cibus ad salutem hominis, hoc est concubitus ad salutem generis, et utrumque non est sine delecta- tione carnali, quae tamen modificata et temperantia refrenante in usum naturalem redacta libido esse non potest.[71] Quod est autem in sustentanda uita illicitus cibus, hoc est in quaerenda prole fornicarius uel adulterinus concubitus; et quod est in luxuria uentris et gutturis illicitus cibus, hoc est in libidine nullam prolem quaerente illicitus concubitus; et quod est in cibo licito nonnullis immoderatior appetitus, hoc est in coniugibus uenialis ille con- cubitus. Sicut ergo satius est emori fame quam idolothytis uesci,[72] ita satius est defungi sine liberis quam ex illicito coitu stirpem quaerere.

Vndecumque autem nascantur homines, si parentum uitia non sectentur et deum recte colant, honesti et salui erunt. Semen enim hominis ex qualicumque homine dei creatura est, et eo male uten- tibus male erit, non ipsum aliquando malum erit. Sicut autem filii

---

[70] 'The wise and just man' is St Paul; the citation is from Phil. 1: 23. The sentence that fol- lows further paraphrases Paul's observations in that passage.

[71] This passage is echoed in Augustine's *Retractationes*; see Appendix 1. The analogy that the sexual act is intended for procreation as the act of eating is for life's preservation becomes familiar in the later history of Christian ethics.

[72] To eat the meat of animals sacrificed to idols was regarded by early Christians as tanta- mount to worship of the deities; hence Paul's warning at 1 Cor. 8 against the practice.

Obviously among the fathers of old a man with the consent of his wife was allowed to take another woman, so that children could be born for them to share from the intercourse and seed of the husband, and the discretion and consent of the wife. Whether this is permissible also today I should not care to claim offhand, for the need to bear children which existed then no longer applies. At that time, even when wives bore children, it was permissible to marry others as well to ensure a greater number of descendants, but this is certainly not licit today. The interval which separates our eras brings such discretion to act rightly or otherwise that nowadays the man who does not take even one wife acts for the better unless he cannot control himself. But in those early days even those who could have controlled themselves much more easily if their devotion at that time had not demanded otherwise, took a number of wives without blame.

Take the example of the wise and just man who longs very much 'to leave this life and be with Christ'.[70] He takes delight in this as the best prospect, but he takes food to remain in the flesh, not out of a desire to live in the here and now, but because of the obligation to look to others' needs. Similarly it was the sense of obligation and not lust impelling holy men of that time to have sexual intercourse with women within the lawful bond of marriage.

18. For as food is to the health of the individual, so sexual intercourse is to the health of the nation. Each is not without its physical pleasure, but if restrained and confined to natural use by the controlling reins of temperance, it cannot be lust.[71] But just as there is food which is unlawful for sustaining life, so fornication or adultery is illicit in the furtherance of offspring. Analogous to the food which is unlawful in pandering to the belly and throat is the illicit intercourse sought in lust without any offspring in view; and the more undisciplined appetite shown by some in taking lawful food has its equivalent in the pardonable intercourse in which married couples indulge. So just as it is better to die of hunger than to eat the food set before idols,[72] so it is better to die childless than to seek offspring from unlawful intercourse. [XVI]

But whatever the source from which individuals are born, so long as they do not imitate the vices of their parents and observe due worship of God, they will gain both honour and salvation. For the human seed which comes from each and every man is God's creation. It will go ill with those who abuse it, but in itself at no time will be evil. Just as the children of adulterers who are good do not justify acts of adultery, so wicked children of married couples are no

boni adulterorum nulla defensio est adulteriorum, sic mali filii
coniugatorum nullum crimen est nuptiarum. Proinde sicut patres
temporis noui testamenti ex officio consulendi alimenta sumentes,
quamuis ea cum delectatione naturali carnis acciperent, nullo
modo tamen comparabantur delectationi eorum qui immolaticio
uescebantur, aut eorum qui quamuis licitas escas tamen immoderatius absumebant, sic patres temporis ueteris testamenti consulendi
officio concumbebant, quorum delectatio illa naturalis nequaquam
usque ad irrationalem aut nefariam libidinem relaxata nec turpitu-
dini stuprorum nec coniugatorum intemperantiae conferenda est.
Eadem quippe uena caritatis nunc spiritaliter, tunc carnaliter,
propter illam matrem Hierusalem propagandi erant filii;[73] sed
diuersa opera patrum non faciebat nisi diuersitas temporum. Sic
autem necesse erat ut carnaliter coirent etiam non carnales
prophetae, sicut necesse erat ut carnaliter uescerentur etiam non
carnales apostoli.

[XVII]   19. Quotquot ergo nunc sunt quibus dicitur *Si se non continent,
nubant,* non comparandae sunt tunc etiam nubentibus sanctis. Ipsae
quidem nuptiae in omnibus gentibus eadem sunt filiorum procreandorum causa, qui qualeslibet postea fuerint, ad hoc tamen
institutae sunt nuptiae ut ordinate honesteque nascantur. Sed
homines qui se non continent tamquam ascendunt in nuptias gradu
honestatis; qui autem se sine dubio continerent, si hoc illius temporis ratio permisisset, quodam modo descenderunt in nuptias gradu
pietatis, ac per hoc quamuis utrorumque nuptiae, in quantum nuptiae sunt quia procreandi causa sunt, aequaliter bonae sint, hi
tamen homines coniugati illis hominibus coniugatis non sunt comparandi. Habent enim isti quod illis propter honestatem nuptiarum, quamuis ad nuptias non pertineat, secundum ueniam
concedatur, id est progressum illum qui excedit generandi necessitatem quod illi non habebant. Sed neque hi, si qui forte nunc inueniuntur, qui non quaerunt in conubio nec appetunt nisi propter
quod institutae sunt nuptiae, coaequari possunt illis hominibus. In
istis enim carnale est ipsum desiderium filiorum, in illis autem
spiritale erat, quia sacramento illius temporis congruebat. Nunc
quippe nullus pietate perfectus filios habere nisi spiritaliter

---

[73] Jerusalem signifies the city of God in this world (and heaven in the next) as Babylon
symbolizes the unconverted world.

indictment of marriage. So too with the fathers of the eras of the New Testament and the Old. Those of the New took food from a sense of duty to consult others' interests; though they consumed it with natural physical pleasure, they are in no way comparable to those who delighted in feasting on food set before idols, or to those who though feasting on lawful food consumed it too intemperately. In the same way the fathers of the Old Testament indulged in intercourse because of their obligation to consult the interests of others. The natural pleasure which they enjoyed certainly did not degenerate into unreasoning or depraved lust, and is not to be compared with foul debauchery or with the lack of discipline of married couples. In fact it was by the same channel of charity that children were to be born for our glorious mother Jerusalem;[73] then it was according to the flesh, but now according to the spirit, but it was merely the difference between eras that made the procedure of the fathers different. Thus it was necessary that the prophets, though not men of the flesh, should have intercourse of the flesh, just as the apostles likewise, though not men of the flesh, should eat food of the flesh.

19. So all the women of today, who are told that if they fail to [xvii] control themselves they should marry, are not to be compared with the holy women of old who were also married. Marriage exists among all nations for the same purpose of begetting children, and however they turn out later, marriage was established so that they would be born with due order and honour. But men who lack self-control mount upwards into marriage, so to say, by the ladder of the honourable, whereas the men of old, who would undoubtedly have controlled themselves had the rationale of the time allowed it, climbed down, so to say, into marriage by the ladder of devotion. Accordingly though the marriages of both, in so far as they are marriages established to beget children are equally good, yet married men of today are not to be compared with those married men of old. For men today, because of the honourable status of marriage, are allowed as pardonable indulgence (though it is not of the essence of marriage) that extended use of sex which goes beyond the necessity to beget children, an indulgence which the men of old did not have. Yet even the men of today (if any chance to be found) who in marriage seek and desire only that end for which marriage was instituted cannot be equated with those men of old; for in modern man the very desire for children lies in the flesh, whereas in those earlier men it lay in the spirit, for it accorded with the sacred

quaerit;[74] tunc uero ipsius pietatis erat operatio etiam carnaliter
filios propagare, quia illius populi generatio nuntia futurorum erat
et ad dispensationem propheticam pertinebat.

20. Ideoque non sicut uni uiro etiam plures habere licebat uxores,
ita uni feminae plures uiros nec prolis ipsius causa, si forte illa parere
posset, ille generare non posset. Occulta enim lege naturae amant
singularitatem quae principantur; subiecta uero non solum singula
singulis sed, si ratio naturalis uel socialis admittit, etiam plura uni
non sine decore subduntur. Neque enim sic habet unus seruus
plures dominos, quomodo plures serui unum dominum. Ita duobus
seu pluribus maritis uiuis nullam legimus seruisse sanctarum; plures
autem feminas uni uiro legimus, cum gentis illius societas sinebat et
temporis ratio suadebat; neque enim contra naturam nuptiarum
est. Plures enim feminae ab uno uiro fetari possunt, una uero a
pluribus non potest (haec est principiorum uis), sicut multae animae
uni deo recte subduntur. Ideoque non est uerus deus animarum nisi
unus; una uero anima per multos falsos deos fornicari potest, non
fecundari.[75]

[XVIII]   21. Sed quoniam ex multis animis una ciuitas futura est haben-
tium *animam unam et cor unum* in deum, quae unitatis nostrae perfectio post hanc peregrinationem futura est, ubi omnium cogitationes
nec latebunt inuicem nec inter se in aliquo repugnabunt,[76]
propterea sacramentum nuptiarum temporis nostri sic ad unum
uirum et unam uxorem redactum est, ut ecclesiae dispensatorem
non liceat ordinari nisi unius uxoris uirum, quod acutius
intellexerunt qui nec eum qui catechumenus uel paganus habuerit
alteram ordinandum esse censuerunt.[77] De sacramento enim agitur, non de peccato. Nam in baptismo peccata omnia dimittuntur,

[74] That is, by welcoming them into the Church at baptism.

[75] The earlier part of this section, in which wives are linked with slaves as naturally subordinate to husbands and lords, derives from scriptural authority (1 Peter 2: 18ff.) and from the
traditional Greek analysis of the household as in Book I of Aristotle's *Politics*. Though in his
conception of marriage Augustine seeks to emancipate women from this subordinate role, he
never shakes off this philosophical influence. It is tellingly exposed in this final sentence, in
which the wife's relation to the husband is compared with the soul's subjection to God (the
image of fornication with false gods is a striking innovation).

[76] The citation is from Acts 4: 32. Augustine develops the notion of 'the one city' in *The City
of God*, which in the world to come will be the new Jerusalem, a name which means 'City of
Peace' or 'Vision of Peace'. See Brown, *Augustine of Hippo*, ch. 21.

[77] Cf. 1 Tim. 3: 2, Tit. 1: 6. These Pauline passages provided the basis for the rule in both
East and West that a man twice married could not be ordained priest. But the Eastern
Church did not take into account any marriage entered upon before baptism, whereas

mystery of that time. Whereas today no one of exemplary devotion seeks to have children except spiritually,[74] in those days the role of that very devotion was to beget children physically, for the procreation of that people was the harbinger of the future, relating to the dispensation which was prophesied.

20. So though it was possible for one man to have several wives, it was not similarly permitted for one woman to have several husbands, even to give birth to children if it so happened that she could bear them and her husband could not father them. By nature's hidden law, things which dominate love to be unique, whereas not inappropriately those which lie below them are subordinated, not merely as one to one, but as several to one, should natural or communal logic allow it. One slave does not have several masters, as several slaves have one master. Similarly we read that none of the holy women served two or more living husbands, whereas we do read that one husband had several wives when the social structure of the nation allowed it and the condition of the time demanded it, for this is not contrary to the nature of marriage. Several women can be made pregnant by one man, but one woman cannot become plurally pregnant by a number of men. Such is the power of the dominant elements. Similarly, many souls are properly subject to the one God. This is why souls have only one true God; a soul can indeed commit fornication with many false gods, but it cannot be made fruitful.[75]

21. In the future, the one city will be composed of many souls who [XVIII] have 'one soul and one heart' in God, and after this earthly pilgrimage it will be the perfection of our unity, in which all men's thoughts will not be hidden from each other, and will in no way be opposed to each other.[76] For this reason the sacrament of marriage has in our time been reduced to one husband and one wife, so that it is not possible for a man to be ordained minister of the Church if he has had more than one wife. This has been more clearly understood by those who have decreed that a man who as catechumen or pagan had a second wife, should not be ordained.[77] The concern here is with the sacrament, not with sinning. In baptism all sins are forgiven, but he who said 'If you have taken a wife, you have not sinned, and if a virgin marries, she does not sin', and 'Let her do

Ambrose (De officiis 1. 247; Ep. 63. 63) maintained that two marriages at any earlier stage in life were a bar to ordination. Jerome (Ep. 69) accepted the view of the Eastern Church; Augustine sided with Ambrose, and their ruling became the norm in the West. See Homes Dudden, Saint Ambrose, 125.

sed qui dixit *Si acceperis uxorem, non peccasti, et si nupserit uirgo, non peccat, et Quod uult faciat, non peccat, nubat,*[78] satis declarauit nuptias nullum esse peccatum. Propter sacramenti autem sanctitatem sicut femina, etiamsi catechumena fuerit, uitiata non potest post baptismum inter dei uirgines consecrari, ita non absurde uisum est eum qui excessit uxorum numerum singularem non peccatum aliquod commisisse, sed normam quamdam sacramenti amisisse, non ad uitae bonae meritum sed ad ordinationis ecclesiasticae signaculum necessariam. Ac per hoc sicut plures uxores antiquorum patrum significauerunt futuras nostras ex omnibus gentibus ecclesias uni uiro subditas Christo, ita noster antistes unius uxoris uir significat ex omnibus gentibus unitatem uni uiro subditam Christo, quae tunc perficietur cum *reuelauerit occulta tenebrarum et manifestauerit cogitationes** *cordis, ut tunc laus sit unicuique a deo.*[79] Nunc autem sunt manifestae, sunt latentes dissensiones, etiam salua caritate, inter eos qui unum et in uno futuri sunt; quae tunc utique nullae erunt. Sicut ergo sacramentum pluralium nuptiarum illius temporis significauit futuram multitudinem deo subiectam in terrenis omnibus gentibus, sic sacramentum nuptiarum singularum nostri temporis significat unitatem omnium nostrum subiectam deo futuram in una caelesti ciuitate.

Itaque sicut duobus pluribusue seruire, sic a uiuo uiro in alterius transire conubium nec tunc licuit nec nunc licet nec unquam licebit. Apostatare quippe ab uno deo et ire in alterius adulterinam superstitionem semper est malum. Nec causa ergo numerosioris prolis fecerunt sancti nostri quod Cato dicitur fecisse Romanus ut traderet uiuus uxorem etiam alterius domum filiis impleturam.[80] In nostrarum quippe nuptiis plus ualet sanctitas sacramenti quam fecunditas uteri.

22. Si ergo et illi, qui propter solam generationem propter quam sunt institutae nuptiae, coniunguntur, non comparantur patribus multo aliter ipsos filios quam isti quaerentibus (quandoquidem filium immolare iussus Abraham intrepidus ac deuotus, quem de tanta desperatione susceperat unico non peperit, nisi eo prohibente [XIX] manum deponeret, quo iubente leuauerat),[81] restat ut uideamus utrum saltem continentes nostri coniugatis illis patribus comparandi

[78] 1 Cor. 7: 28, 36.   [79] 1 Cor. 4: 5.   [80] Cf. Plutarch, *Cato Minor* 25.
[81] Cf. Gen 22: 1 ff.

* cogitationes *cett., Combès*; occulta *C, Zycha*

what she wishes; she does not sin, let her marry',[78] made it sufficiently clear that marriage is no sin. Now to ensure the sacred nature of the sacrament, a woman who has lost her virginity, even if she is a catechumen, cannot after baptism be consecrated among the virgins of God. So similarly it has not seemed out of place that a man who has had more than one wife, though not having committed any sin, has not observed the norm, so to say, of the sacrament, which was required not to gain the reward of a good life, but for the seal of ecclesiastical ordination. Thus just as the plurality of wives of the fathers of old was a sign that there would be churches drawn from all nations made subject to their one husband Christ, so our bishop as husband of one wife signifies the unity of all nations made subject to Christ as their one husband. This will be brought to pass when 'he reveals the things hidden in darkness and discloses the purposes of the heart, so that each may then receive commendation from God'.[79] But at present there are both open and hidden disagreements, even when charity is maintained, amongst those who will later be one and in one; these dissensions will certainly not exist then. So just as the sacrament of marriage with more than one wife in those earlier days was a sign of the great number who would be subject to God in all the nations of the earth, so the sacrament of marriage with one spouse in our own day is a sign of the unity of all of us which is to be made subject to God in the one city of heaven.

Hence passing from one husband still living to marriage with another, the equivalent of serving two or more masters, was not permissible then, is not now, and never shall be; for to apostasize from the one God, and to indulge in adulterous superstition by worshipping another, is always evil. So our holy men did not even for the sake of more numerous offspring do what the Roman Cato is said to have done, namely to pass his wife while he was still alive over to fill the house of another with children;[80] for in the marriages of our Christian women the sanctity of the sacrament takes precedence over the fertility of the womb.

22. So even those who marry to have offspring, the sole purpose for which marriage was established, do not compare with the fathers of old, whose motive in seeking to have children differed so much from that of men today. (Think of Abraham; when bidden to sacrifice his son, in fearless devotion he was not for sparing his only child, obtained after such great despair; only when God vetoed it did he lower the hand raised at His command.[81]) In view of this, it

sint; nisi forte iam isti praeferendi sunt eis quibus nondum quos con-
feramus inuenimus. Maius enim bonum erat in illorum nuptiis
quam est bonum proprium nuptiarum, cui procul dubio bonum
continentiae praeferendum est, quia non tali officio quaerebant illi
filios ex nuptiis, quali ducuntur isti ex quodam sensu naturae mortalis successionem decessioni requirentis. Quod quisquis bonum
negat, ignorat deum omnium bonorum a caelestibus usque ad terrena, ab immortalibus usque ad mortalia creatorem. Hoc autem
sensu generandi nec bestiae penitus carent et maxime alites, quarum
in promptu est cura nidificandi et quaedam coniugiorum similitudo
ad simul procreandum atque nutriendum.

Sed illi homines istum naturae mortalis adfectum, cuius in suo
genere castitas accedente dei cultu, sicut quidam intellexerunt, in
tricenario fructu ponitur,[82] longe sanctiore mente superabant, qui
de suis nuptiis filios propter Christum quaerebant ad genus eius
secundum carnem distinguendum ab omnibus gentibus, sicut deo
disponere placuit, ut hoc prae ceteris ad eum prophetandum
ualeret quod praenuntiabatur, ex quo etiam genere et ex qua gente
esset in carne uenturus. Valde ergo nostrorum fidelium castis nuptiis amplius bonum erat, quod pater Abraham in suo femore
nouerat, cui manum subdere famulum iussit ut de uxore quae a filio
esset ducenda iuraret.[83] Ponens enim manum sub femore hominis
et iurans per deum caeli, quid aliud significabat nisi in ea carne,
quae ex illo femore originem duceret, deum caeli esse uenturum?
Bonum ergo sunt nuptiae in quibus tanto meliores sunt coniugati
quanto castiores et fideliores deum timent, maxime si filios quos
carnaliter desiderant etiam spiritaliter nutriant.

23. Nec quod purificari lex hominem et post coniugalem concubitum iubet, peccatum esse declarat, si non est ille qui secundum
ueniam conceditur, qui etiam nimius impedit orationes.[84] Sed sicut
multa lex ponit in sacramentis et umbris futurorum, quaedam in
semine quasi materialis informitas, quae formata corpus hominis

---

[82] The parable of the sower (Matt. 13. 3 ff.), in which different soils yield different levels of
fruit, was lent an allegorical interpretation by the Fathers; see *De sancta uirginitate* [XLV] 46
(and n.), where one such interpretation equates chastity in Christian marriage with the yield
of thirtyfold.

[83] Cf. Gen. 24: 2 ff.

[84] This chapter rebuts the Manichaeans' claim that the Jewish ceremony of purification
after sexual intercourse indicates the sinfulness of the sexual act. Augustine's gloss on the
passage (Lev. 15: 2 ff.) applies Paul's two qualifications to the approval of sexual intercourse at
1 Cor. 7: 5 f.

remains for us to consider whether the continent if no others among [XIX]
us can be compared with the fathers of old—unless perhaps they
are already to be ranked above them, though we have not as yet
found any to compare with them! For the good which lay in the
marriages of those earlier men was greater than the good which is
proper to marriage (to which the good of continence is undoubtedly
to be preferred). The reason for this is that those men did not seek
children from marriage with the sense of obligation which moti-
vates men today, an obligation arising from a recognition of their
mortal nature, which demands that some succession will follow
their departure. Whoever says that this is not good has no knowledge of God, the Creator of all goods from those in heaven to those
on earth, from things immortal to things mortal. This instinct for
begetting is not lacking even in the brute beasts, and notably in the
birds, whose diligence in nesting and whose approximation to the
married state in both begetting and rearing is plain to see.

But the men of old with far holier intention transcended this attitude of mortal nature, whose chastity of its own kind when rein-
forced by worship of God has been recognized by some as bearing
fruit thirtyfold.[82] For those men of old sought children from their
marriages for Christ's sake, in order to differentiate his fleshly stock
from all nations. This was how it pleased God to ordain, that fore-
telling from what stock and what race he would come in the flesh
would take precedence over all else in prophesying him. So that was
a good, much greater than the chaste marriages of our believers
today, which father Abraham recognized in his thigh, when he
ordered his servant to place his hand under it to swear an oath
about the wife which his son was to marry.[83] For by placing a hand
under a man's thigh and swearing by God in heaven, he signified
nothing other than that the God of heaven would come in the flesh
which originated from that thigh. So marriage is a good, and the
spouses in it are the better as they fear God with greater chastity and
fidelity, especially if they nurture also in the spirit the children which
they desire in the flesh.

23. Again, the fact that the Law orders a man to be purified after
intercourse even with his wife does not pronounce it to be a sin,
unless it is intercourse allowed as pardonable, and which when
excessive hinders prayers.[84] But like many things which the Law
denotes as sacred symbols foreshadowing future events, any
absence of material shape in the seed, which when lent shape will

redditura est, in significatione posita est uitae informis et inerudi-
tae; a qua informitate quoniam oportet hominem doctrinae forma
et eruditione mundari, in huius rei signum illa purificatio praecepta
est post seminis emissionem.[85] Neque enim et in somnis peccato fit;
et tamen etiam ibi praecepta est purificatio. Aut si et hoc peccatum
quisquam putat, non arbitrans accidere nisi ex aliquo huius modi
desiderio, quod procul dubio falsum est,[86] numquid et solita men-
suum peccata sunt feminarum? A quibus tamen eas eadem legis
uetustas praecepit expiari, non nisi propter ipsam materialem
informitatem, quae facto concepto tamquam in aedificationem
corporis additur. Ac per hoc cum informiter fluit, significari per
illam lex uoluit animum sine disciplinae forma indecenter fluidum
ac dissolutum, quem formari oportere significat,[87] cum talem
fluxum corporis iubet purificari. Postremo numquid et mori peccatum est, aut mortuum sepelire non etiam bonum opus humanitatis
est? Et tamen purificatio et inde mandata est, quia et mortuum corpus uita deserente non peccatum est, sed peccatum significat animae desertae a iustitia.[88]

[xx]   24. Bonum, inquam, sunt nuptiae, et contra omnes calumnias
possunt sana ratione defendi. Nuptiis tamen sanctorum patrum
non quas nuptias sed quam continentiam comparem quaero, immo
non nuptiae nuptiis (nam par in omnibus munus est mortali
hominum naturae datum), sed homines qui nuptiis utuntur illis
hominibus qui longe aliter nuptiis usi sunt quos confero quoniam
non inuenio, quinam continentes illis coniugatis conferendi sint
requirendum est—nisi forte Abraham continere se non posset a
nuptiis propter regnum caelorum, qui unicum prolis pignus,
propter quod nuptiae carae sunt, potuit intrepidus immolare
propter regnum caelorum!

[85] Augustine's ingenious explanation, that the post-coital cleansing symbolizes prepar-
ation for the future development of the body and mind of the foetus, is less likely than that the
'wasting' of the semen, visualized as the life-force, demanded purification; the regulation
specifies the cleansing of semen not implanted in the woman but present on the bed or clothing or persons concerned. See P. J. Budd, *The New Century Bible: Leviticus* (London, 1996);
J. Milgrom, *Leviticus 1–16* (Garden City, NY, 1991).

[86] Augustine robustly dismisses the suggestion that involuntary emission in sleep (as distinct from masturbation) is sinful. He mentions it, perhaps drawing on his own experiences,
because of the cleansing demanded at Lev. 15: 16f. See O'Donnell on *Conf.* 10. 30. 41.

[87] In Leviticus, the regulation about cleansing in menstruation follows immediately after
cleansing after intercourse (15: 19–24). The '*impurity*' lasts for seven days, and washing of
clothing and the body is prescribed. Intercourse during menstruation is forbidden (Lev. 18:
19). Augustine offers a justification for ritual cleansing similar to that for emission of semen.

form a human body, is made to signify a life lacking form and schooling. From this formless state man must be cleansed by the shape and education imparted by learning, and so to indicate this, that purification was prescribed after the emission of seed.[85] That emission does not become sinful in sleep either, yet purification is prescribed in those circumstances as well. But should anyone regard this too as sinful, in the belief that it occurs only following a voluntary impulse of this kind (a belief undoubtedly mistaken),[86] are then the regular monthly periods of women also sins? Yet that same ancient Law commanded that women be purified after them, the sole reason adduced being that absence of material shape which when conception occurs is incorporated into the growth of the body. And since the flow is shapeless, the Law intended that this should signify a lack of disciplined shape of the mind, being unfittingly fluid and loose; and when the Law prescribes that such an outflow from the body be purified, it signifies that it must be given shape.[87] And a final example: death is surely not a sin, and is not the burial of a dead person also a good work of human kindness? Yet purification was enjoined for this too, on the grounds that when life quits a dead body there is no sin, but it denotes the sin of the soul abandoned by righteousness.[88]

24. Marriage, I repeat, is a good, and can be defended by sound [xx] reasoning against all calumnies. As for the marriages of the holy fathers, what I look for is not marriage but continence comparable with theirs. Or rather, I am not seeking to compare marriage with marriage (for marriage is a gift bestowed on the mortal nature of man which is equal in all cases), but since I do not find men embracing marriage who are comparable with those who embraced it in a far different spirit, I must investigate what persons who practise continence can be compared with the married couples of old. But perhaps Abraham could not discipline himself to forgo marriage for the sake of the kingdom of heaven, though he fearlessly steeled himself to sacrifice his sole dear offspring whose existence made marriage dear to him, for the sake of the kingdom of heaven!

---

[88] See Num. 19: 11 ff. ('He that touches a dead body shall be unclean for seven days . . .'). Augustine's explanation here brings the regulation close to the Christian practice which invokes Macc. 2. 12. 46: 'It is a holy and wholesome thought to pray for the dead that they may be released from their sins.'

[XXI]   25. Continentia quippe non corporis, sed animi uirtus est. Vir-
tutes autem animi aliquando in opere manifestantur, aliquando in
habitu latent, sicut martyrii uirtus eminuit apparuitque tolerando
passiones. Sed quam multi sunt in eadem uirtute animi quibus
temptatio deest,[89] qua id quod intus est in conspectu dei, etiam in
hominum procedat nec tunc esse incipiat, sed tunc innotescat? Iam
enim erat in Iob patientia, quam nouerat deus et cui testimonium
perhibebat, sed hominibus innotuit temptaminis examine;[90] et
quod latebat intrinsecus per ea quae forinsecus inlata sunt non
natum sed manifestum est. Habebat utique et Timotheus uirtutem
continendi a uino, quam non ei abstulit Paulus monendo *ut uino
modico uteretur propter stomachum et frequentes suas infirmitates*;[91] alioquin
perniciose docebat, ut propter salutem corporis fieret in animo
damnum uirtutis. Sed quia poterat ea uirtute salua fieri quod mon-
ebat, ita relaxata est corpori utilitas bibendi ut maneret in animo
habitus continendi.

Ipse est enim habitus quo aliquid agitur cum opus est; cum
autem non agitur, potest agi sed non opus est. Hunc habitum circa
continentiam quae fit a concubitu non habent illi quibus dicitur *Si
se non continent, nubant*; hunc uero habent quibus dicitur *Qui potest
capere, capiat.*[92] Sic usi sunt perfecti animi bonis terrenis ad aliud nec-
essariis per hunc habitum continentiae, quo eis non obligarentur et
quo possent eis etiam non uti si non opus esset. Nec quisquam eis
bene utitur nisi qui et non uti potest. Multi quidem facilius se abstinent ut non utantur quam temperant ut bene utantur; nemo tamen
potest sapienter uti nisi qui potest et continenter non uti. Ex hoc
habitu et Paulus dicebat: *Scio et abundare et penuriam pati.*[93] Penuriam
quippe pati quorumcumque hominum est, sed scire penuriam pati
magnorum est. Sic et abundare quis non potest? Scire autem abundare nonnisi eorum est quos abundantia non corrumpit.

26. Verum ut apertius intellegatur quomodo sit uirtus in habitu
etiamsi non sit in opere, loquor de exemplo de quo nullus dubitat

---

[89] By AD 400, martyrdom for the Christian faith was a distant memory, but 'enthusiasm
for the cult and its phenomenal growth in the fourth century can only be understood when
it is firmly anchored in the historical consciousness of post-Constantinian Christians . . .
The age of the martyrs retained something of the flavour of a heroic age' (Markus, *The End
of Ancient Christianity*, 24). In a society no longer threatened by such persecution 'monasticism
came to absorb the ideal of the martyr' (ibid. 71). But Augustine contrasts the heroism of
the martyrs with the untried virtue of consecrated virgins; see esp. *De sancta uirginitate*
[XLIV] 45.

[90] Cf. Job 1 ff.   [91] 1 Tim. 5: 23.   [92] 1 Cor. 7: 9.   [93] Phil. 4: 12.

25. For continence is a virtue not of the body but of the mind. Now [XXI]
virtues of mind are sometimes displayed in action, but sometimes lie
hidden in everyday behaviour. So, for example, the virtue of martyrdom has become clear and conspicuous in endurance of sufferings;
but how many are there who possess the same virtue of mind but are
not put to the test?[89] In that trial what is visible to God advances also
before men's eyes; it does not originate at that time, but only then
makes itself known. Job already possessed patience; it was known to
God who bore witness to it, but it became clear to men when he was
tested by trial.[90] What lay hidden within did not originate in the
trials imposed from without, but it became visible then. Again, Timothy undoubtedly possessed the virtue of abstention from wine. Paul
did not deprive him of this when he advised him to 'take a little wine
for his stomach's sake and for his frequent ailments';[91] otherwise
Paul's admonition, that he should suffer loss of virtue in mind for the
sake of health of body, would have been wicked. But because that
advice could be given without prejudice to his virtue, the value of
drinking was made available to the body in such a way that his
practice of restraint remained in the mind.

This very cast of mind indeed ensures that something is done
when required; when it is not done, it is possible to do it, but there is
no need. Such a habit of restraint in the matter of sexual intercourse
is not the way of those to whom it is said 'If they do not control themselves, let them marry'; but those persons do possess it who are told:
'Let this be accepted by one who can.'[92] This is how those who
attained spiritual perfection treated earthly goods necessary for
another purpose in this habit of continence, thus ensuring that they
were not bound by them, and they could further refrain from the use
of them if the need was not there. No one uses these goods well except
the person who can also refrain from using them. There are indeed
many who more readily practise abstinence by non-use rather than
show restraint by good use, but no one can use them wisely except the
person who can also exercise self-control to refrain from using them.
Paul commented also on this practice: 'I know both how to enjoy
plenty and to endure poverty.'[93] Endurance of poverty is within the
scope of any persons whatsoever, but to know how to endure it is the
mark of great men. Similarly anyone can enjoy plenty, but to know
how to enjoy it is the mark only of those whom it does not corrupt.

26. But to promote a clearer understanding of how virtue resides
in habit even if not evinced in action, I cite an example on which no

catholicorum Christianorum. Dominus enim noster Iesus Christus quod in ueritate carnis esurierit ac sitierit, manducauerit et biberit, nullus ambigit eorum qui ex eius euangelio fideles sunt. Num igitur non erat in illo continentiae uirtus a cibo et potu quanta erat in Iohanne Baptista? *Venit enim Iohannes non manducans neque bibens, et dixerunt: 'Daemonium habet.' Venit filius hominis manducans et bibens, et dixerunt: 'Ecce uorax et uinaria, amicus publicanorum et peccatorum.'*[94] Numquid non talia dicuntur in domesticos eius, patres nostros, ex alio genere utendi terrenis quantum ad concubitum pertinet: 'Ecce homines libidinosi et immundi, amatores feminarum et lasciuiarum'? Et tamen sicut in illo illud non erat uerum (quamuis uerum esset quod non sicut Iohannes abstineret a manducando et bibendo; ipse enim apertissime uerissimeque ait: *Venit Iohannes non manducans neque bibens, uenit filius hominis manducans et bibens*), sic nec hoc in illis patribus uerum est (quamuis uenerit modo apostolus Christi non coniugatus nec generans, quem dicant pagani 'Magus erat', uenerit autem tunc propheta Christi nuptias faciens et filios procreans, quem dicant Manichaei 'Mulierosus erat').[95]

Et iustificata est sapientia a filiis suis quod dominus ibi subiecit cum de Iohanne et de se illa dixisset, *Iustificata est* inquit *sapientia a filiis suis,*[96] qui uident continentiae uirtutem in habitu animi semper esse debere, in opere autem pro rerum ac temporum oportunitate manifestari, sicut uirtus patientiae sanctorum martyrum in opere apparuit, ceterorum uero aeque sanctorum in habitu fuit. Quocirca sicut non est impar meritum patientiae in Petro qui passus est et in Iohanne qui passus non est,[97] sic non est impar meritum continentiae in Iohanne qui nullas expertus est nuptias et in Abraham qui filios generauit. Et illius enim celibatus et illius conubium pro temporum distributione Christo militauerunt; sed continentiam Iohannes et in opere, Abraham uero in solo habitu habebat.

---

[94] Matt. 11: 18f.

[95] As becomes clear in the next paragraph, Augustine here contrasts the apostle John with Abraham. For John as model of virginity in Augustine, see *In Ioannis euangelium* 124: 7; Abraham was condemned by the Manichees because he fathered a child by the slave-girl Hagar (Gen. 16: 3ff.).

[96] Matt. 11: 19.

[97] The tradition that Peter was martyred at Rome under Nero was universally accepted in the West by this date, and his feast-day shared with St Paul (June 29) was an occasion of mass pilgrimage to Rome; see e.g. Paulinus of Nola, *Ep.* 17. 2. For the obscure traditions of John's

Catholic Christian has doubts. No faithful believer in Christ's gospel is non-committal about whether our Lord Jesus Christ in the flesh truly hungered and thirsted, ate and drank. So did he not possess the virtue of abstinence from food and drink equally with John the Baptist? 'For John came, neither eating nor drinking, and they said "He has a demon". The Son of Man came both eating and drinking, and they said, "Look, a glutton and a wine-bibber, a friend of tax-collectors and sinners."'[94] Are not such things said against our fathers, the members of his household, because of their different ways of employing earthly things relating to sexual intercourse? 'See these lustful and unclean men,' they say, 'lovers of women and of wanton behaviour!' Yet just as the previous allegation was untrue of Christ (though it was true that he did not abstain as John did from eating and drinking; for he himself said quite openly and truthfully, 'John came neither eating nor drinking; the Son of man came eating and drinking'), so this description is not true of the fathers of old (though now an apostle of Christ has come who is neither married nor fathering children, causing the pagans to say of him, 'He was a magician,' whereas at that earlier time Christ's prophet came, marrying and fathering offspring, rousing the Manichees to say of him, 'He was a womanizer.')[95]

'Yet Wisdom was vindicated in her children.'[96] This is what the Lord appended after he had spoken those words about John and himself. 'Wisdom', he said, 'was vindicated in her children,' for they see that the virtue of continence must always reside in the disposition of the mind, and be visible in action according as the circumstances and the times allow. This was how the virtue of patience shown by the martyrs was made manifest in action, while that of the rest, equally holy persons, lay in their disposition. So just as the merit of patience in Peter who suffered and that of John who did not were not dissimilar,[97] so the merit of continence in John who had no experience of marriage and that of Abraham who fathered offspring was much the same; for the celibacy of the one and the marriage of the other both campaigned for Christ according to the allocation of the times. But whereas John demonstrated his continence in action as well, Abraham maintained his solely in his disposition.

---

death, see *ODCC*, 'John, St., Apostle'; Augustine clearly rejects here reports of his martyrdom.

27. Illo itaque tempore, cum et lex dies patriarcharum subsequens maledictum dixit qui non excitaret semen in Israhel, et qui poterat non promebat sed tamen habebat. Ex quo autem uenit plenitudo temporis ut diceretur *Qui potest capere, capiat*,[98] ex illo usque adhuc et deinceps usque in finem qui habet, operatur; qui operari noluerit, non se habere mentiatur. Ac per hoc ab eis qui corrumpunt bonos mores colloquiis malis[99] inani et uana uersutia dicitur homini Christiano continenti et nuptias recusanti: 'Tu ergo melior quam Abraham?' Quod ille cum audierit, non perturbetur nec audeat dicere 'Melior', nec a proposito delabatur (illud enim non uere dicit, hoc non recte facit), sed dicat: 'Ego quidem non sum melior quam Abraham, sed melior est castitas celibum quam castitas nuptiarum; quarum Abraham unam habebat in usu, ambas in habitu. Caste quippe coniugaliter uixit; esse autem castus sine coniugio potuit, sed tunc non oportuit. Ego uero facilius non utor nuptiis quibus est usus Abraham, quam sic utor nuptiis quemadmodum est usus Abraham; et ideo melior sum illis qui per animi incontinentiam non possunt quod ego, non illis qui propter temporis differentiam non fecerunt quod ego. Quod enim ego nunc ago, melius illi egissent si tunc agendum esset; quod autem illi egerunt, sic ego non agerem etsi nunc agendum esset.' Aut si talem se iste sentit et nouit, ut salua et permanente in habitu animi sui uirtute continentiae, si ad usum nuptiarum ex aliquo religionis officio descendisset, talis maritus et talis pater esset qualis fuit Abraham, audeat plane respondere illi captioso interrogatori, et dicere: 'Non sum quidem melior quam Abraham in hoc dumtaxat genere continentiae, qua ille non carebat etsi non apparebat; sed sum talis non aliud habens, sed aliud agens.'

Dicat plane ista, quia etsi uoluerit gloriari, non erit insipiens; ueritatem enim dicit.[100] Si autem parcit, ne quis eum existimet super id quod eum uidet aut audit aliquid ex illo, auferat a persona sua nodum quaestionis et non de homine sed de re ipsa respondeat et dicat: 'Qui tantum potest, talis est qualis fuit Abraham.' Potest autem fieri ut minor sit continentiae uirtus in animo eius qui non utitur nuptiis quibus est usus Abraham; sed tamen maior est quam

[98] Matt. 19: 12.
[99] Augustine refers to Jovinian and those who subsequently endorsed his views; see *Retractationes* 2. XXII. 1 (Appendix 1).
[100] Cf. 2 Cor. 12: 6.

27. Thus at that time, when the Law which succeeded the era of [XXII]
the patriarchs declared as accursed any man who did not raise children in Israel, even the man who could have practised continence
did not do so, but he none the less possessed it. But ever since the
fullness of time came to bring forth the words 'Let this be accepted
by one who can',[98] from then until now, and from now on until the
world's end, he who possesses it practises it. As for him who refuses
to practise it, he must not falsely claim that he possesses it. So those
men who corrupt good manners by wicked gossip[99] employ empty
and fruitless guile when they say to the Christian who practises continence and rejects marriage: 'So are you better than Abraham?'
When the Christian hears this, he should not be discomfited, but he
must not presume to say, 'Yes, better.' Nor must he abandon his purpose (for such a claim is untrue, but such action is misguided), but
his response should be: 'I am certainly not better than Abraham,
but the chastity of celibates is better than the chastity of marriage;
Abraham practised one of these, but his disposition embraced both.
For his life in marriage was chaste, but he could have lived chastely
unmarried; at that time, however, it was not fitting. As for myself, I
find it easier not to engage in marriage as Abraham did rather than
participate in it as Abraham did; and therefore I am better than
those who through incontinence of mind cannot do what I do. But
I am not better than those who because they lived at a different time
did not do what I do. In fact, what I now do they would have done
better, if that had then been their duty; however, what they did I
would not now do, even if that were what I should now do.' Or if the
Christian feels and knows that he is the kind of person who, while
preserving the virtue of continence intact and enduring in his disposition, would be the sort of husband and father that Abraham
was if he had to stoop to marriage because of some religious obligation, he should have the courage to make a frank response to that
captious questioner, and to say: 'So far as this issue of continence
goes, I am no better than Abraham was. He did not lack it, even if it
was not apparent. But I am not the sort of person whose action runs
contrary to his disposition.'

He can say this frankly, for even if his intention is to boast, he will
not be stupid since he speaks the truth.[100] But if he holds back for fear
that anyone should think that there is more to him than the appearance he presents or anything he hears him say, he should detach the
nub of the issue from his personal involvement, and concentrate his

in animo eius, qui propterea tenuit coniugii castitatem, quia non potuit ampliorem. Sic et femina innupta quae *cogitat ea quae sunt domini, ut sit sancta et corpore et spiritu,*[101] cum audierit impudentem* illum percunctatorem dicentem 'Tu ergo melior quam Sarra?', respondeat 'Ego melior sum, sed his quae uirtute huius continentiae carent, quod de Sarra non credo. Fecit ergo illa cum ista uirtute quod illi tempori congruebat, a quo ego sum immunis, ut in meo etiam corpore appareat quod illa in animo conseruabat.'

[XXIII]   28. Res ergo ipsas si comparemus, nullo modo dubitandum est meliorem esse castitatem continentiae quam castitatem nuptialem, cum tamen utrumque sit bonum; homines uero cum comparamus, ille est melior qui bonum amplius quam alius habet. Porro qui amplius eiusdem generis habet, et id quod minus est habet; qui autem tantummodo quod minus est habet, id quod est amplius non utique habet. In sexaginta enim sunt et triginta, non in triginta sunt et sexaginta. Non operari autem ex eo quod habet in distributione officiorum positum est, non in egestate uirtutum, quia nec bono misericordiae caret qui non inuenit miseros quibus possit misericorditer subuenire.

29. Huc accedit quia non recte comparantur homines hominibus ex uno aliquo bono. Fieri enim potest ut alius non habeat aliquid quod alius habet, sed aliud habeat quod pluris aestimandum est. Maius enim bonum est oboedientiae quam continentiae.[102] Nam conubium nusquam nostrarum scripturarum auctoritate damnatur, inoboedientia uero nusquam absoluitur. Si ergo proponatur uirgo permansura sed tamen inoboediens, et maritata quae uirgo permanere non posset sed tamen oboediens, quam meliorem dicamus? Minus laudabilem quam si uirgo esset, an damnabilem sicut uirgo est? Ita si conferas ebriosam uirginem

[101] 1 Cor. 7: 34.
[102] For Augustine, obedience ('in a sense the mother of all commandments . . . compliance with the commandments', [XXIII] 30 below) and humility are the paramount virtues. His mentor Ambrose had underlined the importance of obedience for those who follow Christ, the perfect pattern of obedience (*De fide* 5. 109f.). In the context of an Africa riven by the Donatist schism, Augustine the bishop trumpeted the role of the Catholic Church as the bastion of obedience at all levels of society, including the married state (*De moribus eccl. cath.* 30. 63; Brown, *Augustine of Hippo*, 225). In the present context he is concerned especially with obedience in the monastic life; later in his *Ordo monasterii* and his *Rule*, he visualises it as 'solidarity with the community'. See G. Lawless, *Augustine of Hippo and his Monastic Rule* (Oxford, 1987), 74ff.; Markus, *The End of Ancient Christianity*, 162ff.

* impudentem *cett.*, *Combès*: imprudentem *CB, Zycha*

answer on the subject itself, not the person. He should say: 'Anyone who can achieve as much is a second Abraham.' It is however possible that the virtue of continence is less in evidence in the mind of the person who does not embrace marriage as Abraham did, yet is greater than that in the mind of the person who embraced the chastity of marriage because he could not attain that which was greater. Likewise the unmarried woman too, who 'ponders the things of the Lord, that she may be holy in both body and spirit',[101] when she hears that shameless questioner asking 'So are you better than Sara?', should reply: 'I am better, better that is than those who lack this virtue of continence, but I do not believe this of Sara. The reason is that she exercised that virtue as was appropriate at that time. But I am not subject to those circumstances, so what she preserved in mind is conspicuous in my body as well.'

28. So if we compare the issues themselves, we can be in no doubt whatever that the chastity of continence is better than the chastity of marriage, though both are a good. But when we compare persons, the better of the two is the one who possesses a greater good than the other. Further, when the goods are of the same kind, he who possesses the greater also possesses the lesser, whereas he who possesses only the lesser certainly does not possess the greater. The number sixty contains also the number thirty, but the number thirty does not include also the number sixty. A person's failure to put his powers into action is the result of how he allocates his obligations, and does not spell poverty of virtues; so, for example, the man who does not come across people in misery to whom he can offer merciful help does not lack the good of mercy. [XXIII]

29. There is the further point that it is not right to compare individuals by the criterion of a particular good. It can happen that one man does not possess a quality which another has, but has another which is to be considered of greater worth. For example, the good of obedience is more important than the good of continence,[102] for whereas marriage is nowhere condemned on the authority of our scriptures, disobedience is nowhere condoned. So if confronted by one who intends to remain a virgin but is disobedient and a married woman who cannot retain her virginity but is obedient, which are we to pronounce the better, the one who is less praiseworthy than if she were a virgin, or the one who merits condemnation in her life as a virgin? Or again, in contrasting a drunken virgin with a sober matron, who would hesitate to make the same judgement? For

sobriae coniugatae, quis dubitet eandem ferre sententiam? Nuptiae quippe et uirginitas duo bona sunt quorum alterum maius; sobrietas autem et ebriositas, sicut oboedientia et contumacia, illa bona sunt, haec mala. Melius est autem habere omnia bona uel minora quam magnum bonum cum magno malo, quia et in corporis bonis melius est habere Zachaei staturam cum sanitate quam Goliae cum febro.[103]

30. Recte plane quaeritur non utrum omnimodis inoboediens uirgo coniugatae oboedienti, sed minus oboediens oboedientiori comparanda sit, quia et illa nuptialis castitas est et ideo bonum est, sed minor quam uirginalis. Tanto ergo minor in bono oboedientiae quanto minor in bono castitatis, si altera alteri comparetur, quae praeponenda sit iudicat qui primo ipsam castitatem et oboedientiam comparans uidet omnium uirtutum quodam modo matrem esse oboedientiam. Ac per hoc ideo potest esse oboedientia sine uirginitate, quia uirginitas ex consilio est, non ex praecepto. Oboedientiam uero illam dico qua praeceptis obtemperatur. Ideoque oboedientia praeceptorum sine uirginitate quidem potest, sed sine castitate esse non potest.

Ad castitatem namque pertinet non fornicari, non moechari, nullo illicito concubitu maculari; quae qui non obseruant, contra praecepta dei faciunt et ob hoc extorres sunt a uirtute oboedientiae. Virginitas autem propterea potest esse sine oboedientia quia potest femina consilio uirginitatis accepto et custodita uirginitate praecepta contemnere; sicut multas sacras uirgines nouimus uerbosas curiosas ebriosas litigiosas auaras superbas;[104] quae omnia contra praecepta sunt et sicut ipsam Euam inoboedientiae crimine occidunt. Quapropter non solum oboediens inoboedienti, sed oboedientior coniugata minus oboedienti uirgini praeponenda est.

31. Ex hac oboedientia pater ille, qui sine uxore non fuit, esse sine unico filio et a se occiso paratus fuit.[105] Vnicum enim non immerito dixerim, de quo audiuit a domino: *In Isaac uocabitur tibi semen.*[106] Quanto ergo citius ut etiam sine uxore esset, si hoc iubere-

[103] Cf. Luke 19: 2ff.; 1 Kings 17: 4ff.

[104] This vehement repetition of the frailties of some consecrated virgins (see [XII] 14 above) indicates that Augustine's establishment of conventual houses for women was attracting some unsuitable candidates. Later in AD 424 *Ep.* 211 rebukes the rebelliousness and wrangling of virgins in community life.

[105] For Augustine's later revision of his views of the attempted sacrifice of Isaac, see *Retract.* 2. XXII.2 (Appendix 1).

marriage and virginity are two goods, of which the second is the greater; but as for sobriety and drunkenness, and obedience and defiance, the first in each case is a good, and the second an evil. Now it is better to possess nothing but goods, even lesser ones, than to possess a great good combined with a great evil; for in the goods of the body too, it is better to be a dwarf like Zachaeus and in good health than to be a giant like Goliath with a fever.[103]

30. Clearly the right question is not whether a totally disobedient virgin is to be compared with an obedient matron, but the less obedient woman with the more obedient, for nuptial chastity also exists and is a good, but a lesser good than that of the virgin. Suppose, therefore, that the one who is inferior in the good of obedience as she is superior in the good of chastity is compared with the other. Judgement about which is to be preferred is made by the person who first compares chastity itself with obedience, and realises that obedience is in a sense the mother of all virtues. So for this reason there can be obedience without virginity, because virginity falls under counsel and not under commandment. By obedience I mean compliance with the commandments. So obedience can exist without virginity, but not without chastity.

The reason for this is that chastity forbids fornication, adultery, or defilement by unlawful intercourse. Those who do not observe these prohibitions contravene God's commandments, and thus are banished from the virtue of obedience. But virginity can exist without obedience, because a woman can adopt the counsel of virginity and preserve it, but spurn the commandments. We know many consecrated virgins who exemplify this, for they are garrulous, inquisitive, drunken, argumentative, greedy, and arrogant.[104] All these faults contravene the commandments and impose death through the sin of disobedience as they did on the person of Eve. So not only is the obedient person to be preferred to the disobedient, but the matron who is more obedient is to be preferred to the virgin who is less so.

31. It was by virtue of this obedience that the patriarch, not without a wife, was ready to dispense with his only son and to kill him with his own hand.[105] I say 'only son' advisedly, for Abraham heard the Lord say of him: 'Through Isaac your offspring will bear your name.'[106] How much more readily, then, would he have heard that

---

[106] Gen. 21: 12. 'Only son' indicates that the Christian community does not recognize the child which Abraham fathered by the slave-girl Hagar (n. 96 above).

tur, audiret! Vnde non frustra saepe miramur nonnullos utriusque
sexus ab omni concubitu continentes neglegenter oboedire praeceptis, cum tam ardenter arripuerint non uti concessis. Vnde quis
dubitat et excellentiae sanctorum illorum patrum atque matrum filios generantium non recte comparari mares et feminas nostri temporis, quamuis ab omni concubitu immunes in uirtute oboedientiae
minores, etiamsi illis hominibus et in habitu animi defuisset quod in
istorum opere manifestum est?

Sequantur ergo agnum pueri cantantes canticum nouum, sicut
in Apocalypsi scriptum est, *Qui cum mulieribus se non contam-
inauerunt*,[107] non ob aliud nisi quia uirgines permanserunt. Nec ideo
se arbitrentur meliores esse primis patribus sanctis, qui nuptiis ut ita
dicam nuptialiter usi sunt. Earum quippe usus ita se habet ut, si
quid in eis per carnis commixtionem quod excedat generandi
necessitatem, quamuis uenialiter factum fuerit, contaminatio sit.
Nam quid expiat uenia si omnino non contaminat illa progressio? A
qua contaminatione mirum si immunes essent pueri sequentes
agnum nisi uirgines permanerent.

[XXIV]   32. Bonum igitur nuptiarum per omnes gentes atque omnes
homines in causa generandi est et in fide castitatis; quod autem ad
populum dei pertinet, etiam in sanctitate sacramenti,[108] per quam
nefas est etiam repudio discedentem alteri nubere, dum uir eius
uiuit, nec saltem ipsa causa pariendi; quae cum sola sit qua nuptiae
fiunt, nec ea re non subsequente propter quam fiunt soluitur
uinculum nuptiale nisi coniugis morte. Quemadmodum si fiat ordinatio cleri ad plebem congregandam, etiamsi plebis congregatio
non subsequatur, manet tamen in illis ordinatis sacramentum
ordinationis; etsi aliqua culpa quisquam ab officio remoueatur,
sacramento domini semel imposito non carebit, quamuis ad iudi-
cium permanente.[109] Generationis itaque causa fieri nuptias
apostolus ita testis est: *Volo* inquit *iuniores nubere*, et quasi ei diceretur

---

[107] Apoc. 14: 4.

[108] As climax to the treatise, Augustine summarizes the three goods of marriage. The first
two, offspring and fidelity, are to apply to all marriages, Christian and non-Christian alike;
the third, *sacramentum* or the life-long vow, binds Christians alone.

[109] In the developing theology of the sacraments in the West, ordination, like baptism and
confirmation, is said to imprint and indelible seal or 'character' on the soul, so that once conferred it cannot be rescinded. This view of priesthood was already traditional by Augustine's
time; see e.g. Cyprian, *Ep.* 67, and in general see B. Leeming, 'The Sacramental Character',
Principles of Sacramental Theology (2nd edn. London, 1960), 129 ff.

he was also to be without a wife, if this had been enjoined on him! So we are often surprised, and not without good reason, that a number of persons of both sexes abstain from all sexual intercourse but are slothful at obeying the commandments, in spite of having so zealously embraced abstinence from things permitted. So does anyone doubt that it is not right to compare the men and women of our own time with the pre-eminence of the holy fathers and the mothers of children of those early days? For though these persons of today have no part in any sexual intercourse, they are inferior in the virtue of obedience, and this would be true even if the mental dispositions of those persons of old had lacked what is conspicuous in the active life of those of today.

So the boys who follow the Lamb are to sing their new song derived from the words of the Apocalypse, 'They have not defiled themselves with women',[107] for no reason other than that they have remained virgins. They are not to imagine that on that account they are better than those holy fathers of yore who lived out their marriages, to coin a phrase, 'as marriages should be'. For the proper use of marriage is such that if sexual intercourse in marriage seeks something more than what is necessary for procreation, defilement is involved though the sin is venial. For if such trespass does not defile at all, what does the forgiveness expiate? It would be surprising if the boys who follow the Lamb were free of such defilement, if they did not remain virgins.

32. Therefore the good of marriage in every nation and throughout mankind lies in the purpose of procreation and in the fidelity of chastity; but so far as the people of God are concerned, it lies also in the sanctity of the sacrament,[108] by reason of which it is forbidden for a woman, for so long as her husband lives, to marry another, even if she has been put away by her husband, and not even in order to have children. Though procreation is the sole purpose of marriage, even if this does not ensue and is the only reason why it takes place, the nuptial bond is loosed only by the death of a spouse. There is a parallel in the ordination of clergy to assemble a congregation; even if no such congregation is later established, the sacrament of ordination remains implanted in those ordained. Even if an individual were relieved of his office because of some defect, he will not forfeit the sacrament of the Lord once it is bestowed, but it will continue with him until the Judgement.[109] To revert to marriage, the Apostle attests that its purpose is procreation in these words: 'I would have the younger ones marry', and as if he were being

[XXIV]

'Vt quid?', continuo subiecit: *Filios procreare, matres familias esse.*[110] Ad fidem autem castitatis illud pertinet, *Uxor non habet potestatem corporis sui, sed uir; similiter et uir non habet potestatem corporis sui, sed mulier.*[111] Ad sacramenti sanctitatem illud: *Vxorem a uiro non discedere; quodsi discesserit, manere innuptam aut uiro suo reconciliari, et uir uxorem non dimittat.*[112]

Haec omnia bona sunt, propter quae nuptiae bonum sunt, proles fides sacramentum. Nec prolem autem carnalem iam hoc tempore quaerere ac per hoc ab omni tali opere immunitatem quamdam perpetuam retinere atque uni uiro Christo spiritaliter subdi melius est utique et sanctius; si tamen ea uacatione sic utantur homines, quomodo scriptum est, ut cogitent *quae sunt domini, quomodo placeant deo,*[113] id est ut perpetuo cogitet, continentia ne quid minus habeat oboedientia; quam uirtutem tamquam radicalem atque ut dici solet matricem et plane generalem sancti antiqui patres in opere exercuerunt, illam uero continentiam in animi habitu tenuerunt, qui profecto per oboedientiam, quia iusti et sancti erant et ad omne opus bonum semper parati, etiamsi ab omni concubitu abstinere iuberentur, efficerent. Quanto enim facilius possent uel iussione uel exhortatione dei non concumbere, qui prolem, cui uni propagandae concumbendo seruiebant, oboediendo poterant immolare?

[xxv]   33. Quae cum ita sint, haereticis quidem, siue Manichaeis siue quicumque alii patribus ueteris testamenti de pluribus calumniantur uxoribus, hoc esse argumentum deputantes quo eorum conuincant incontinentiam, satis superque responsum est, si tamen capiunt non esse peccatum, quod neque contra naturam committitur quia non lasciuiendi sed gignendi causa illi* feminis utebantur; neque contra morem, quia illis temporibus ea factitabantur; neque contra praeceptum, quia nulla lege prohibebantur. Illos uero, qui illicite feminis usi sunt, uel arguit in scripturis illis diuina sententia uel nobis lectio iudicandos atque uitandos, non adprobandos imitandosue proponit.

---

[110] 1 Tim. 5: 14; Paul refers specifically to young widows here.
[111] 1 Cor. 7: 4.
[112] 1 Cor. 7: 10 f.; thus the three texts are adduced to underpin the three goods of marriage.
[113] 1 Cor. 7: 32.

---

* illi *Combès*: illis *codd., Zycha*

asked why, he at once added: 'To bear children, and to manage the household.'[110] So far as fidelity in chastity is concerned, what he says is: 'A woman does not have domination over her body; her husband does. Likewise a husband does not have dominion over his body; his wife does.'[111] On the sanctity of the sacrament he says: 'A wife must not leave her husband, but if she does, she must either remain unmarried, or be reconciled to her husband; and a husband must not put away his wife.'[112]

All these things which make a marriage good—offspring, fidelity, sacrament—are goods. But in our day it is certainly better and holier not to aspire to offspring in the flesh, and in forgoing them to maintain a permanent renunciation of all such activity, and to become spiritually subject to Christ as sole husband—provided, however, that individuals exploit that freedom to ponder, in scripture's words, 'the things of the Lord, how to please God',[113] which means pondering constantly that obedience should not take second place to continence. The holy fathers of old practised the virtue of obedience, which is, as it were, the root virtue, or as it is often termed, the matrix; it is clearly of universal application. As for continence, the fathers preserved it as an attitude of mind. Even if commanded to abstain from all intercourse, they would certainly have managed this through obedience, for they were just and holy people, always ready to perform every good work. How much more readily could they have renounced sexual intercourse at God's command or urging, when in obedience they braced themselves to sacrifice the child for whose begetting alone they made themselves slaves to intercourse?

33. Since these are the facts, my rejoinder to the heretics, [xxv] whether Manichees or any others, is enough and more than enough. They make false charges against the fathers of the Old Testament because of their having several wives. They believe that this constitutes proof by which to convict them of incontinence. My reply is sufficient as long as they grasp that no sin was committed against nature (for their intimacy with these women was in order to beget children, not for wanton play), nor against custom (for such behaviour was common in those days), nor against any commandment (for their conduct was forbidden by no law). But as for men who abused women unlawfully, God's verdict in those very scriptures condemns them, or our reading recommends that we judge and disregard them, rather than approve and imitate them.

[XXVI]　　34. Nostros autem qui coniuges habent, quantum possumus admonemus ne secundum suam infirmitatem de illis sanctis patribus audeant iudicare, comparantes, ut ait apostolus, *semet ipsos sibimet ipsis*,[114] et ideo non intellegentes quantas uires habeat animus iustitiae contra libidines seruiens, ne carnalibus huiusce modi motibus acquiescat eosque in concubitum ultra generandi necessitatem prolabi aut progredi sinat, quantum ordo naturae, quantum morum consuetudo, quantum legum scita praescribunt. Hoc quippe ideo de illis patribus homines suspicantur, quia ipsi per incontinentiam uel nuptias elegerunt uel coniugibus intemperanter utuntur. At uero continentes, uel mares qui defunctis uxoribus uel feminae quae defunctis uiris uel utrique qui pari consensu continentiam deo uouerunt, sciant sibi quidem mercedis amplius deberi quam coniugalis castitas poscit; sed sanctorum patrum nuptias, qui prophetice coniungebantur, qui neque in concubitu nisi prolem neque in ipsa prole nisi quod in carne uenturo Christo proficeret requirebant, non solum prae suo proposito non contemnant, uerum etiam suo proposito sine dubitatione praeponant.

35. Pueros quoque ac uirgines integritatem ipsam deo dicantes multo maxime commonemus ut tanta norint humilitate tuendum esse quod in terra interim uiuunt, quanto magis caeli est quod uouerunt. Nempe scriptum est: *Quanto magnus es, tanto humila te in omnibus*.[115] Nostrum ergo est de magnitudine eorum aliquid dicere, illorum de magna humilitate cogitare. Exceptis igitur quibusdam, illis coniugatis patribus et matribus sanctis, quibus ideo isti meliores non sunt, quamuis coniugati non sint, qui* si coniugati essent pares non essent, ceteros omnino huius temporis coniugatos, uel post expertum concubitum continentes, a se superari non dubitent, non quantum ab Anna Susanna, sed quantum ambae a Maria superantur. Quod ad ipsam pertinet, sanctam carnis integritatem loquor; nam quae alia sint Mariae merita quis ignorat?

[114] 2 Cor. 10: 12.
[115] Ecclus. 3: 20. Augustine resumes his exhortation to virgins on humility in *De sancta uirginitate* [XXXI] 31–[LVI] 57.

* qui *scripsi*; quia *codd*.

34. As for our contemporaries with wives, we urge them with [XXVI]
all the force we can muster not to presume to pass judgement on
those holy fathers by the criterion of their own weakness, in the
Apostle's words 'comparing themselves with themselves'.[114] By so
doing they fail to understand the great strength which the mind dis-
plays in serving righteousness against lusts. This enables it not to
acquiesce in such motions of the flesh, and not to slip or advance
into intercourse beyond the need to beget children, according as the
order of nature, the norm of custom, and the decrees of the laws
prescribe. For men entertain such suspicions of the fathers because
they themselves have either opted for marriage through incontinence, or they exploit their wives sexually with lack of restraint. But
those who are continent (whether men whose wives have died, or
women whose husbands have died, or couples who by mutual
agreement have vowed their continence to God) are to realize that
a greater reward is indeed owed to them than the chastity of marriage demands. But as for the holy fathers whose marriages performed a prophetic role, who sought nothing from sexual
intercourse except offspring, and from their offspring only what was
of service to Christ who was to come in the flesh, not only should
our continent contemporaries not despise their marriages by
unfavourable comparison with their own commitment, but they
should not hesitate to rank them higher than their own commitment to virginity.

35. Further, and much the most pressingly of all, we urge the
boys and maidens who dedicate their virginity to God to realize that
their transitory lives on earth must be invested with a humility in
keeping with the more heavenly vows which they have taken. Does
not scripture say 'The greater you are, the more you must humble
yourself in all things'?[115] Therefore it is for us to touch upon their
greatness, but for them to ponder the greatness of humility. So if we
except certain people (I refer to those holy fathers and mothers who
were married; the people of today though unmarried are not better
than they were, and if they had married they would not be their
equals), they should not doubt that they rise superior to all married
persons, especially those of today, and even to those who remain
continent after experience of intercourse—not so much as Susanna
is surpassed by Anna, but as both are surpassed by Mary. In referring to her, I speak of the sacred virginity of her flesh; for who is
unaware of Mary's other merits?

Mores itaque congruos huic tanto proposito adiungant ut de praepollenti praemio certam securitatem gerant, scientes sane sibi atque omnibus fidelibus dilectis et electis Christi membris multis ab oriente et occidente uenientibus, etsi inter se distante pro meritis gloriae luce fulgentibus, hoc tamen magnum in commune praestari, ut cum Abraham et Isaac et Iacob recumbant in regno dei, qui non propter hoc saeculum sed propter Christum coniuges, propter Christum patres fuerunt.

They must therefore join appropriate behaviour to their lofty commitment, so that they may feel certain assurance of their surpassing reward, for they will surely realise that to themselves as to all the faithful beloved and chosen members of Christ coming from east and west, even though the light of glory with which they gleam differs in accordance with their merits, the great boon is granted of reclining with Abraham, Isaac, and Jacob in God's kingdom; for they have been spouses for Christ, and fathers too for Christ, not for this world.

DE SANCTA VIRGINITATE

ON HOLY VIRGINITY

[I]   1. Librum de bono coniugali nuper edidimus, in quo etiam Christi uirgines commonuimus atque monuimus ne propter excellentiam muneris amplioris quod diuinitus acceperunt contemnant in sui comparatione patres et matres populi dei, hominesque illos quos tamquam oliuam commendat apostolus ne superbiat insertus oleaster,[1] qui uenturo Christo etiam filiorum propagatione seruiebant, ideo meriti inferioris esse arbitrentur, quia iure diuino continentia conubio et nuptiis pia uirginitas anteponitur. In illis quippe parabantur et parturiebantur futura quae nunc impleri mirabiliter et efficaciter cernimus, quorum etiam uita coniugalis prophetica fuit; unde non consuetudine humanorum uotorum atque gaudiorum sed ualde profundo consilio dei in quibusdam eorum fecunditas honorari, in quibusdam etiam fecundari sterilitas meruit.[2]

Hoc uero tempore quibus dictum est *Si se non continent, nubant*[3] non adhibenda est exhortatio sed consolatio; quibus autem dictum est *Qui potest capere, capiat*,[4] exhortandi sunt ne terreantur, et terrendi ne extollantur. Non solum ergo praedicanda est uirginitas ut ametur, uerum etiam monenda ne infletur.

[II]   2. Hoc isto sermone suscepimus. Adiuuet Christus, uirginis filius et uirginum sponsus, uirginali utero corporaliter natus, uirginali conubio spiritaliter coniugatus. Cum igitur ipsa uniuersa ecclesia uirgo sit desponsata uni uiro Christo,[5] sicut dicit apostolus, quanto digna sunt honore membra eius quae hoc custodiunt etiam in ipsa carne, quod tota custodit in fide quae imitatur matrem uiri sui et domini sui? Nam ecclesia quoque et mater et uirgo est; cuius enim integritati consulimus, si uirgo non est? Cuius prolem adloquimur, si mater non est?[6]

Maria corporaliter caput huius corporis peperit; ecclesia

---

[1] 'The fathers and mothers' are the Patriarchs and wives of the Old Testament. Paul's designation of them at Rom. 11: 17ff. as the olive-tree is an injunction to the Gentiles ('the engrafted wild olive') to acknowledge that they now share the strong spiritual life of the Jews. They are to refrain from boasting that they had supplanted the Jews, 'for if God did not spare the natural branches, perhaps he will not spare you'.

[2] Augustine here echoes a notion earlier elaborated in his *Contra Faustum* (AD 397–8) 22. 24: 'Their lives as well as their words were prophetic.' In developing this thought, he argues that their marriages presaged the union of Christ and his Church, and that their children were forerunners of the Christian offspring which result from that union. The fecundity which 'deserved to win honour' was that of Abraham, Isaac, and Jacob (Gen. 12: 2, 26: 4, 35: 11); their wives Sara, Rebecca, and Rachel were initially barren but later bore children (Gen. 18: 10, 25: 21, 30: 23).

[3] 1 Cor. 7: 9.   [4] Matt. 19: 12.

1. I recently issued a book on the good of marriage. In it I have also [I] reminded and warned the virgins of Christ not to hold up the eminence of that higher gift conferred on them by heaven as a reason for disparaging the fathers and mothers of the people of God by comparison with themselves. Nor should they, because by divine law continence is preferred to marriage and holy virginity to wedlock, regard those persons as inferior in merit. The Apostle approvingly designates them as the olive-tree in order to deter the engrafted wild olive from boasting.[1] They ministered to the Christ who was to come also by multiplying their offspring; in them were prepared and brought to birth those future events which we now see wondrously and effectively fulfilled. Their married life too was prophetic; so it was that in some of them their fecundity deserved to win honour, and in others barrenness deserved to become fruitful, not in the usual way through human aspirations and pleasures, but by the most profound of God's designs.[2]

But at the present time, those who have been told 'If they do not control themselves, let them marry'[3] are not to be urged to do so, but consoled. On the other hand, those who have been told 'Let this be accepted by one who can'[4] are to be encouraged not to be fearful, yet to be fearful so as not to become arrogant. So virginity is not only to be praised that it may be loved, but also counselled not to be puffed up.

2. Such is the task that I have undertaken in this discourse. I pray [II] that Christ, son of a virgin and bridegroom of virgins, born in the flesh of a virgin's womb and wedded in the spirit in a virgin marriage, may come to my aid. So since the whole Church, as the Apostle has it, is herself a virgin espoused to Christ her only husband,[5] how great is the distinction which her members deserve who maintain in their very flesh what the whole Church maintains in faith, in imitation of the mother of her husband and her lord? For the Church too is both mother and virgin. To whose chastity do we look, if she is no virgin? Whose offspring do we address, if she is no mother?[6]

Mary brought forth the head of this body in the flesh; the Church brings forth the members of that head in the spirit. In both, virginity is

---

[5] See Eph. 5: 25 ff; 2 Cor. 11: 2 (the Church at Corinth). Augustine develops the teaching at greater length in *In Ioannis euangelium* (completed AD 416–17) 8. 4.

[6] The influence of Ambrose is clear here, especially his *Expos. in Luc.* 2. 7 and *De uirginibus* 1. 31; for this and other citations, see Homes Dudden, *Saint Ambrose*, 636 ff.

spiritaliter membra illius capitis parit. In utraque uirginitas fecunditatem non impedit, in utraque fecunditas uirginitatem non
adimit. Proinde cum ecclesia uniuersa sit sancta et corpore et spiritu, nec tamen uniuersa sit corpore uirgo sed spiritu, quanto sanc-
tior est in his membris, ubi uirgo est et corpore et spiritu![7]

[III]   3. Scriptum est in euangelio quod mater et fratres Christi, hoc
est consanguinei carnis eius, cum illi nuntiati fuissent et foris
exspectarent, quia non possent eum adire prae turba, ille respondit:
*'Quae est mater mea, aut qui sunt fratres mei?' Extendens manum super discip-
ulos suos ait: 'Hi sunt fratres mei; et quicumque fecerit uoluntatem patris mei,
ipse mihi frater et mater et soror est',*[8] quid aliud nos docens nisi carnali
cognationi genus nostrum spiritale praeponere, nec inde beatos
esse homines si iustis et sanctis carnis propinquitate iunguntur, sed
si eorum doctrinae ac moribus oboediendo atque imitando
cohaerescunt? Beatior ergo Maria percipiendo fidem Christi quam
concipiendo carnem Christi. Nam et dicenti cuidam *Beatus uenter qui
te portauit* ipse respondit *Immo, beati qui audiunt uerbum dei, et custodiunt.*[9]
Denique fratribus eius (id est, secundum carnem cognatis) qui non
in eum crediderunt quid profuit illa cognatio? Sic et materna
propinquitas nihil Mariae profuisset nisi felicius Christum corde
quam carne gestasset.

[IV]   4. Ipsa quoque uirginitas eius ideo gratior et acceptior, quia non
eam conceptus Christus uiro uiolaturo quam conseruaret ipse
praeripuit, sed priusquam conciperetur iam deo dicatam de qua
nasceretur elegit. Hoc indicant uerba quae sibi fetum adnuntianti
angelo Maria reddidit. *Quomodo* inquit *fiet instud, quoniam uirum non
cognosco?*[10] Quod profecto non diceret nisi deo uirginem se ante
uouisset. Sed quia hoc Israhelitarum mores adhuc recusabant,
desponsata est uiro iusto non uiolenter ablaturo sed potius contra
uiolentos custodituro quod illa iam uouerat. Quamquam etiamsi
hoc solum dixisset *Quomodo fiet istud*? nec addidisset *quoniam uirum non
cognosco*, non quaesisset utique, promissum sibi filium quomodo
femina paritura esset, si concubitura nupsisset.

Poterat et iuberi uirgo permanere, in qua dei filius formam serui

---

[7] Throughout this section Augustine appears to have Ambrose, *De uirginibus* I at his elbow
or in his mind.
[8] Matt. 12: 48 ff.   [9] Luke 11: 27 f.   [10] Luke 1: 34.

no obstacle to fecundity; in both, fecundity does not dispense with virginity. So since the Church as a whole is both body and spirit, whereas she is not wholly virgin in body but in spirit, how much holier she is in these members in which she is a virgin in both body and spirit![7]

3. The gospel records that when the arrival of the mother and [III] brothers of Christ (that is, his blood-relatives) had been reported to him, and they were waiting on the fringes because they could not get close to him because of the crowd, his rejoinder was: 'Who is my mother, or who are my brothers?' Then stretching out his hands over his disciples, he said: 'These are my brothers; and whoever does the will of my father is my brother and mother and sister.'[8] What was he teaching us but to rank our spiritual kinship above relatives in the flesh? And that men are blessed not through association with just and holy men as blood-relatives, but through our attachment to them by obeying their teaching and by imitating their behaviour? So Mary was more blessed by her grasp of faith in Christ than by conceiving Christ in the flesh; for when someone remarked 'Blessed is the womb that bore thee', Christ himself replied: 'No, blessed are they that hear the word of God, and keep it.'[9] And finally, what benefit accrued from this relationship to those brothers (that is, blood-relatives) who did not believe in him? In the same way Mary's kinship as mother would have been of no benefit to her if she had not borne Christ more blessedly in her heart than in the flesh.

4. Her virginity itself was also all the more pleasing and [IV] acceptable because after Christ was conceived he did not himself first arrogate it in order to preserve it from violation by man, but before his conception he chose it, when it was already dedicated to God, from which to be born. This is shown in the words which Mary used to answer the angel when he told her of the child she was to bear. 'How can that be', she asked, 'since I know no man?'[10] She would certainly not have said this if she had not already vowed her virginity to God. But because the customs of the Israelites were at that time still opposed to this, she was espoused to a righteous man, not one who would forcibly deprive her of what she had already vowed to God, but rather would safeguard it against men of violence. Yet even had she merely asked 'How can that be?' and had not added 'since I know no man', if she had married intending to indulge in sexual intercourse, she would not have inquired expressly how as a woman she would bear the son promised to her.

Again, she could have been ordered to remain a virgin so that by

congruenti miraculo acciperet;[11] sed exemplo sanctis futura uirginibus, ne putaretur sola uirgo esse debuisse quae prolem etiam
sine concubitu concipere meruisset, uirginitatem deo dicauit cum
adhuc quid esset conceptura nesciret, ut in terreno mortalique corpore caelestis uitae imitatio uoto fieret, non praecepto, amore eli-
gendi non necessitate seruiendi. Ita Christus nascendo de uirgine
quae, antequam sciret quis de illa fuerat nasciturus, uirgo statuerat
permanere, uirginitatem sanctam adprobare maluit quam imper-
are, Ac sic etiam in ipsa femina in qua forman serui accepit uirginitatem esse liberam uoluit.

[v]   5. Non est ergo cur dei uirgines contristentur quod etiam ipsae
uirginitate seruata matres carnis esse non possunt; illum enim
solum decenter uirginitas parere posset, qui in sua natiuitate parem
habere non posset. Verumtamen ille unius sanctae uirginis partus
omnium sanctarum uirginum est decus, et ipsae cum Maria matres
Christi sunt, si patris eius faciunt uoluntatem. Hinc enim et Maria
laudabilius atque beatius Christi mater est secundum supra memo-
ratam eius sententiam: *Quicumque facit uoluntatem patris mei qui in caelis
est, ipse mihi frater et soror et mater est.* Has sibi omnes propinquitates in
populo quem redemit spiritaliter exhibet; fratres et sorores habet
sanctos uiros et sanctas feminas, quoniam sunt illi in caelesti hered-
itate coheredes.[12] Mater eius est tota ecclesia quia membra eius, id
est fideles eius, per dei gratiam ipsa utique parit. Item mater eius est
omnis anima pia, faciens uoluntatem patris eius fecundissima caritate in his quos parturit, donec in eis ipse formetur.[13] Maria ergo
faciens uoluntatem dei corporaliter Christi tantummodo mater est,
spiritaliter autem et soror et mater.

[vi]   6. Ac per hoc illa una femina non solum spiritu uerum etiam corpore et mater et uirgo. Et mater quidem spiritu non capitis nostri,
quod est ipse saluator, ex quo magis illa spiritaliter nata est, quia
omnes qui in eum crediderint, in quibus et ipsa est, recte filii sponsi
appellantur,[14] sed plane mater membrorum eius, quod nos sumus,
quia cooperata est caritate ut fideles in ecclesia nascerentur, quae
illius capitis membra sunt, corpore uero ipsius capitis mater. Oportebat enim caput nostrum propter insigne miraculum secundum

[11] Phil. 2: 7.   [12] Cf. Rom. 8: 17.
[13] Augustine echoes Paul at Gal. 4: 19, where Paul in his evangelizing describes himself as
'like a mother in the pains of childbirth, until Christ is formed in you'.
[14] Matt. 9: 15.

an apt miracle the son of God could assume 'the form of a slave'.[11] But her intention was to serve as an example for holy virgins; and so to avoid giving the impression that she alone ought to be a virgin as one who had deserved to conceive a child even without sexual intercourse, she dedicated her virginity to God while as yet unaware of what she was to conceive. This was so that the imitation of heavenly life in an earthly and mortal body would be fulfilled by vow and not under command, by eagerness to choose rather than by compulsion to serve. So Christ, by being born of a virgin who had decided to remain such before becoming aware who was to be born of her, chose to approve rather than to impose her holy virginity. In this way he willed that the virginity of the woman in whom he accepted 'the form of a slave' should be freely chosen.

5. There is accordingly no reason for God's virgins to be [v] despondent because they cannot like Mary become mothers in the flesh while preserving their virginity. Virginity could fittingly bring forth only him who in his birth could have no peer. None the less, the parturition of that holy virgin alone is the glory of all holy virgins; they too in company with Mary are mothers of Christ as long as they do the will of the Father. This indeed is why Mary too is Christ's mother in a more praiseworthy and blessed sense; as his words cited earlier have it, 'Whoever does the will of my father in heaven is my brother and sister and mother.' He reveals all these relationships in the spiritual sense in the people whom he redeemed. He regards as brothers and sisters holy men and holy women, for they are coheirs in that heavenly inheritance.[12] The entire Church is his mother, because by God's grace she assuredly brings forth his members, in other words his faithful ones. Again, every devoted soul is his mother, when they carry out the will of the Father with a love most fruitful in those they bring to birth until Christ himself can be fashioned in them.[13] So Mary in doing God's will is physically merely Christ's mother, whereas spiritually she is both sister and mother.

6. In this sense, that woman alone is both mother and virgin not [vi] only in spirit but also in body. In fact she is not the mother of our Head, who is our Saviour, in the spirit; instead, in the spiritual sense she is his daughter, for all who have shown belief in him, Mary herself included, are rightly called 'children of the bridegroom'.[14] But she is clearly the mother of his members (which is what we are) because in love she co-operated so that the faithful children who are

carnem nasci de uirgine, quo significaret membra sua de uirgine
ecclesia secundum spiritum nascitura. Sola ergo Maria et spiritu et
corpore mater et uirgo, et mater Christi et uirgo Christi; ecclesia
uero in sanctis regnum dei possessuris spiritu quidem tota mater
Christi est, tota uirgo Christi, corpore autem non tota, sed in
quibusdam uirgo Christi, in quibusdam mater, sed non Christi. Et
coniugatae quippe fideles feminae et deo uirgines dicatae sanctis
moribus et caritate *de corde puro et conscientia bona et fide non ficta,*[15] quia
uoluntatem patris faciunt, Christi spiritaliter matres sunt; quae
autem coniugali uita corporaliter pariunt, non Christum sed Adam
pariunt, et ideo currunt ut sacramentis imbuti Christi membra fiant
partus earum, quoniam quid pepererint norunt.[16]

[VII]   7. Hoc dixi ne forte audeat fecunditas coniugalis cum uirginali
integritate contendere atque ipsam Mariam proponere ac uirginibus dei dicere: 'Illa in corpore duas res habuit honorandas, uirginitatem et fecunditatem, quia et integra permansit et peperit;
hanc felicitatem quoniam totam utraeque* habere non potuimus,
partitae sumus ut uos sitis uirgines, nos simus matres; uobis quod
defit in prole consoletur seruata uirginitas, nobis prolis lucro amissa
compensetur integritas.' Haec uox fidelium coniugatarum ad
sacras uirgines utcumque ferenda esset si Christianos corpore par-
erent, ut hoc solo esset Mariae fecunditas carnis excepta uirginitate
praestantior, quod illa ipsum caput horum membrorum, hae autem
membra illius capitis procrearent; nunc uero etiamsi tales hac uoce
contendant, quae ad hoc tantum uiris iunguntur atque miscentur ut
filios habeant, nihilque aliud de filiis cogitant nisi ut eos Christo
lucrentur, atque id mox ut potuerint faciunt, non tamen Christiani

---

[15] 1 Tim. 1: 5.
[16] In company with other Christians and some pagans, Augustine believed that 'some
great sin lay behind the misery of the human condition' (so Brown, *Augustine of Hippo*, 388,
with further bibliography on the 4th-cent. preoccupation with original sin). Hence his
emphasis here as elsewhere on the importance of child-baptism for fear that untimely death
would deny an infant life in heaven. There is evidence for the practice of such early baptism
from the 2nd cent. onwards in Justin Martyr, Tertullian, and Origen (who claims that the
custom was handed down from the apostles). During the 4th cent. postponement of baptism
into adult life became frequent; Basil and John Chrysostom in the East, and Ambrose, Paulinus of Nola, and Augustine himself in the West, exemplify this. Augustine's preoccupation
with original sin led him to argue strongly for infant baptism. See J. Jeremias, *Infant Baptism in
the First Four Centuries* (London, 1960); J. J. Cunningham, *Aquinas, Summa Theologiae*, vol. 57
(Blackfriars, London, 1975), App. 3.

---

* utraeque *MSS*: utraque *C*[1], *Zycha*

members of that Head could be born within the Church; whereas in the flesh she is the mother of the Head himself. For it was necessary that our Head by a striking miracle should be born of the flesh of a virgin, to indicate that his members would be born spiritually of the virgin Church. So Mary alone is both mother and virgin in both the spirit and the flesh; she is both Christ's mother and Christ's virgin. The Church on the other hand, in the persons of the saints who will possess the kingdom of God, is in sum Christ's mother and in sum Christ's virgin in spirit but not wholly in the flesh; in some she is Christ's virgin, and in others a mother, but not Christ's mother. For both married women in the faith and virgins consecrated to God are Christ's mother spiritually, by reason of their holy manners and their love 'from a pure heart, a good conscience, and faith unfeigned',[15] for they do the will of the father; but those who in married life bear children in the flesh are mothers not of Christ but of Adam. They make haste to ensure that their offspring are steeped in the sacraments and become Christ's members, for they are well aware of the nature of what they have brought forth.[16]

7. My purpose in saying this is to ensure that the fruitfulness of marriage may not perhaps presume to vie with virgin chastity, instancing Mary herself and saying to God's virgins: 'She had two things in the flesh worthy of honour, virginity and fecundity, for she both remained inviolate and bore a child. Since each of the two of us could not enjoy this blessing in its entirety, we have divided it out, so that you are virgins and we are mothers. Your preservation of virginity is to be a consolation for lack of offspring, whereas our loss of virginity is to be set against our gain of children.' Such words of married women in the faith addressed to consecrated virgins would certainly be tolerable if the children to whom they gave birth were Christians. Mary's fecundity in the flesh (if we discount her virginity) would in that case be more outstanding only in her having given birth to the Head himself of these members, whereas they give birth to the members of that Head. But as things stand, even if such married women who argue on these lines marry and have intercourse with husbands solely to bear children, with no other purpose in mind for these children other than winning them for Christ, and they carry this through as soon as they can, even so those born of their flesh are not Christians, but they become so later, when the Church gives birth to them. This is because the Church is the mother of Christ's members spiritually, as she is also the virgin of Christ spiritually. Though the mothers have

[VII]

ex earum carne nascuntur, sed postea fiunt ecclesia pariente per
hoc quod membrorum Christi spiritaliter mater est, cuius etiam
spiritaliter uirgo est. Cui sancto partui cooperantur et matres, quae
non Christianos corpore pepererunt, ut fiant quod se corpore
parere non potuisse nouerunt; per hoc tamen cooperantur, ubi et
ipsae uirgines matresque Christi sunt, in fide scilicet *quae per dilec-
tionem operatur*.[17]

[VIII]   8. Nulla ergo carnis fecunditas sanctae uirginitati etiam
carnis comparari potest. Neque enim et ipsa quia uirginitas est sed
quia deo dicata est honoratur, quae licet in carne seruetur spiritus
tamen religione ac deuotione seruatur. Ac per hoc spiritalis est
etiam uirginitas corporis, quam uouet et seruat continentia pietatis.
Sicut enim nemo impudice utitur corpore nisi spiritu prius con-
cepta nequitia, ita nemo pudicitiam seruat in corpore nisi spiritu
prius insita castitate. Porro autem si pudicitia coniugalis, quamuis
custodiatur in carne, animo tamen non carni tribuitur, quo prae-
side atque rectore nulli praeter proprium coniugium caro ipsa miscetur, quanto magis quantoque honoratius in animi bonis illa
continentia numeranda est, qua integritas carnis ipsi creatori animae et carnis uouetur consecratur seruatur!

[IX]   9. Nec illarum ergo fecunditas carnis, quae hoc tempore
nihil aliud in coniugio quam prolem requirunt quam mancipent
Christo, pro amissa uirginitate compensari posse credenda est. Pri-
oribus quippe temporibus uenturo secundum carnem Christo
ipsum genus carnis in ampla quadam et prophetica gente necessarium fuit;[18] nunc autem cum ex omni hominum genere atque
omnibus gentibus ad populum dei et ciuitatem regni caelorum
membra Christi colligi possint, sacram uirginitatem *qui potest capere,
capiat*, et ea tantum quae se non continet nubat.[19] Quid enim? Si
aliqua mulier diues multam pecuniam huic bono operi impendat ut
emat ex diuersis gentibus seruos quos faciat Christianos, nonne
uberius atque numerosius quam uteri quantalibet feracitate Christi
membra gignenda curabit? Nec ideo tamen pecuniam suam
comparare muneri sacrae uirginitatis audebit. At si propter facien-
dos qui nati fuerint Christianos fecunditas carnis pro amissa

---

[17] Gal. 5: 6.   [18] See *De bono coniugali* [IX] 9 above.
[19] Cf Matt. 19: 12; 1 Cor. 7: 9.

not borne Christians in the flesh, they co-operate with the Church in this holy birth, so that their children may become what they know they could not have borne in the flesh. Their co-operation, however, lies in the fact that they are themselves Christ's virgins and mothers, that is in the faith 'which is made effective through love'.[17]

8. Therefore no fruitfulness of the flesh can be compared with the holy virginity even of the flesh, for this is not honoured in itself as virginity, but because it is consecrated to God; and though preserved in the flesh, it is maintained by scrupulousness and devotion of the spirit. In this sense even physical virginity is spiritual, for devoted continence vows and preserves it. Just as no one abuses his body unless such evil behaviour has first been entertained in the spirit, so no one preserves chaste behaviour in the body unless chastity is implanted earlier in the spirit. Moreover, if chastity in marriage though maintained in the flesh is the responsibility of the mind and not of the flesh, and under its governance and guidance the flesh has no sexual relations with anyone outside its own marriage, how much the more, indeed how much the more honourably must we reckon among the goods of the mind that continence by which virginity of body is vowed, consecrated, and maintained for the Creator of both soul and body! [VIII]

9. It follows, then, that the physical fruitfulness even of women who at this time seek nothing from marriage except offspring to commit to Christ cannot possibly be thought to compensate for loss of virginity. It is true that in earlier days, when Christ was still to come in the flesh, offspring of the flesh were essential in a populous and prophetic nation.[18] But today, since Christ's members can be gathered from every race of men and from all nations to form the people of God and the city of heaven's kingdom, the person who can embrace virginity should embrace it, and only the woman who does not contain herself should marry.[19] Suppose some wealthy woman were to devote a lot of money to the worthy project of purchasing from various nations slaves to convert into Christians; will she not ensure that Christ's members are brought to birth more abundantly and in greater numbers than any born from a womb however fruitful? Yet she will not on that account presume to equate what her money achieves with the role of holy virginity. But if the loss of holy virginity is deservedly compensated by the fertility of the flesh, in the interests of making Christians out of those who are born, the transaction will be more fruitful should virginity be [IX]

uirginitate merito compensabitur, fructuosius erit hoc negotium, si
magno pecuniario pretio uirginitas amittatur, quo pueri faciendi
Christiani multo plures emantur quam unius utero quamlibet fertili
nascerentur.

[x]   Quod si stultissime dicitur, habeant fideles nuptae bonum suum,
de quo in alio uolumine quantum uisum est disseruimus; et hon-
orent amplius, sicut rectissime consuerunt, in sacris uirginibus
melius earum, de quo isto sermone disserimus.

10. Nam ne illo quidem debent continentium meritis se conferre
coniugia, quod ex eis uirgines procreantur; hoc enim non coniugii
bonum est, sed naturae, quae sic diuinitus instituta est ut ex quolibet humano utriusque sexus concubitu, siue ordinato et honesto
siue turpi et illicito, nulla femina nisi uirgo nascatur, nulla tamen
sacra uirgo nascitur; ita fit ut uirgo nascatur etiam de stupro, sacra
autem uirgo nec de coniugio.

[xi]   11. Nec nos hoc in uirginibus praedicamus, quod uirgines sunt, sed
quod deo dicatae pia continentia uirgines. Nam, quod non temere
dixerim, felicior mihi uidetur nupta mulier quam uirgo nuptura;
habet enim iam illa quod ista adhuc cupit, praesertim si nondum
uel sponsa cuiusquam sit. Illa uni studet placere cui data est, haec
multis, incerta cui danda est;[20] hoc uno pudicitiam cogitationis
defendit a turba, quod non adulterum sed maritum quaerit in
turba. Illa igitur uirgo coniugatae merito praeponitur quae nec
multitudini se amandam proponit, cum amorem unius ex multitu-
dine inquirit, nec se uni iam componit inuento, *cogitans quae sunt
mundi, quomodo placeat uiro*,[21] sed *speciosum forma prae filiis hominum*[22] sic
amauit ut, quia eum sicut Maria concipere carne non posset, ei
corde concepto etiam carnem integram custodiret.

[xii]   Hoc genus uirginum nulla corporalis fecunditas protulit; non
est haec proles carnis et sanguinis. Si harum quaeritur mater, ecclesia est. Non parit uirgines sacras nisi uirgo sacra, illa quae desponsata est uni uiro, casta exhiberi Christo.[23] Ex illa non tota corpore
sed tota uirgine spiritu, nascuntur sanctae uirgines et corpore et
spiritu.

---

[20] Though in Classical law the woman's consent to marriage was essential, her tender age
(12–16) and the social conventions made it inevitable that a husband was chosen for her
(Gillian Clark, *Women in Late Antiquity* (Oxford, 1993), 1 ff.)
    [21] 1 Cor. 7: 34.   [22] Ps. 44 (45): 3.   [23] Cf. 2 Cor. 11: 2.

surrendered in return for a great financial reward, so that with it many more children can be purchased to be made Christians than can be born from one woman's womb, however fertile.

On the assumption that this suggestion is utterly foolish, married [x] women in the faith must adhere to their own good (which I discussed as seemed appropriate in another work), and so far as sacred virgins are concerned ascribe greater distinction to theirs as being better; this is the subject of my present discussion.

10. Married couples ought not to equate their merits with those of celibates, even on the grounds that virgins are born from them, for this is a good of nature not of marriage. Nature has been established by God in such a way that from all human intercourse between the two sexes, whether lawful and honourable or debased and forbidden, no woman except a virgin is born. Yet none is born a consecrated virgin; accordingly a virgin is born even from fornication, whereas no consecrated virgin is born even from a marriage.

11. But in discussing virgins we do not praise their being virgins, [xi] but rather that they are virgins dedicated by devoted continence to God. Indeed, and I do not make this claim lightly, a married woman seems to me to be more happily placed than a virgin looking to marry, because the married woman already has what the virgin is eager still to attain, especially if she is not yet betrothed to anyone. The married woman's concern is to please the one man to whom she has been consigned, whereas the virgin is eager to please many, for she is uncertain to whom she is to be consigned.[20] She defends the purity of her intention from the crowd solely by the fact that she seeks not an adulterer but a husband. So rightly ranked higher than the married woman is the virgin who in seeking the love of one from the many, neither offers herself to the many for loving nor adorns herself for one when she has found him, 'pondering on worldly things, how to please her husband'.[21] Instead she has loved 'one handsome in beauty beyond the sons of men',[22] and because unlike Mary she could not conceive him in the flesh, her purpose is to conceive him in her heart, and also to keep her body virgin for him.

No fertility of body brought forth this species of virgins; it is no [xii] offspring of flesh and blood. If we seek out their mother, it is the Church. Only a sacred virgin brings forth sacred virgins, one who is espoused to the one husband, to be presented a chaste virgin to Christ.[23] From her who is not wholly virgin in body but is wholly virgin in spirit, are born sacred virgins in both body and spirit.

12. Habeant coniugia bonum suum, non quia filios procreant sed quia honeste, quia licite, quia pudice, quia socialiter procreant et procreatos pariter salubriter instanter educant, quia tori fidem [XIII] inuicem servant, quia sacramentum conubii non uiolant. Haec tamen omnia humani officii sunt munera; uirginalis autem integritas et per piam continentiam ab omni concubitu immunitas angelica portio est,²⁴ et in carne corruptibili incorruptionis perpetuae meditatio. Cedat huic omnis fecunditas carnis, omnis pudicitia coniugalis; illa non est in potestate, illa non est in aeternitate; fecunditatem carnalem non habet liberum arbitrium, pudicitiam coniugalem non habet caelum. Profecto habebunt magnum aliquid praeter ceteros in illa communi immortalitate, qui habent aliquid iam non carnis in carne.

13. Vnde mirabiliter desipiunt qui putant huius continentiae bonum non esse necessarium propter regnum caelorum sed propter praesens saeculum, quod scilicet coniugia terrenis curis pluribus atque artioribus distenduntur, qua molestia uirgines et continentes carent; quasi ob hoc tantum melius sit non coniugari, ut huius temporis relaxentur angustiae, non quod in futurum saeculum aliquid prosit! Hanc uanam sententiam ne cordis propria uanitate protulisse uideantur, adhibent ex apostolo testimonium ubi ait: *De uirginibus autem praeceptum domini non habeo, consilium autem do, tamquam misericordiam consecutus a deo ut fidelis essem. Existimo itaque hoc bonum esse propter praesentem necessitatem, quia bonum est homini sic esse.*²⁵ Ecce, inquiunt, ubi manifestat apostolus hoc propter praesentem necessitatem bonum esse, non propter futuram aeternitatem. Quasi praesentis necessitatis rationem haberet apostolus nisi prouidens et consulens in futurum, cum omnis eius dispensatio non nisi ad uitam aeternam uocet!

[XIV]   14. Praesens ergo est uitanda necessitas, sed tamen quae aliquid bonorum impedit futurorum; qua necessitate uita cogitur coniugalis cogitare quae mundi sunt, quomodo placeat uir uxori uel uxor uiro, non quod ea separent a regno dei, sicut sunt peccata quae ideo praecepto non consilio cohibentur, quia domino praecipienti non oboedire damnabile est; sed illud, quod in ipso dei regno

---

²⁴ Cf. Matt. 22: 30, also evoked below in 'there is no married chastity in heaven'.
²⁵ 1 Cor. 7: 25f.

12. Marriages are to possess their own good, not because they bring forth children, but because they bring them forth honourably, lawfully, and chastely, for the good of society; and once they are begotten, they likewise bring them up in a wholesome and purposeful way. Marriage is a good also because the partners preserve for each other the fidelity of the marriage-bed, and because they do not violate the sacrament of marriage.

All these, however, are duties of human obligation, whereas [XIII] unsullied virginity and abstention from all intercourse by devoted continence is the role assigned to angels,[24] the intention to preserve enduring incorruption while in the corruptible flesh. All physical fertility, all marital chastity must yield precedence to this, for the first does not lie within men's power, and the second does not abide in eternity; free will does not control bodily fertility, and there is no married chastity in heaven. It is certain that those who already in the flesh possess something not of the flesh will attain a grandeur beyond the rest in that immortality which is shared by all.

13. So those who believe that the efficacy of this continence is essential not for life in the kingdom of heaven but for that in the present world are strangely misguided. They argue that marriages are a source of tension, because of the quite numerous and constricting earthly cares, and that virgins and those who practise continence are free of such troubles. As if it were better not to marry solely to be released from today's hardships, and not because there will be some advantage for the age to come! So as not to appear to have advanced this empty doctrine from their own emptiness of heart, they adduce evidence from the Apostle, where he says: 'So far as virgins are concerned, I have no commandment from the Lord, but I offer this counsel as one who has obtained from God the mercy of being trustworthy. I think, then, that in view of the present necessity it is good for a man to remain as he is'.[25] Observe, they say, that the Apostle here reveals that this is good for the present necessity, not for the eternity to come. As if the Apostle was taking stock of the present necessity without foresight and thought for the future, whereas the entire ordering of his thought summons us solely to eternal life!

14. We must accordingly skirt 'the present necessity', but only that [XIV] which impedes any of our future blessings. It is this necessity which compels those in married life to take thought for the things of the world—how a husband is to please his wife, or a wife her husband. Not that such things cut us off from God's kingdom, as do sins

amplius haberi posset, si amplius cogitaretur quomodo placendum esset deo, minus erit utique, cum hoc ipsum minus coniugii necessitate cogitatur.

Ideo *De uirginibus* inquit *praeceptum domini non habeo*; praecepto enim quisquis non obtemperat, reus est et debitor poenae. Proinde quia uxorem ducere uel nubere peccatum non est, si autem peccatum esset praecepto uetaretur, propterea praeceptum domini de uirginibus nullum est.

Sed quoniam deuitatis remissisue peccatis adeunda est uita aeterna, in qua est quaedam egregia gloria non omnibus in aeternum uicturis, sed quibusdam ibi tribuenda, cui consequendae parum est liberatum esse a peccatis, nisi aliquid ipsi liberatori uoueatur, quod non sit criminis non uouisse sed uouisse ac reddidisse sit laudis, '*Consilium* inquit *do, tamquam misericordiam consecutus a deo ut fidelis essem*; neque enim inuidere debeo fidele consilium qui non meis meritis sed dei misericordia sum fidelis; *existimo itaque hoc bonum esse propter praesentem necessitatem.*'²⁶ 'Hoc', inquit, 'unde praeceptum domini non habeo, sed consilium do, hoc est, de uirginibus existimo bonum esse propter praesentem necessitatem. Noui enim quid praesentis temporis, cui coniugia seruiunt, necessitas cogat ut ea quae dei sunt minus cogitentur quam sufficit adipiscendae illi gloriae quae non erit omnium quamuis in aeterna uita ac salute manentium; *Stella enim ab stella differt in gloria. Sic et resurrectio mortuorum. Bonum est ergo homini sic esse.*'²⁷

[xv]   15. Deinde adiungit idem apostolus et dicit: *Adligatus es uxori? Ne quaesieris solutionem. Solutus es ab uxore? Ne quaesieris uxorem.*²⁸ Horum duorum quod prius posuit ad praeceptum pertinet, contra quod non licet facere. Non enim licet dimittere uxorem nisi ex causa fornicationis, sicut in euangelio ipse dominus dicit.²⁹ Illud autem quod addidit, *Solutus es ab uxore? Ne quaesieris uxorem*, consilii sententia est, non praecepti; licet itaque facere, sed melius est non facere. Denique continuo subiecit: *Et si acceperis uxorem, non peccasti; et si nupserit uirgo, non peccat.*³⁰ Illud autem prius cum

---

²⁶ See n. 25. Augustine thus interprets 'the present necessity' (which Paul relates to the imminence of the Parousia) as the need to consider the welfare of a spouse, which virgins forgo to serve the Lord.
²⁷ 1 Cor. 15: 41 f., 7: 26.   ²⁸ 1 Cor. 7: 27.   ²⁹ Cf. Matt. 19: 9.
³⁰ 1 Cor. 7: 28.

forbidden by commandment and not counsel (for it is a cause of condemnation not to heed the Lord's commandment); but that greater possible reward in God's kingdom, which is consequent upon giving greater thought to how to please God, will certainly be diminished when less thought is given to this because of the requirements of marriage.

So when Paul says 'So far as virgins are concerned, I have no commandment from the Lord', the point is that if someone disobeys a commandment, he is guilty and subject to punishment. So because it is not a sin to take a wife or marry a husband (for if it were a sin, it would be forbidden by a commandment), there is no commandment of the Lord which binds virgins.

However, in the eternal life which is to be attained by avoidance or forgiveness of sins, there is an illustrious glory which is to be assigned not to all who will dwell in eternity, but to certain individuals there, and to obtain this it is not sufficient to have been freed from sins; some vow must also be made to him who has delivered us. (It is not a sin to have failed to make such a vow, but it is praiseworthy to have made and delivered it.) It is for this reason that Paul says: 'I offer this counsel as one who has obtained from God the mercy of being trustworthy, for I must not begrudge faithful counsel because I am trustworthy not by my own merits, but by God's mercy. I therefore think that this good is for the present necessity.'[26] What he is saying is: 'I offer counsel on an issue on which I have no commandment from the Lord; so far as virgins are concerned, I think that their state is good because of the present necessity. For I know that the needs of the present time, to which marriage-partners are subject, compel them to devote less thought to the things of God than is enough to attain that glory not attained by all who will abide in eternal life and salvation. "For star differs from star in glory, and it is the same with the resurrection of the dead." It is therefore good for a man to remain as he is.'[27]

15. The Apostle then develops the point in these words: 'Are you bound to a wife? Do not seek to free yourself. Are you unattached to a wife? Do not seek one.'[28] The first of the two statements is part of a commandment which it is not permitted to transgress; for it is not permitted to put away a wife except for fornication, as the Lord himself states in the gospel.[29] As for Paul's further statement, 'Are you unattached to a wife? Do not seek one', this expresses counsel, not commandment, so it is permitted to take a wife, but it is better not to do so. Finally, he there and then added, 'And if you have taken a wife, you have not sinned; and if a virgin marries, she does not sin'.[30] But

[xv]

dixisset, *Adligatus es uxori? Ne quaesieris solutionem,* numquid addidit 'Et si solueris, non peccasti'? Iam enim supra dixerat: *His autem qui sunt in coniugio praecipio non ego sed dominus, uxorem a uiro non discedere; quodsi discesserit, manere innuptam aut uiro suo reconciliari.*[31] Fieri enim potest ut non sua culpa sed mariti discedat. Deinde ait *Et uir uxorem ne dimittat,* quod nihilominus ex praecepto domini posuit, nec ibi addidit 'Et si dimiserit, non peccat'. Praeceptum est enim hoc, cui non oboedire peccatum est, non consilium quo si uti nolueris minus boni adipisceris, non mali aliquid perpetrabis. Propterea cum dixisset *Solutus es ab uxore? Ne quaesieris uxorem,* quia non praecipiebat ne malum fieret, sed consulebat ut melius fieret, continuo subiunxit: *Et si acceperis uxorem, non peccasti; et si nupserit uirgo, non peccat.*

[XVI]   16. Addidit tamen: *Tribulationem autem carnis habebunt huius modi, ego autem uobis parco,*[32] hoc modo exhortans ad uirginitatem continentiamque perpetuam ut aliquantulum a nuptiis etiam deterreret, modeste sane, non tamquam a re mala et illicita, sed tamquam ab onerosa ac molesta. Aliud est enim admittere carnis turpitudinem, aliud habere carnis tribulationem; illud est criminis facere, hoc laboris est pati, quem plerumque homines etiam pro officiis honestissimis non recusant. Sed pro habendo coniugio iam hoc tempore, quo non per carnis propaginem uenturo Christo ipsius prolis propagatione seruitur, istam tribulationem carnis, quam nupturis praedicit apostolus, suscipere tolerandam perstultum esset, nisi metueretur incontinentibus ne temptante Satana in peccata damnabilia laberentur. Quod autem se dicit eis parcere quos ait tribulationem carnis habituros, nihil mihi interim sanius occurrit quam eum noluisse aperire et explicare uerbis eandem ipsam carnis tribulationem quam praenuntiauit eis qui eligunt nuptias in suspicionibus zeli coniugalis, in procreandis filiis atque nutriendis, in timoribus et maeroribus orbitatis. Quotus enim quisque, cum se conubii uinculis adligauerit, non istis trahatur atque agitetur adfectibus? Quos neque nos exaggerare

---

[31] 1 Cor. 7: 10 f.   [32] 1 Cor. 7: 28.

earlier, after saying 'Are you bound to a wife? Do not seek to free yourself', he did not add 'And if you do free yourself, you have not sinned',
did he? In fact he had already said earlier: 'To the married it is not I
but the Lord who gives this command, that a wife should not separate
from her husband; but if she does separate, she must remain unmarried, or be reconciled to her husband.'[31] For it can be the case that her
leaving is the husband's fault, and not hers. Next he says: 'Nor must a
husband put away his wife', which he equally expressed as the Lord's
commandment without the qualification 'And if he does put her
away, he does not sin.' For this is a commandment which it is sinful not
to obey, and not a counsel the refusal to follow which means you will
choose the lesser good but do nothing wrong. So after saying 'Are you
unattached to a wife? Do not seek one', since he was not command-
ing the avoidance of evil but counselling that something better be
done, he immediately added: 'And if you have taken a wife, you have
not sinned; and if a virgin marries, she does not sin.'

16. However, he did add: 'But those who marry will have [XVI]
tribulation of the flesh of this kind, but I would spare you that.'[32] In
this way he was urging virginity and lasting continence, with the
additional intention of expressing slight discouragement of marriage, quite mildly, as from something burdensome and troublesome, not from something evil and forbidden. For it is one thing to
perform disgraceful acts of the flesh, and another to experience
tribulation of the flesh; the first is sinful behaviour, whereas the second is endurance of hardship which people for the most part do not
refuse to undertake when they also shoulder the most honourable
obligations. It would be utterly foolish to undergo this burdensome
tribulation of the flesh, which the Apostle presages for those about
to marry, by indulging in marriage in this day and age, when no service is done to Christ's future coming by begetting offspring for him
through the progeny of the flesh, unless those with lack of self-
control should fear that at Satan's prompting they may fall into sins
which incur damnation. As for Paul's statement that he spares those
who he says will have tribulation of the flesh, at present no more sensible suggestion strikes me other than that he refused to divulge and
describe that tribulation of the flesh which he prophesied for those
who choose marriage; he means suspicions aroused by marital jeal-
ousy, problems in bearing and nurturing children, and the fears and
pains of childlessness. For how very few of those who bind themselves in the chains of marriage are not tugged and troubled by such

debemus, ne ipsis non parcamus, quibus parcendum existimauit apostolus.[33]

[XVII]   17. Tantum per hoc, quod breuiter posui, cautum fieri lectorem oportuit aduersus eos qui in hoc quod scriptum est, *tribulationem autem carnis habebunt huiusmodi, ego autem uobis parco*,[34] nuptiis calumniantur, quod eas ex obliquo sententia ista damnauerit; uelut ipsam damnationem noluerit dicere, cum ait *Ego autem uobis parco*, ut uidelicet cum istis parcit animae suae non pepercerit, si mentiendo dixit *Et si acceperis uxorem, non peccasti; et si nupserit uirgo, non peccat*. Quod qui de sancta scriptura credunt uel credi uolunt, tamquam uiam sibi muniunt ad mentiendi licentiam uel ad defensionem suae peruersae opinionis, ubicumque aliud sentiunt quam sana doctrina postulat. Si quid enim manifestum de diuinis libris prolatum fuerit quo eorum confutentur errores, hoc ad manum habent uelut scutum quo se aduersus ueritatem quasi tuentes nudent a diabolo uulnerandos, ut dicant hoc auctorem libri non uerum dixisse, alias ut infirmis parceret, alias ut contemptores terreret, sicut occurrerit causa qua eorum peruersa sententia defendatur. Atque ita dum ea quae opinantur defendere quam corrigere malunt, scripturarum sanctarum auctoritatem frangere conantur, qua una omnes ceruices superbae duraeque franguntur.

[XVIII]   18. Vnde sectatores et sectatrices perpetuae continentiae et sacrae uirginitatis admoneo ut bonum suum ita praeferant nuptiis ne malum iudicent nuptias, neque fallaciter sed plane ueraciter ab apostolo dictum nouerint: *Qui dat nuptum bene facit, et qui non dat nuptum melius facit. Et si acceperis uxorem, non peccasti; et si nupserit uirgo, non peccat*. Et paulo post: *Beatior autem erit si sic permanserit, secundum meam sententiam*. Et ne humana sententia putaretur, adiungit: *Puto autem, et ego spiritum dei habeo*.[35] Haec dominica, haec apostolica, haec uera, haec sana doctrina est sic eligere dona maiora ne minora damnentur.

Melior est in scriptura dei ueritas dei quam in cuiusquam mente aut carne uirginitas hominis. Quod castum est sic ametur ut quod uerum est non negetur. Nam quid mali non possunt etiam de sua

---

[33] This passage demonstrates Augustine's constant attempt to elucidate the meaning of the scriptures ('at present no more sensible suggestion . . .') and his scrupulous fidelity to their guidance ('we must not overemphasize . . .').
[34] n. 32. He refers to the Manichees' attacks on marriage.
[35] 1 Cor. 7: 38, 28, 40.

emotions? But we must not overemphasize these in case we fail to spare those who the Apostle considered should be spared.[33]

17. On these grounds alone which I have briefly outlined the [XVII] reader ought to have been put on his guard against those who exploit these words of scripture, 'They will have tribulation of the flesh of this kind, but I would spare you that.'[34] They use them to make false charges against marriage, arguing that this statement implicitly condemns it. As if Paul, when he says 'But I would spare you that', was unwilling to express explicit condemnation! In other words, when sparing them he did not spare his own soul's integrity, seeing that he had lied in saying, 'And if you have taken a wife, you have not sinned; and if a virgin marries, she does not sin.' Those who adopt this view of holy scripture, or want it to be adopted, are paving the way, so to speak, to give them freedom to lie or to defend their own misguided opinions whenever they take a view differing from what sound teaching demands. If any clear statement emerges from the divinely inspired books which refutes their wrong-headed belief, they keep this at hand to serve as a shield to protect themselves against the truth, and in so doing they leave themselves exposed to be wounded by the devil. They claim that the author of the book did not speak the truth, on some occasions to spare the weak, and at others to deter sceptics, according as the situation allowed them to defend their own misguided judgement. In this way, in seeking to defend rather than correct their views, they attempt to break down the authority of the sacred scriptures, by which alone all arrogant and obstinate necks are forced down.

18. Therefore my advice to men and women who opt for [XVIII] lasting continence and sacred virginity is this: they must rank the good that is theirs above that of marriage, but without regarding marriage as an evil. They should also realize that the following words of the Apostle are not false but clearly true: 'He who gives a daughter in marriage does well, and he who does not give her in marriage does better. And if you have taken a wife, you have not sinned; and if a virgin marries, she does not sin.' Then a little later: 'In my opinion she will be more blessed if she remains as she is.' To ensure that this is not taken as a human judgement, he adds: 'This is my thinking, and I also possess the spirit of God.'[35] This is the teaching of the Lord, the teaching of the Apostle, this is the true and sound teaching: to opt for the greater gift in such a way as not to condemn the lesser.

The truth of God in God's scripture is better than the virginity of man displayed in the mind or the body of any individual. What is

carne cogitare, qui credunt apostolicam linguam eo ipso loco ubi
uirginitatem corporis commendabat, a corruptione mendacii uirginem non fuisse? Primitus ergo ac maxime qui bonum uirginitatis
eligunt scripturas sanctas firmissime teneant nihil esse mentitas, ac
per hoc etiam illud uerum esse quod dictum est: *Et si acceperis uxorem,
non peccasti; et si nupserit uirgo, non peccat.* Nec putent minui tam magnum integritatis bonum si nuptiae non erunt malum. Immo uero
hinc sibi potius maioris gloriae palmam praeparatam esse confidat
quae non damnari si nuberet timuit, sed honoratius coronari quia
non nuberet concupiuit. Qui ergo sine coniugio permanere
uoluerint, non tamquam foueam peccati nuptias fugiant, sed
tamquam collem minoris boni transcendant ut in maioris continentiae monte requiescant. Ea quippe lege collis iste inhabitatur ut
non cum uoluerit quis emigret: *Mulier* enim *adligata est quamdiu uir
eius uiuit.*[36] Verumtamen ad continentiam uidualem ab ipso
tamquam gradu conscenditur; propter uirginalem uero uel decli-
nandus est non consentiendo petitoribus uel transiliendus praeue-
niendo petitores.

[XIX]   19. Ne quis autem putaret duorum operum, boni atque
melioris, aequalia fore praemia, propterea contra eos disserendum
fuit, qui quod ait apostolus, *Existimo autem hoc bonum esse propter praesentem necessitatem,*[37] ita interpretati sunt ut non propter regnum
caelorum sed propter saeculum praesens uirginitatem utilem dicer-
ent; tamquam in illa uita aeterna nihil ceteris amplius habituri
essent qui hoc melius elegissent! In qua disputatione cum ad illud
ueniremus quod idem apostolus ait, *Tribulationem autem carnis
habebunt huiusmodi, ego autem uobis parco,* in alios litigatores incurrimus,
qui non aequales perpetuae continentiae nuptias facerent, sed eas
omnino damnarent.[38] Nam cum error uterque sit, uel aequare
sanctae uirginitati nuptias uel damnare, nimis inuicem fugiendo
duo isti errores aduersa fronte confligunt, quia ueritatis medium
tenere noluerunt; quo et certa ratione et sanctarum scripturarum

[36] 1 Cor. 7: 39. In the sentence that follows Augustine ranks virginity, widowhood, and marriage on a descending scale of merit; see [XLV] 46 below.
[37] 1 Cor. 7: 26. Augustine refers to the followers of Jovinian, who argued that those in the married state are as meritorious as virgins, and accordingly attain equal honour in heaven.
[38] 1 Cor. 7: 28; the Manichees advance this argument.

chaste must be loved in such a way that truth is not denied. Can those who believe that the Apostle's tongue was not free of defilement by the corruption of lying, in that very passage where he was extolling physical virginity, put no limit on the evil thoughts which they entertain about their own flesh? First and foremost, then, those who choose the good of virginity must most firmly hold that the sacred scriptures have told no lies, and that this statement accordingly is also true: 'And if you take a wife, you have not sinned; and if a virgin marries, she does not sin.' But they must not think either that the great good of virginity is demeaned if marriage is not an evil. On the contrary, the virgin must rest assured that the palm of greater glory lies in wait for her precisely because she did not fear condemnation had she married, but was eager to obtain a more honourable crown because she did not marry. So those who have decided to remain unmarried should not avoid marriage as if it were a cesspool of sin, but they should mount above it as though it were the hillock of the lesser good, to take their rest on the mountain-peak of continence, which is higher. For residence on that hillock is governed by the law that none may leave it at will, for 'As long as her husband lives, a wife is bound by it'.[36] From that rung a woman mounts to continence in widowhood; but to attain the continence of virginity, that rung is either to be avoided by refusing the advances of suitors, or is to be surmounted by forestalling them.

19. I did not however want anyone to think that there will be equal [XIX] rewards for the two modes of life, the good and the better, and accordingly it was necessary to argue against those who interpreted that statement of the Apostle, 'I think, however, that this is good for the present necessity',[37] as a declaration that virginity was useful not for life in the kingdom of heaven, but for the present age. As if those who had chosen the better way would not in the eternal life to come enjoy greater honour than the rest! When in the course of this debate we came to the further statement of the Apostle, 'They will have tribulation of the flesh of this kind, but I spare you that', we encountered other disputants who did not regard marriage as equal to permanent continence, but condemned it utterly.[38] Both views are erroneous, making marriage equal to sacred virginity and condemning it; the two errors in their excessive eagerness to avoid each other end up by locking horns with each other through their unwillingness to hold the middle path of truth. That middle way enables us both by sure reason and by the authority of holy scripture to establish that

auctoritate nec peccatum esse nuptias inuenimus nec eas bono uel uirginalis continentiae uel etiam uidualis aequamus.

[xx]   Alii quippe adpetendo uirginitatem, nuptias tamquam adulterium detestandum esse putauerunt; alii uero defendendo conubium excellentiam perpetuae continentiae nihil mereri amplius quam coniugalem pudicitiam uoluerunt. Quasi uel Susannae bonum Mariae sit humiliatio, uel Mariae maius bonum Susannae debeat esse damnatio![39]

20. Absit ergo ut ita dixerit apostolus nuptis siue nupturis *Ego autem uobis parco*, tamquam noluerit dicere quae poena coniugatis in futuro saeculo debeatur; absit ut a Daniele de temporali iudicio liberatam Paulus mittat in gehennam; absit ut maritalis torus ei poena sit ante tribunal Christi cui fidem seruando elegit sub falsa accusatione adulterii uel periclitari uel mori. Quid egit uox illa, *Melius est mihi incidere in manus uestras quam peccare in conspectu dei*,[40] si deus eam fuerat non quia pudicitiam nuptialem seruabat liberaturus, sed quia nupserat damnaturus? Et nunc quotiens castitas coniugalis aduersus calumniatores criminatoresque nuptiarum scripturae sanctae ueritate munitur, totiens cum sancto spiritu contra falsos testes Susanna defenditur, totiens a falso crimine liberatur et multo maiore negotio. Tunc enim uni coniugatae, nunc omnibus; tunc de occulto et falso adulterio, nunc de uero et manifesto conubio crimen intenditur; tunc una mulier ex eo quod iniqui seniores dicebant, nunc omnes mariti et uxores ex eo quod apostolus dicere noluit accusantur. Damnationem quippe uestram, inquiunt, tacuit cum ait *Ego autem uobis parco*. Quis hoc? Nempe ille qui superius dixerat: *Et si acceperis uxorem, non peccasti; et si nupserit uirgo, non peccat.* Cur igitur in eo quod modeste tacuit coniugiorum suspicamini crimen, et in eo quod aperte dixit coniugiorum non agnoscitis defensionem? An eos damnat tacitus quos locutus absoluit? Nonne iam mitius accusatur Susanna non de coniugio sed de ipso adulterio quam doctrina apostolica de mendacio? Quid in tanto periculo faceremus

---

[39] For Susanna, chaste wife of Joachim at Babylon, see Dan. 13. She was falsely accused of adultery by two lascivious elders, and saved from execution by Daniel's intervention at her trial. She became for Christians the traditional model of marital chastity. For the virgin Mary as model of perpetual continence, see [IV] 4 above.

[40] Dan. 13: 23.

marriage is not a sin, yet also to refuse to rank it as equal to the good
of continence exercised by virgins and by widows too.

Some indeed in espousing virginity have believed that we should [xx]
stigmatize marriage as adultery; others in defending marriage
would have it that the pre-eminence of perpetual continence
deserves no greater honour than marital chastity. This is to argue
that the good of Susanna demeans Mary, or that the greater good of
Mary must spell condemnation for Susanna![39]

20. So let it not be said that the Apostle stated 'But I spare you
that' to those who were married or about to marry with the impli-
cation that he was unwilling to specify the punishment in store for
married persons in the age to come. Let it not be said that Paul con-
signs to hell the woman whom Daniel freed from condemnation in
this passing world; let it not be said that the marriage-bed brings
punishment at Christ's judgement-seat to the woman who in maintaining fidelity opted for condemnation or death on the false charge
of adultery. What was the point of her words 'It is better for me to
fall into your hands than to sin in God's sight'[40] if God's intention
was not to free her because she preserved the chastity of her marriage, but to condemn her for having married? Even today, whenever conjugal chastity is defended by the truth of holy scripture
against those who tell lies and bring charges against marriage,
Susanna in company with the holy Spirit is being defended on those
occasions against false witnesses, and acquitted on that false charge
in a situation much more troublesome. For in her case the charge
was against one married person, but now it is against all; then the
charge levelled was of secret and untruthful adultery, but now it is of
true and open marriage; then the one woman was arraigned upon
the allegation of wicked elders, but now all husbands and wives are
accused on what the Apostle refused to state. They claim that when
Paul said 'But I spare you', he suppressed mention of your damnation. Yet who was he who uttered those words? Why, the very
person who had earlier said, 'And if you take a wife, you have not
sinned; and if a virgin marries, she does not sin.' Why then do you
people suspect an accusation against marriages from his disciplined
silence, yet fail to acknowledge a defence of them in his explicit
statement? So is his silence a condemnation of those whom his
words exonerate? Is the accusation against Susanna—not of being
married, but of adultery itself—not milder than the indictment of
Paul's teaching on a charge of lying? How would we react to judicial

nisi tam certum apertumque esset pudicas nuptias non debere
damnari, quam certum apertumque est sanctam scripturam non
posse mentiri?

[XXI]   21. Hic dicet aliquis: quid hoc pertinet ad sacram uirginitatem
uel perpetuam continentiam, cuius praedicatio isto sermone suscepta est? Cui respondeo primo quod superius commemoraui, ex
hoc gloriam maioris illius boni esse maiorem, quod eius adipiscendae causa bonum coniugale transcenditur, non peccatum
coniugii deuitatur. Alioquin perpetuae continentiae non praecipue
laudari, sed tantum non uituperari sufficeret, si propterea teneretur
quoniam nubere crimen esset. Deinde quia non humana sententia
sed diuina scripturae auctoritate ad tam excellens donum homines
exhortandi sunt, non mediocriter neque praetereunter agendum est,
ne cuiquam ipsa diuina scriptura in aliquo mentita uideatur.
Dehortantur enim potius quam exhortantur uirgines sacras qui eas
sic permanere nuptiarum damnatione compellunt. Vnde enim
confidant uerum esse quod scriptum est *Et qui non dat nuptum melius
facit,* si falsum putant esse quod iuxta superius nihilominus scriptum
est *Et qui dat uirginem suam bene facit*?[41] Si autem loquenti scripturae
de nuptiarum bono indubitanter crediderint, eadem caelestis
eloquii ueracissima auctoritate firmatae ad melius suum feruenti ac
fidenti alacritate transcurrent.

Vnde iam satis pro suscepto negotio diximus, et quantum potuimus demonstrauimus nec illud quod ait apostolus, *Existimo autem
hoc bonum esse propter praesentem necessitatem,* sic esse accipiendum,
tamquam in hoc saeculo meliores sint sacrae uirgines fidelibus coniugatis, in regno autem caelorum atque in futuro saeculo pares sint,
nec illud ubi ait de nubentibus *Tribulationem autem carnis habebunt
huiusmodi, ego autem uobis parco,* ita intellegendum tamquam nuptiarum peccatum et damnationem maluerit tacere quam dicere.
Harum quippe duarum sententiarum singulas duo errores sibimet
contrarii non eas intellegendo tenuerunt. Illam enim *de praesenti
necessitate* illi pro se interpretantur qui nubentes non nubentibus
aequare contendunt, hanc uero ubi dictum est *Ego autem uobis parco*
illi qui nubentes damnare praesumunt. Nos autem secundum scripturarum sanctarum fidem sanamque doctrinam nec peccatum
esse dicimus nuptias, et earum tamen bonum non solum infra

danger like hers, if it were not as certain and crystal-clear that marriage should not be condemned as it is certain and crystal-clear that
scripture cannot lie?

21. At this point someone will say: what relevance has this to [XXI]
sacred virginity or lifelong continence, praise of which was the initial theme of this discourse? My first reply to this is the point I made
earlier: the glory of the greater good is greater not because its attainment means that marriage is shunned as a sin, but that its good is
transcended. Otherwise it would be enough for lifelong continence
not to be accorded special praise, but merely to avoid blame if it
were embraced because marriage was a serious sin. Secondly, since
people are to be urged to grasp so pre-eminent a gift on the divine
authority of scripture and not by human judgement, we must act in
no mealy-mouthed or dismissive fashion to ensure that divine scripture itself does not seem to anyone to have lied in any respect. For
those who urge sacred virgins to remain so by condemning marriage are a source of discouragement rather than encouragement to
them. How are they to be sure that those words of scripture 'And he
who does not give his daughter in marriage, does better' are true, if
they hold that the words preceding are false, which none the less
state 'And he who gives his daughter in marriage does well'?[41] On
the other hand, if they put unhesitating belief in what scripture says
about the good of marriage, they will be sustained by the authority
of the divine utterance in all its truth, and they will hasten over to
their own better good with glowing and confident eagerness.

So we have now said enough on the task undertaken. We have
shown to the best of our ability that the Apostle's words 'But I think this
good is for the present necessity' are not to be interpreted as meaning
that sacred virgins are better than faithful spouses in this world but
equal to them in the kingdom of heaven in the age to come. Again,
when Paul says of married people, 'But they will have tribulation of the
flesh of this kind, but I spare you', we are not to understand it as imply-
ing that he preferred to leave unspoken rather than to specify that marriage incurred sin and condemnation. Two errors which contradict
each other have manipulated each of these two passages through a failure to understand them. Those who seek to put married people on a
level with the unmarried interpret the phrase 'for the present necessity' in support of their position; those who take it upon themselves to
condemn married people interpret 'But I spare you' to support theirs.
We, however, follow the reliable and sound teaching of the holy

uirginalem uerum etiam infra uidualem continentiam constitu-
imus, praesentemque necessitatem coniugatorum non quidem ad
uitam aeternam, uerumtamen ad excellentem gloriam et honorem
qui perpetuae continentiae reseruatur, impedire eorum meritum
dicimus, neque hoc tempore nisi eis qui se non continent nuptias
expedire, tribulationemque carnis ex affectu carnali uenientem,
sine quo nuptiae incontinentium esse non possunt, nec tacere
uoluisse apostolum uera praemonentem nec plenius explicare
hominum infirmitati parcentem.

[XXII]   22. Nunc iam scripturarum diuinarum euidentissimis testi-
moniis, quae pro nostrae memoriae modulo recordari ualuerimus,
clarius appareat non propter praesentem huius saeculi uitam, sed
propter futuram quae in regno caelorum promittitur, perpetuam
continentiam deligendam. Quis autem hoc non aduertat in eo
quod paulo post idem apostolus ait: *Qui sine uxore est, cogitat ea quae
sunt domini, quomodo placeat domino; qui autem matrimonio iunctus est, cogitat ea quae sunt mundi, quomodo placeat uxori. Et diuisa est mulier innupta et
uirgo; quae innupta est sollicita est quae sunt domini, ut sit sancta et corpore et
spiritu; quae autem nupta est sollicita est quae sunt mundi, quomodo placeat
uiro?*[42] Non utique ait: 'Cogitat ea quae securitatis sunt in hoc
saeculo, ut sine grauioribus molestiis tempus transigat'; neque ad
hoc diuisam dicit innuptam et uirginem ab ea quae nupta est, id est
distinctam atque discretam, ut innupta in hac uita secura sit propter
temporales molestias euitandas quibus nupta non caret, sed *Cogitat*
inquit *quae sunt domini, quomodo placeat domino*, et *Sollicita est quae sunt
domini, ut sit sancta et corpore et spiritu*. Nisi forte usque adeo quisque
insipienter contentiosus est ut conetur adserere non propter regnum caelorum sed propter praesens saeculum domino placere nos
uelle, aut propter uitam istam non propter aeternam esse sanctas et
corpore et spiritu. Hoc credere quid est aliud nisi miserabiliorem
esse omnibus hominibus? Sic enim apostolus ait: *Si in hac uita tantum
in Christo sperantes sumus, miserabiliores sumus omnibus hominibus.*[43] An
uero qui frangit panem suum esurienti, si tantum propter hanc

---

[42] 1 Cor. 7: 32 ff. For the variant reading from the Vulgate in Augustine's text, see *De bono
coniugali* [X] 10 with n. 47 there.
[43] 1 Cor. 15: 19.

scriptures to state that marriage is no sin, but on the other hand to rank the good of marriage below not only the continence of virgins, but also that of widows. We also say that 'the present necessity' of married people is an obstacle not indeed to their attaining eternal life, but to gaining that pre-eminent glory and honour reserved for lifelong continence; and further, that in this day and age marriage is a useful course only for those who lack self-control; and that the Apostle, in his forewarning of the truth, sought neither to be reticent about the tribulation of the flesh (which results from the bodily emotions which are an essential feature of marriages between partners lacking self-control), nor in his concern for human weakness to explain it more fully.

22. It must now be more clearly evident, from the most conspicuous testimonies of the divine scriptures which we have been able to recall within the modest limits of our recollection, that lifelong continence is to be chosen not for the present life in this world but for the future life promised in the kingdom of heaven. Who could not observe this from the comment that the self-same Apostle makes a little later: 'He that is without a wife ponders the things of the Lord, how to please the Lord; but he who is joined in marriage ponders the things of the world, how to please his wife. The unmarried woman and virgin is set apart; she who is unmarried is concerned for the things of the Lord, that she may be holy in both body and spirit. But the married woman is concerned for the things of the world, how to please her husband'?[42] He certainly does not say: 'She takes thought for the things which promote freedom from the cares in this world, that she may pass her time free of heavier troubles.' Nor does he say that the unmarried virgin is 'set apart' (in other words, distinct and separated) from the married woman so that being unmarried she may live an untroubled life, because she is free from the temporal worries which are the lot of the married woman. No; 'She ponders', he says, 'the things of the Lord' and 'She is concerned for the things of the Lord, that she may be holy in both body and spirit.' But perhaps all are so foolishly argumentative as to endeavour to maintain that we seek to please the Lord not for life in the kingdom of heaven, but for that of the present world; or that virgins are holy in both body and spirit for this life, and not for the eternal life to come. What does such a belief imply except being more wretched than all mankind? That is certainly what the Apostle states: 'If our hope in Christ is for this life only, we are more wretched than all men.'[43] Surely the man who breaks bread to share with one who is hungry is a fool if he does it only with

uitam facit, stultus est, et ille erit prudens qui castigat corpus suum usque ad continentiam qua nec coniugio misceatur, si ei nihil proderit in regno caelorum?

[XXIII] 23. Postremo ipsum dominum audiamus euidentissimam hanc sententiam proferentem. Nam cum de coniugibus non separandis nisi causa fornicationis diuine ac terribiliter loqueretur, dixerunt ei discipuli: *Si talis est causa cum uxore, non expedit nubere.* Quibus ille *Non omnes* inquit *capiunt uerbum hoc. Sunt enim spadones qui ita nati sunt; sunt autem alii qui ab hominibus facti sunt; et sunt spadones qui se ipsos castrauerunt propter regnum caelorum. Qui potest capere, capiat.*[44] Quid ueracius, quid lucidius dici potuit? Christus dicit, Veritas dicit, Virtus et Sapientia dei dicit eos qui pio proposito ab uxore ducenda se continuerint, castrare se ipsos propter regnum caelorum, et contra humana uanitas impia temeritate contendit eos qui hoc faciunt praesentem tantummodo necessitatem molestiarum coniugalium deuitare, in regno autem caelorum amplius quidquam ceteris non habere.

[XXIV] 24. De quibus autem spadonibus loquitur deus per Esaiam prophetam, quibus se dicit daturum in domo sua et in muro suo locum nominatum meliorem multo quam filiorum atque filiarum, nisi de his qui se ipsos castrant propter regnum caelorum?[45] Nam illis quibus ipsum uirile membrum debilitatur ut generare non possint sicut sunt eunuchi diuitum et regum, sufficit utique, cum Christiani fiunt et dei praecepta custodiunt, eo tamen proposito sunt ut coniuges si potuissent haberent, ceteris in domo dei coniugatis fidelibus adaequari, qui prolem licite pudiceque susceptam in dei timore nutriunt, docentes filios suos ut ponant in deo spem suam, non autem accipere meliorem locum quam est filiorum atque filiarum. Neque enim uxores animi uirtute sed carnis necessitate non ducunt. Contendat sane qui uoluerit de his prophetam spadonibus hoc praenuntiasse qui corpore abscisi sunt; iste quoque error causae quam suscepimus suffragatur. Neque enim spadones

---

[44] Matt. 19: 10 ff.

[45] Isa. 56: 5. The prophet (Trito-Isaiah) is concerned to modify the harsh proscription of eunuchs at Deut. 23: 1, where they are excluded from the assembly; the prophet states that if such men are righteous they will have an honoured place in the Temple and in the eyes of posterity. The Fathers interpreted 'eunuchs' as a mystical allusion to consecrated virgins; see Jerome, *In Esaiam* 15: 21 (this treatise appeared after AD 408, and Jerome's putative sources have not survived, but it seems certain that this interpretation was a commonplace among Christian exegetes by Augustine's time).

this life in mind; and will that man be wise who disciplines his body to embrace even the continence which foregoes sexual intercourse in marriage, if he is to gain no benefit in the kingdom of heaven?

23. Finally, let us listen to the Lord himself as he delivers this [XXIII] clearest of judgements. When he stated in divine and awe-inspiring tones that married couples should not part except for fornication, his disciples said to him: 'If such is the situation with a wife, it is better not to marry.' But he said to them: 'Not everyone can accept this teaching. For there are eunuchs who have been so from birth; there are others who have been made so by men; and there are eunuchs who have castrated themselves for the kingdom of heaven. Let anyone accept this who can.'[44] What could be said with greater truth and clarity? Christ states, Truth states, the Power and Wisdom of God states that those who with devoted resolve have refrained from taking a wife castrate themselves for the sake of the kingdom of heaven. By contrast, the empty minds of men with a rashness which is sacrilegious maintain that those who act in this way are merely avoiding 'the present necessity' of marital difficulties, and that in the kingdom of heaven they do not obtain any greater honour than the rest.

24. But when God speaks of these eunuchs through his [XXIV] prophet Isaiah, saying that he will grant them a place of renown much higher than that of his sons and daughters in his house and within his walls, to which of them does he refer but those who castrate themselves for the sake of the kingdom of heaven?[45] As for those such as the eunuchs of plutocrats and kings, whose male organ is so enfeebled that they cannot father children, it is certainly enough, once they become Christians and keep God's commandments, and would have planned to take wives had they been able to do so, that they become equal in God's house to the other faithful who are married, that is, to the couples who raise and nurture their offspring lawfully and chastely in the fear of God, and teach their children to put their hope in God; but that they do not occupy a place higher than those sons and daughters. For it is not their strength of mind but physical constraints that cause them not to marry. Those who wish can argue if they like that the prophet made his declaration in reference to those physically mutilated, for this misconception lends further support to the case I have mounted; for God has not advanced those eunuchs above those who find no place in his house, but specifically above those who uphold the merit of

istos eis qui in domo eius non habent locum praetulit deus, sed eis utique qui in filiis generandis coniugalis uitae meritum seruant. Nam cum dicit *Dabo eis locum multo meliorem*, ostendit et coniugatis dari, sed multo inferiorem.

Vt ergo concedamus in domo dei praedictos futuros eunuchos secundum carnem, qui in populo Israhel non fuerunt,[46] quia et ipsos uidemus cum Iudaei non fiant tamen fieri Christianos, nec de illis dixisse prophetam qui proposito continentiae coniugia non quaerentes se ipsos castrant propter regnum caelorum, itane tanta dementia quisquam est contrarius ueritati ut in carne factos eunuchos meliorem quam coniugati locum in domo dei habere credat, et pio proposito continentes, corpus usque ad contemptas nuptias castigantes, se ipsos non in corpore sed in ipsa concupiscentiae radice castrantes, caelestem et angelicam uitam in terrena mortalitate meditantes, coniugatorum meritis pares esse contendat, et Christo laudanti eos qui se ipsos castrauerunt non propter hoc saeculum sed propter regnum caelorum Christianus contradicat, adfirmans hoc uitae praesenti esse utile, non futurae?

Quid aliud istis restat nisi ut ipsum regnum caelorum ad hanc temporalem uitam in qua nunc sumus asserant pertinere? Cur enim non et in hanc insaniam progrediatur caeca praesumptio? Et quid hac assertione furiosius? Nam etsi regnum caelorum aliquando ecclesia etiam quae hoc tempore est appellatur, ad hoc utique sic appellatur quia futurae uitae sempiternaeque colligitur. Quamuis ergo *promissionem habeat uitae praesentis et futurae*, in omnibus tamen bonis operibus suis non respicit *quae uidentur, sed quae non uidentur. Quae enim uidentur, temporalia sunt; quae autem non uidentur, aeterna.*[47]

[xxv]   25. Nec sane spiritus sanctus tacuit quod contra istos impudentissime ac dementissime peruicaces apertum atque inconcussum ualeret, eorumque beluinum impetum ab ouili suo inexpugnabili munitione repelleret. Cum enim dixisset de spadonibus *Dabo eis in domo mea et in muro meo locum nominatum, meliorem multo quam filiorum atque filiarum*, ne quis nimium carnalis existimaret aliquid in his uerbis temporale sperandum, continuo subiecit: *Nomen aeternum dabo eis, nec unquam deerit,*[48] tamquam diceret: Quid tergiuersaris,

---

[46] The citation from Isaiah continues with the promise of similar favour to foreigners who are like the eunuchs devout; Augustine seems to assume that they too are 'eunuchs'.

[47] 1 Tim. 4: 8; 2 Cor. 4: 18.

[48] Isa. 56: 5.

their married life by begetting children. For by his words "I will give them a place much higher", he shows that married people are also awarded a place, but one much lower.

Therefore, even granted that those mentioned as eunuchs physically not belonging to the people of Israel[46] will be in God's house, because we see that they too without becoming Jews become Christians; granted too that the prophet did not speak of those who eschew marriage and castrate themselves for the kingdom of heaven; is anyone imbued with such madness and is so hostile to the truth as to believe that those who have become eunuchs physically have a higher place in God's house than married people? And to maintain that those who with devoted resolve remain continent, disciplining their bodies to the point of spurning marriage, castrating themselves not physically but at the very root of concupiscence, pondering the life of heaven and of angels in their mortal life on earth, are merely equal to the merits of married people? And should the Christian argue against Christ, when he praises those who have castrated themselves not for this world but for the kingdom of heaven, and maintain that such a course is useful for the present and not the future life?

What remains for these persons except to argue that the kingdom of heaven itself lies in this transient life in which we now live? Why should blind presumption not advance as far as that madness? What is more lunatic than such a claim? True, the Church as it also exists here and now is sometimes called the kingdom of heaven, but it is so called specifically for the reason that it is being assembled for the eternal life to come. So though 'it possesses the promise of present and future life', in all its good works it looks not to 'the things seen but the things not seen, for the things which are seen are transient, but those unseen are eternal'.[47]

25. And indeed the holy Spirit has not refrained from an [xxv] effective response, open and unshakeable, against those most shamefully and crazily perverse individuals, nor from repulsing their bestial assault from his sheepfold, the defences of which cannot be stormed. For after his statement about the eunuchs 'I will give them in my house and within my walls a place of renown much higher than that of my sons and daughters', he sought to ensure that no one who was preoccupied with the flesh should have any worldly expectation from these words, so he at once added: 'I will give them fame everlasting which will never perish.'[48] It was as if he were saying: Why, unholy blindness, do you equivocate? Why do you

impia caecitas? Quid tergiuersaris? Quid serenitati ueritatis nebulas tuae peruersitatis offundis? Quid in tanta scripturarum luce tenebras unde insidieris inquiris? Quid temporalem tantummodo utilitatem promittis continentibus sanctis? *Nomen aeternum dabo eis.* Quid ab omni concubitu immunes et eo quoque ipso quo hinc sese abstinent, ea quae sunt domini cogitantes, quomodo placeant domino, ad terrenam commoditatem referre conaris? *Nomen aeternum dabo eis.* Quid regnum caelorum, propter quod se castrauerunt sancti spadones, in hac tantum uita intellegendum esse contendis? *Nomen aeternum dabo eis.* Et si forte hic ipsum aeternum pro diuturno conaris accipere, addo, accumulo, inculco *Nec unquam deerit.* Quid quaeris amplius? Quid dicis amplius? Aeternum hoc nomen quidquid illud est spadonibus dei, quod utique gloriam quamdam propriam excellentemque significat, non erit commune cum multis, quamuis in eodem regno et in eadem domo constitutis. Nam ideo fortassis et nomen dictum est quod eos quibus datur distinguit a ceteris.[49]

[XXVI] 26. 'Quid sibi ergo uult' inquiunt 'ille denarius qui opere uineae terminato aequaliter omnibus redditur, siue iis qui ex prima hora siue iis qui una hora operati sunt?'[50] Quid utique, nisi aliquid significat quod omnes communiter habebunt, sicuti est ipsa uita aeterna, ipsum regnum caelorum, ubi erunt omnes quos deus praedestinauit uocauit iustificauit glorificauit?[51] *Oportet enim corruptibile hoc induere incorruptionem, et mortale hoc induere immortalitatem.*[52] Hic est ille denarius, merces omnium; *Stella* tamen *ab stella differt in gloria; sic et resurrectio mortuorum.* Haec sunt merita diuersa sanctorum. Si enim caelum significaretur illo denario, nonne in caelo esse omnibus est commune sideribus? Et tamen *Alia est gloria solis, alia gloria lunae, alia stellarum.*[53]

Si denarius ille pro sanitate corporis poneretur, nonne, cum recte ualemus omnibus membris, communis est sanitas, et si usque in mortem permaneat, pariter et aequaliter omnibus inest? Et tamen *Posuit deus membra singulum quodque eorum in corpore prout uoluit,*[54] ut nec totum sit oculus nec totum auditus nec totum odoratus, et quidquid

---

[49] In the citation from Isaiah, I translate *nomen* as 'fame'; here it is used in the literal sense of 'term' or 'name', referring to the title 'eunuch' which marks out consecrated virgins from other Christians.

[50] Cf. Matt. 20: 9 ff.   [51] Cf. Rom. 8: 30.   [52] 1 Cor. 15: 53.

[53] 1 Cor. 15: 41 f.   [54] 1 Cor. 12: 18.

equivocate? Why do you shroud the clear sky of truth with the
clouds of your debased thinking? Why do you search for darkness in
the dazzling light of the scriptures to lay an ambush there? Why do
you promise merely transient benefit to the holy ones who practise
continence? "I will give them fame everlasting." Why do you seek to
direct towards temporal profit those who have no truck with any
sexual intercourse, and who moreover in abstaining from it "ponder the things of the Lord, how to please the Lord"? "I will give
them fame everlasting." Why do you claim that the kingdom of
heaven, for which these holy eunuchs have castrated themselves, is
to be understood only in the context of this life? "I will give them
fame everlasting." If by any chance at this juncture you try to interpret this word 'everlasting' as merely long-lasting, I add, I append, I
emphasize: "Which will never perish." What more do you seek?
What more have you to say? As applied to God's eunuchs this term
'everlasting', however interpreted, certainly denotes some unique
and outstanding glory; it will not be shared with the many, though
they will be set in the same kingdom and the same house. It is perhaps for this reason that the term 'eunuch' was employed, because
it marks out those to whom it is given from the rest.[49]

26. 'So what relevance', they ask, 'has that denarius which is
bestowed equally upon all, once the work in the vineyard is done,
whether on those who worked from the first hour or on those who
worked for a single hour?'[50] What indeed does it signify but something which all will have in common, namely eternal life itself, the
kingdom of heaven itself, where all will abide whom God has pre-
destined, summoned, justified, and glorified?[51] 'For this corruptible
body must put on incorruption, and this mortal body must put on
immortality.'[52] This is what the denarius is, the reward gained by all;
but 'Star differs from star in glory, and likewise with the resurrection
of the dead.' Such are the varying rewards of the saints; for should
heaven be denoted by the denarius, surely it is existence in the heavens that all the stars share? Yet 'There is one glory for the sun, and
another for the moon, and another for the stars.'[53]

Supposing the denarius signified health of body. That health is
surely shared by all its limbs as long as we remain physically fit in all
of them; and should that health continue until death, it persists
equally and alike in all of them. Yet 'God has so disposed each of the
limbs in the body as he willed',[54] so that it is not all eye, nor all ear,
nor all nose, and the other parts all have their individuality, though

[XXVI]

aliud habet suam proprietatem, quamuis aequaliter habeat cum omnibus sanitatem. Ita quia ipsa uita aeterna pariter erit omnibus sanctis, aequalis denarius omnibus attributus est; quia uero in ipsa uita aeterna distincte fulgebunt lumina meritorum, *Multae mansiones sunt* apud patrem.[55] Ac per hoc in denario quidem non impari non uiuet alius alio prolixius; in multis autem mansionibus honoratur alius alio clarius.

XXVII]   27. Pergite itaque sancti dei, pueri ac puellae, mares ac feminae, caelibes et innuptae, pergite perseueranter in finem; laudate dominum dulcius quem cogitatis uberius; sperate felicius cui seruitis instantius; amate ardentius cui placetis attentius; lumbis accinctis et lucernis ardentibus exspectate dominum quando ueniat a nuptiis.[56]. Vos adferetis ad nuptias agni canticum nouum, quod cantabitis in citharis uestris. Non utique tale quale cantat uniuersa terra, cui dicitur *Cantate domino canticum nouum, cantate domino, uniuersa terra,*[57] sed tale quale nemo poterit dicere nisi uos. Sic enim uos uidit in Apocalypsi quidam prae ceteris dilectus ab agno, qui discumbere super pectus eius solitus erat,[58] et bibebat et eructuabat mirabilia super caelestia uerbum dei. Ipse uos uidit duodecies duodena milia sanctorum citharoedorum illibatae uirginitatis in corpore, inuiolatae ueritatis in corde; et quia sequimini agnum quocumque ierit, scripsit ille de uobis.

Quo ire putamus hunc agnum, quo nemo eum sequi uel audeat uel ualeat nisi uos? Quo putamus eum ire? In quos saltus et prata? Vbi credo sunt gramina gaudia; non gaudia saeculi huius uana, insaniae mendaces, nec gaudia qualia in ipso regno dei ceteris non uirginibus, sed a ceterorum omnium gaudiorum sorte distincta, gaudia uirginum Christi, de Christo, in Christo, cum Christo, post Christum, per Christum, propter Christum. Gaudia propria uirginum Christi non sunt eadem non uirginum, quamuis Christi; nam sunt aliis alia, sed nullis talia. Ite in haec, sequimini agnum, quia et agni caro utique uirgo. Hoc enim in se retinuit auctus, quod matri non abstulit conceptus et natus. Merito eum sequimini uirginitate cordis et carnis, quocumque ierit. Quid est enim sequi nisi

[55] John 14: 2. For the suggestion here that virgins will get first-class accommodation in heaven, see Cyprian, *De habitu uirginis* 33.
[56] Cf. Luke 12: 35f.   [57] Ps. 95(96): 1.
[58] Cf. Apoc. 14: 1ff. John is regularly identified as 'the apostle loved before all others, who was wont to recline on his breast' (John 13: 23).

each shares good health with all the rest. In the same way eternal life will itself be shared alike by all the saints, and so the denarius has been allotted equally to all. But because in that eternal life the lights of their merits will shine differently, 'There are many dwelling-places' in the Father's house.[55] Accordingly, since the value of the denarius remains the same, one of us will not live longer than another, but in those numerous dwelling-places one will obtain brighter glory than another.

27. So press on, holy ones of God, boys and girls, males and females, unmarried men and women; press on unremittingly to the end. Praise the Lord in tones sweeter as your thoughts centre on him more fruitfully. Hope in him more blessedly as you serve him more urgently; love him more glowingly as you please him more diligently. With loins girt and lamps alight await the Lord's arrival from the wedding.[56] You will bring to the marriage of the Lamb a new song to play on your harps—not indeed one such as the whole earth sings when it is bidden 'Sing a new song to the Lord, sing to the Lord, the whole earth',[57] but one such as none but you will be able to sing. For in the *Apocalypse* this is how you were seen by the man beloved of the Lamb before all others, who was wont to recline on his breast,[58] who imbibed and vomited forth God's description of the wonders of heaven. That man saw you, twelve times twelve thousand blessed harpists, your virginity of body undefiled, your truth of heart inviolate, and he wrote these words about you because you follow the Lamb wherever he goes. [XXVII]

Where do we imagine this Lamb goes, when no one but you presumes or is able to follow him there? Into what glades and meadows? Where, I believe, the pasture is one of joys—not the empty joys of this world for they are deceitful lunacies, nor those joys in God's kingdom which accrue to the rest who are not virgins, but joys distinct from the portion of those allotted to all the rest. These are the joys of Christ's virgins, issuing from Christ, in Christ, with Christ, following Christ, through Christ, because of Christ. The joys peculiar to Christ's virgins are not the same as those of non-virgins, though these too are of Christ; for there are different joys for different persons, but no others obtain such as these. Advance towards them, follow the Lamb, for the Lamb in the flesh is assuredly virginal as well; for this he preserved for himself when he was full-grown, and he did not deprive his mother of it when he was conceived and born. Follow him as you deserve, because of

imitari? Quia *Christus pro nobis passus est relinquens nobis exemplum*, sicut ait apostolus Petrus, *ut sequamur uestigia eius*.[59] Hunc in eo quisque sequitur, in quo imitatur; non in quantum ille filius dei est unus per quem facta sunt omnia, sed in quantum filius hominis quae* oportebat in se praebuit imitanda. Et multa in illo ad imitandum omnibus praeponuntur, uirginitas autem carnis non omnibus; non enim habent quid faciant ut uirgines sint, in quibus iam factum est ut uirgines non sint.

[XXVIII]   28. Sequantur itaque agnum ceteri fideles, qui uirginitatem corporis amiserunt, non quocumque ille ierit sed quousque ipsi potuerint. Possunt autem ubique praeter cum in decore uirginitatis incedit. *Beati pauperes spiritu*;[60] imitamini eum *qui propter uos pauper factus est, cum diues esset. Beati mites*; imitamini eum qui dixit *Discite a me, quoniam mitis sum et humilis corde. Beati lugentes*; imitamini eum qui fleuit super Hierusalem. *Beati qui esuriunt et sitiunt iustitiam*; imitamini eum qui dixit *Meus cibus est ut faciam uoluntatem eius qui misit me. Beati misericordes*; imitamini eum qui uulnerato a latronibus et in uia iacenti semiuiuo desperatoque subuenit. *Beati mundicordes*; imitamini eum *qui peccatum non fecit, nec inuentus est dolus in ore eius. Beati pacifici*; imitamini eum qui pro suis persecutoribus dixit *Pater, ignosce illis, quia nesciunt quid faciunt. Beati qui persecutionem patiuntur propter iustitiam*; imitamini eum qui *pro uobis passus est, relinquens uobis exemplum ut sequamini uestigia eius*. Haec qui imitantur, in his agnum sequuntur. Sed certe etiam coniugati possunt ire per ista uestigia, etsi non perfecte in eadem forma ponentes pedem, uerumtamen in eisdem semitis gradientes.

[XXIX]   29. Sed ecce ille agnus graditur itinere uirginali. Quomodo post eum ibunt qui hoc amiserunt quod nullo modo recipiunt? Vos ergo, uos ite post eum, uirgines eius; uos et illuc ite post eum, quia propter hoc unum quocumque ierit sequimini eum. Ad quodlibet enim aliud sanctitatis donum quo eum sequantur, hortari possumus coniugatos praeter hoc quod irreparabiliter amiserunt.

---

[59] 1 Pet. 2: 21.
[60] For the sequence of the Beatitudes enumerated here, see Matt. 5: 3ff. Augustine had already composed a commentary verse by verse in his *De sermone Domini in monte* 1. 3 (AD 394). Here he more pithily glosses each of the eight with an apt citation from scripture. The references are: 2 Cor. 8: 9; Matt. 11: 29; Luke 19: 41; John 4: 34; Luke 10: 30ff.; 1 Pet. 2: 22: Luke 23: 34; 1 Pet, 2: 21.

---

* quae *PK*: quia *CB, Zycha*

your virginity in heart and flesh, wherever he goes, for what does 'follow' mean but 'imitate'? For as the apostle Peter says, 'Christ suffered for us, leaving us an example to follow in his steps.'[59] Each of us follows him in as much as we imitate him, not as the son of God through whom alone all things were made, but as the son of man who revealed in himself all that we must imitate. Many things in him are revealed for all to imitate, but bodily virginity is not set forth for all, for those who have already lost their virginity have not the means of being virgins.

28. So the rest of the faithful, who have lost their virginity, [XXVIII] must follow the Lamb not wherever he goes, but so far as they themselves can go. They can in fact follow everywhere except where he has advanced into the glory of virginity. 'Blessed are the poor in spirit';[60] imitate him 'who became poor for your sake, when he was rich'. 'Blessed are the meek'; imitate him who said 'Learn from me, for I am meek and humble of heart.' 'Blessed are they that mourn'; imitate him who wept over Jerusalem. 'Blessed are they that hunger and thirst after justice'; imitate him who said, 'My food is to do the will of him who sent me.' 'Blessed are the merciful'; imitate him who lent assistance to the man who was wounded by footpads, and lay on the road half-dead and beyond hope. 'Blessed are the merciful'; imitate him who 'committed no sin, nor was guile found in his mouth'. 'Blessed are the peace-makers'; imitate him who said on behalf of his persecutors, 'Father, forgive them, for they know not what they do.' 'Blessed are they that suffer persecution for justice's sake'; imitate him who 'suffered on your behalf, leaving you an example to follow in his footsteps'. Those who imitate him in these ways thereby follow the Lamb. But what is beyond doubt is that married people too can walk in his footsteps. Though they do not plant their feet perfectly in the same traces, they none the less tread the same paths.

29. But see, that Lamb treads the virgins' path, so how will [XXIX] those who have lost it follow him when they never recover it? So you who are his virgins, you must follow him on that path as well, for it is on this score alone that you follow him wherever he goes. We can encourage those who are married to advance towards any other gift of sanctity to which they can follow him, except to this, which they have lost beyond hope of recovery. Follow him therefore, maintaining with constancy the course which you vowed with burning zeal to take. While you can, ensure that you do not lose the good of

Vos itaque sequimini eum tenendo perseueranter quod uouistis ardenter. Facite cum potestis ne uirginitatis bonum a uobis pereat, cui facere nihil potestis ut redeat. Videbit uos cetera multitudo fidelium, quae agnum ad hoc sequi non potest. Videbit, nec inuidebit; et conlaetando uobis, quod in se non habent habebunt in uobis. Nam et illud canticum nouum proprium uestrum dicere non poterit; audire autem poterit et delectari uestro tam excellenti bono. Sed uos, qui et dicetis et audietis, quia et hoc quod dicetis a uobis audietis, felicius exultabitis iucundiusque regnabitis. De maiore tamen uestro gaudio nullus maeror erit quibus hoc deerit. Agnus quippe, quem uos quocumque ierit sequimini, nec eos deseret qui eum quo uos non ualent sequi. Omnipotentem agnum loquimur. Et uobis praeibit et ab eis non abibit, cum erit deus *omnia in omnibus*;[61] et qui minus habebunt a uobis non adhorrebunt. Vbi enim nulla est inuidentia, consors* est differentia. Praesumite itaque, fidite, roboramini, permanete, qui uouetis et redditis domino deo uestro uota perpetuae continentiae, non propter praesens saeculum sed propter regnum caelorum.

[XXX] 30. Vos etiam qui hoc nondum uouistis, qui potestis capere, capite; perseueranter currite *ut comprehendatis*.[62] *Tollite hostias* quisque suas *et introite in atria* domini,[63] non ex necessitate, potestatem habentes uestrae uoluntatis. Neque enim sicut *Non moechaberis, non occides*[64] ita dici potest 'Non nubes'; illa exiguntur, ista offeruntur. Si fiant ista, laudantur; nisi fiant illa, damnantur. In illis dominus debitum imperat uobis; in his autem si quid amplius supererogaueritis, in redeundo reddet uobis.[65] Cogitate quidquid illud est *In muro eius locum nominatum meliorem multo quam filiorum atque filiarum*.[66] Cogitate illic nomen aeternum. Quis explicat quale nomen erit? Quidquid tamen erit, aeternum erit. Hoc credendo et sperando et amando potuistis coniugia non deuitare prohibita sed transuolare concessa.

[XXXI] 31. Vnde huius muneris magnitudo, ad quod capessendum pro nostris uiribus hortati sumus, quanto est excellentius atque diuinius, tanto magis admonet sollicitudinem nostram non

---

[61] 1 Cor. 15: 28.   [62] Cf. 1 Cor. 9: 24.   [63] Ps. 95 (96): 8.
[64] Exod. 20: 14, 13.   [65] Cf. Luke 10: 35.   [66] n. 45 above.

* consors *codd., Zycha*: concors *Saint-Martin*

virginity, for you can do nothing to regain it. The rest of the crowd of the faithful who cannot follow on this path will observe you. They will observe you, but they will not envy you, and by sharing the joy with you they will possess in you what they do not possess in themselves. They will not be able to sing that new song which belongs to you alone, but they will be able to hear it and to take delight in that good of yours which is so surpassing. But you who are virgins will both sing and hear it, for you will also hear it from your own lips as you sing it; your joy will be the more blessed and your dominion sweeter. Those who do not attain your greater joy will experience no grief, for the Lamb whom you follow wherever he goes will not abandon those either who cannot follow him where you can. The Lamb of whom we speak is almighty; he will both go before you yet not desert them, for he will be the God who is 'all in all'.[61] Those who will possess less will not turn in disgust from you, for where there is no envy, distinction is shared. Have confidence, then; show trust, be strong, endure as you swear and keep vows of lifelong continence to your Lord, for the sake not of the present world but of the kingdom of heaven.

30. As for you who have not yet taken this vow, take it if you can. Persevere in running the race, that you may gain the prize.[62] Each and all of you must 'bring an offering, and enter into the courts'[63] of the Lord, not out of necessity, but as demonstrating the force of your will. The words 'Thou shalt not marry' cannot have the same sense as 'Thou shalt not commit adultery', or 'Thou shalt not kill',[64] for these last are demanded of us, whereas the first is freely offered. If the first is observed, it is praised; if the others are not, they merit condemnation. In these the Lord lays an obligation on you, whereas in the first whatever you add over and above he will on his return repay you.[65] Ponder what is meant by 'The place of honour within his wall, better by far than that of his sons and daughters'.[66] Think on the eternal fame which awaits there; who can explain the nature of it? Whatever it will be, it will last for ever. It is through believing, hoping, and loving this that you have been able not to forgo marriage as something forbidden, but to transcend it as something permitted. [XXX]

31. So the great importance of this gift of virginity, which I have encouraged you as best I can to embrace (the more so as the gift is more outstanding and heaven-sent) prompts my concern to say something not merely about the high glory of chastity, but also [XXXI]

solum de gloriosissima castitate, uerum etiam de tutissima humilitate aliquid loqui. Cum ergo perpetuae continentiae professores se
coniugatis comparantes secundum scripturas compererint eos infra
esse et opere et mercede, et uoto et praemio, statim ueniat in
mentem quod scriptum est: *Quanto magnus es, tanto humila te in omnibus,
et coram deo inuenies gratiam.*[67] Mensura humilitatis cuique ex mensura
ipsius magnitudinis data est; cui est periculosa superbia, quae
amplius amplioribus insidiatur, hanc sequitur inuidentia tamquam
filia pedisequa; eam quippe superbia continuo parit, nec umquam
est sine tali prole atque comite. Quibus duobus malis, hoc est superbia et inuidentia, diabolus diabolus est. Itaque contra superbiam,
matrem inuidentiae, maxime militat uniuersa disciplina christiana.
Haec enim docet humilitatem, qua et acquirat et custodiat caritatem. De qua cum dictum esset *Caritas non aemulatur,* uelut si
causam quaereremus unde fiat ut non aemuletur, continuo subdidit
Non inflatur,[68] tamquam diceret 'ideo non habet inuidentiam quia
nec superbiam'. Doctor itaque humilitatis Christus primo *Semet
ipsum exinaniuit formam serui accipiens, in similitudine hominum factus et
habitu inuentus ut homo; humilauit semetipsum, factus oboediens usque ad
mortem, mortem autem crucis.*[69]

Ipsa uero doctrina eius, quam attente insinuet humilitatem atque
huic praecipiendae uehementer insistat, quis explicare facile possit
atque in hanc rem demonstrandam testimonia cuncta congerere?
Hoc facere conetur uel faciat quisquis seorsum de humilitate
uoluerit scribere.[70] Huius autem operis aliud propositum est, quod
de tam magna re susceptum est ut ei maxime sit cauenda superbia.

[XXXII]   32. Proinde pauca testimonia quae dominus in mentem dare
dignatur ex doctrina Christi de humilitate commemoro, quae
ad id quod intendi fortasse sufficiant. Sermo eius, quem primum
prolixiorem ad discipulos habuit, inde coepit: *Beati pauperes spiritu,*

---

[67] Augustine resumes the theme of humility from *De bono coniugali* [XXXI] 35, where the
same citation of Ecclus. 3: 20 appears.

[68] 1 Cor. 13: 4.

[69] Phil. 2: 7 f.

[70] This is Augustine's modest exordium to what is virtually a mini-treatise on humility
([XXXII] 32–[LVI] 57); he claims that his assemblage of scriptural passages and the commentary on them is his own work. It seems likely, however, that he recalled Cyprian, *De lapsis* 31 on the three children in the fiery furnace 'who persevered in humility and in making
sacrifice to the Lord in the midst of these tortures'; compare the peroration ([LVI] 57) to this
work. He certainly knew Jovinian's exhortation to virgins as cited by Jerome (*Adv. Iov.* 1. 7):

about the most trustworthy virtue of humility. So when those who pledge themselves to lifelong continence compare themselves with married people, and according to the testimony of the scriptures find that married people rank below them in their way of life and its recompense, in their vow and its reward, these words of scripture should at once strike home: 'The greater you are, the more you must humble yourself in all things, and you will obtain favour before God.'[67] The measure of a person's humility is dictated by the measure of his greatness. The greatness embodied by that hazardous pride, which sets traps greater for greater persons, is attended by envy as by a daughter in its train; for pride at once engenders it, and is never without such a daughter and companion. These two evils, pride and envy, each possess a devil. For this reason Christian teaching in its entirety wars above all on pride, the mother of envy, for that discipline seeks humility as the means of obtaining and preserving charity. Following upon the words 'Charity is not envious', as if we were asking why it is not envious, Paul immediately added 'It is not puffed up',[68] as though he were saying 'There is no envy in it because there is no pride either'. So it was that Christ as teacher of humility first 'emptied himself, taking the form of a servant, made in the likeness of men, and being found with the appearance of man; he humbled himself, becoming obedient unto death, even the death of the cross'.[69]

Who could readily explain and assemble all the testimonies to demonstrate how carefully this teaching of his prescribes humility, and how emphatically it harps on this instruction? Whoever wishes to write a separate treatise on humility should attempt or perform this task.[70] But the purpose of this present work is different; it is an undertaking on an issue so great that one must beware of pride above all in essaying it.

32. So I cite a few testimonies of Christ's teaching on humility [XXXII] which the Lord thinks fit to present to my mind; these may perhaps be enough for my purpose. That first discourse of some length which he delivered to the disciples began with these words:

'Be not proud; you are members of the same Church as the married.' Above all, he would recall the frequent admonitions to humility of his mentor Ambrose: 'Why do you consider yourself more important than another, when a Christian ought to put others before himself?' (*Off.* 3. 28). For this and other relevant citations in Ambrose, see Homes Dudden, *Saint Ambrose*, 531 f.

quoniam ipsorum est regnum caelorum;[71] quos sine ulla controuersia humiles intellegimus. Fidem centurionis illius ideo praecipue laudauit, nec se inuenisse in Israhel dixit tantam fidem, quia ille tam humiliter credidit ut diceret *Not sum dignus ut sub tectum meum intres;* unde nec Matthaeus ob aliud eum dixit accessisse ad Iesum, cum apertissime Lucas insinuet quod non ad eum ipse uenerit, sed amicos suos miserit, nisi quia fidelissima humilitate magis ipse accessit quam illi quos misit.[72]

Vnde et illud propheticum est: *Excelsus est dominus et humilia respicit; excelsa autem a longe cognoscit,*[73] utique tamquam non accedentia. Hinc et illi mulieri Chananaeae dicit: *O mulier, magna est fides tua; fiat tibi sicut uis;* quam superius canem appellauerat, nec ei panem filiorum proiciendum esse responderat. Quod illa humiliter accipiens dixerat: *Ita, domine; nam et canes edunt de micis quae cadunt de mensa dominorum suorum.* Ac sic quod adsiduo clamore non impetrabat, humili confessione promeruit.[74]

Hinc illi duo proponuntur orantes in templo, unus Pharisaeus et alter publicanus, propter eos qui sibi iusti uidentur et spernunt ceteros, et enumerationi meritorum praefertur confessio peccatorum. Et utique deo gratias agebat Pharisaeus ex his in quibus multum sibi placebat: *Gratias* inquit *tibi ago, quia non sum sicut ceteri homines, iniusti raptores adulteri, sicut et publicanus iste. Ieiuno bis in sabbato, decimas do omnium quaecumque possideo. Publicanus autem de longinquo stabat, nec oculos ad caelum audebat leuare, sed percutiebat pectus suum, dicens: Propitius esto mihi peccatori.* Sequitur autem diuina sententia: *Amen dico uobis, descendit iustificatus de templo publicanus magis quam ille Pharisaeus.* Deinde causa ostenditur cur hoc iustum sit: *Quoniam is qui se exaltat humilabitur, et qui se humilat exaltabitur.*[75]

Fieri ergo potest ut quisque et mala uera deuitet et uera bona in se consideret, et de his *patri luminum* gratias agat a quo *descendit omne datum optimum et omne donum perfectum,*[76] et tamen elationis vitio reprobetur si aliis peccatoribus maximeque peccata in oratione confiten-

---

[71] Matt. 5: 3.
[72] Matt. 8: 5ff.; Luke 7: 3ff. A year previously (AD 400) Augustine had published his comparison between the gospels, *De consensu euangelistarum*; at 2. 20. 48ff. he explains away the difference by suggesting that in Matthew the centurion 'came towards him but did not reach him'. Humility is not mentioned.
[73] Ps. 137 (138): 6.
[74] Cf. Matt. 15: 22ff., esp. 28, 27.
[75] Luke 18: 10ff.
[76] James 1: 17.

'Blessed are the poor in spirit, for theirs is the kingdom of heaven.'[71] There is no dispute about our regarding them as humble. He gave particular praise to the faith of the famous centurion. He said that he had not found such great faith in Israel, because the centurion believed with such humility as to say: 'I am not worthy that you should enter under my roof.' Thus though Luke most clearly claims that he did not approach Jesus personally but sent his friends, Matthew stated that his coming to him was for no other reason than that he came to Jesus himself rather than those he sent because of his most faithful humility.[72]

This is the point, too, of that prophetic utterance: 'The Lord is raised high, and looks on things that are lowly, but things raised high he perceives from afar',[73] meaning specifically that they do not draw near him. For this reason too he says to the Canaanite woman: 'Woman, great is your faith; be it done to you as you will.' Earlier he had called her a dog, and his response to her had been that the bread of children was not to be thrown before her. But she had greeted these words with humility, saying: 'True, Lord; yet even dogs eat the crumbs that fall from the table of their masters.' So what she failed to obtain by her persistent cries she deserved to gain by her humble confession.[74]

The reason why the two men, the one a Pharisee and the other a tax-collector, are portrayed as praying in the temple is to confront those who regard themselves as just and despise the rest; confession of sins is preferred to a catalogue of merits. The Pharisee was thanking God precisely for the things in which he took great self-satisfaction: 'I give thanks to you', he said, 'because I am not as other men unjust, extortioners, adulterers, as also is this tax-collector. I fast twice a week, I give tithes of all that I possess.' But the tax-collector, standing afar off, did not presume even to lift his eyes to heaven, but was beating his breast, saying: 'God be merciful to me a sinner!' Then follows heaven's judgement: 'Amen I say to you, the tax-collector went down from the temple justified more than the Pharisee.' The reason is then given why this is just: 'For he who exalts himself will be humbled, and he who humbles himself will be exalted.'[75]

So it can be the case that a person both avoids real evils and contemplates real goods within himself, and gives thanks for these to 'the father of lights, from whom comes down every best gift and every perfect gift',[76] yet is none the less rebuked for the vice of pride if even in thought alone (that is, before God's eyes) he haughtily

110 DE SANCTA VIRGINITATE

tibus uel sola cogitatione, quae coram deo est, superbus insultat, quibus non exprobratio cum inflatione sed miseratio sine desperatione debetur.

Quid illud quod quaerentibus inter se discipulis quisnam eorum maior esset, puerum paruulum constituit ante oculos eorum, dicens *Nisi fueritis sicut puer iste, non intrabitis in regnum caelorum?*[77] Nonne humilitatem maxime commendauit et in ea meritum magnitudinis posuit? Vel cum filiis Zebedaei latera eius in sedium sublimitate concupiscentibus ita respondit, ut passionis eius calicem potius bibendum cogitarent, in quo *se humilauit usque ad mortem, mortem autem crucis,*[78] quam superbo adpetitu praeferri ceteris postularent, quid ostendit nisi eis se futurum altitudinis largitorem, qui eum doctorem humilitatis antea sequerentur?

Iam uero quod exiturus ad passionem lauit pedes discipulis, monuitque apertissime ut hoc facerent condiscipulis atque conseruis quod eis fecisset magister et dominus,[79] quantum commendauit humilitatem! Cui commendandae etiam tempus illud elegit, quo eum proxime moriturum cum magno desiderio contuebantur, hoc utique praecipue memoria retenturi quod magister imitandus ultimum demonstrasset. At ille hoc fecit illo tempore quod utique potuit et aliis ante diebus quibus cum eis fuerat conuersatus; quando si fieret, hoc ipsum quidem traderetur, sed utique non sic acciperetur.

[XXXIII]   33. Cum ergo Christianis omnibus custodienda sit humilitas, quandoquidem a Christo Christiani appellantur, cuius euangelium nemo diligenter intuetur qui non eum doctorem humilitatis inueniat, tum maxime uirtutis huius sectatores et conseruatores eos esse conuenit, qui magno aliquo bono ceteris eminent ut magnopere curent illud quod primitus posui *Quanto magnus es, tanto humila te in omnibus, et coram deo inuenies gratiam.* Proinde quia perpetua continentia maximeque uirginitas magnum bonum est in sanctis dei, uigilantissime cauendum est ne superbia corrumpatur.

34. Curiosas et uerbosas malas innuptas Paulus apostolus notat et hoc uitium uenire dicit ex otio. *Simul autem* inquit *et otiosae esse*

[77] Matt. 18: 3.
[78] Cf. Matt. 20: 20ff.; Phil. 2: 8.
[79] Cf. John 13: 1ff.; the washing of the feet took place 'before the festival of the Passover' (13: 1).

disparages others who are sinners, and especially those who confess their sins in prayer; for what these sinners merit is not arrogant censure, but pity without loss of hope.

Again, there was the occasion when the disciples were enquiring amongst themselves which of them was the greater. Jesus set a small child before their eyes, and said: 'Unless you become as this child, you will not enter the kingdom of heaven.'[77] Did he not thereby recommend humility above all, and embody in it the merit of greatness? Or again, consider the answer which he gave to the sons of Zebedee who were eager to be seated aloft at his side. They should think, he said, of the cup of suffering which was to be drunk, the cup 'in which he humbled himself unto death, even the death of the cross',[78] rather than with arrogant insistence demand preferment over the rest. What did he reveal here but that he would bestow high position on those who earlier followed his teaching of humility?

Then again, what a great recommendation he gave to humility when before proceeding to his passion he washed the feet of his disciples, and gave them the clearest instruction to do for their fellow-disciples and fellow-servants what he their master and lord had done for them.[79] In order to recommend it further, he chose the time when they looked on him with great longing immediately before his death, so that they would certainly keep vividly in their memory the final lesson which the master whom they were to imitate had taught them. What he did on that occasion he could certainly have done on other days previously, when he had associated with them; but if it had been done then, the same message would indeed have been passed to them, but it would surely not have been taken to heart so earnestly.

33. All Christians, then, should hold fast to humility because [xxxiii] they derive their name Christians from Christ; and no person who studies his gospel carefully fails to find him to be the teacher of humility. But it is above all appropriate that those who excel the rest in some great good should pursue and preserve this virtue, so as to pay close attention to that passage which I cited at the outset: 'The greater you are, the more you must humble yourself in all things, and you will obtain favour before God.' Therefore since lifelong continence and above all virginity are a great good among God's saints, we must be especially watchful that we are not corrupted by pride.

34. The apostle Paul marks down as wicked unmarried women who pry and prattle; this fault he says is the outcome of idleness. 'As

discunt, circuire domos; non solum autem otiosae, uerum etiam curiosae et uer-
bosae, loquentes quae non oportet.[80] De his superius dixerat: *Iuniores autem*
uiduas euita; cum enim in deliciis egerint, in Christo nubere uolunt, habentes
damnationem quoniam primam fidem inritam fecerunt,[81] id est in eo quod
primum uouerant non steterunt.

[XXXIV]   Nec tamen ait 'nubunt', sed 'nubere uolunt'; multas enim earum
reuocat a nubendo non amor praeclari propositi, sed aperti
dedecoris timor, ueniens et ipse a superbia qua formidatur magis
hominibus displicere quam deo. Hae igitur quae nubere uolunt et
ideo non nubunt quia impune non possunt, quae melius nuberent
quam urerentur,[82] id est quam occulta flamma concupiscentiae in
ipsa conscientia* uastarentur, quas paenitet professionis et piget
confessionis, nisi correctum cor dirigant et dei timore rursus
libidinem uincant, in mortuis deputandae sunt siue in deliciis agant
(unde dicit apostolus *quae autem in deliciis agit, uiuens mortua est*)[83] siue
in laboribus atque ieiuniis nulla cordis correctione superfluis et
magis ostentationi quam emendationi seruientibus.

Non ego talibus magnam curam humilitatis ingero, in quibus
superbia ipsa confunditur et conscientiae uulnere cruentatur. Nec
ebriosis aut auaris aut alio quolibet damnabili morbi genere iacen-
tibus, cum habeant corporalis continentiae professionem
moribusque peruersis a suo nomine dissonent, hanc magnam sollicitudinem piae humilitatis impono, nisi forte in his malis etiam
ostentare se audebunt, quibus non sufficit quod eorum supplicia
differuntur. Nec de his ago in quibus est quidam placendi appetitus
aut elegantiore uestitu quam tantae professionis necessitas postulat,
aut capitis ligamento notabili siue protumidis umbonibus capillorum siue tegminibus ita teneris ut retiola subter posita appareant;[84]

---

* conscientia *codd.*: concupiscentia *Dycha*

[80] 1 Tim. 5: 13, 11 Augustine echoes Ambrose's strictures (*Expos. in Luc.* 2. 21; *Exhort. Virginitatis* 72).
[81] 1 Tim. 5: 11f. The punctuation here, and accordingly the sense, is uncertain. Paul's Greek clearly means 'For when their wanton ways alienate them from Christ, they wish to marry'; and the Vulgate rendering, 'Cum enim luxuriatae fuerint in Christo nubere uolunt', is taken in the same sense. But Paul's advice to avoid younger widows is addressed to Timothy, an earnest Christian; Augustine probably interpreted his text as meaning "they wish to marry in Christ, that is, in the Church", in the spirit of 1 Cor. 7: 39 ('if the husband dies, she is free to marry anyone she wishes, only in the Lord').
[82] Cf. 1 Cor. 7: 9.   [83] 1 Tim. 5: 6.
[84] Condemnation of women's elegant clothing and jewellery was an obsessive motif in the Fathers. Tertullian's *De cultu feminarum* 2. 6 (attacking such ornamentation as the work of the

soon as they learn to be idle', he says, 'they gad about from house to house. Not merely are they idle; they pry and prattle, saying what they should not say.'[80] Earlier he had said of these women: 'Avoid younger widows, for once they involve themselves in sensual pleasures, they wish to marry in Christ, and incur damnation for having violated their earlier pledge',[81] in other words they have not abided by the vow which they had first taken.

Yet he does not say 'They marry', but 'They wish to marry', for many of them are deterred from marriage not by love of their noble vocation, but by fear of manifest shame, which itself stems from pride whereby people fear the displeasure of men more than of God. These women, then, would like to marry, and the reason why they do not marry is because they cannot do so with impunity. They would do better to marry rather than to burn,[82] that is than be ravaged in their inmost hearts by the hidden flame of lust; they regret the pledge they have made but are ashamed to admit it. Unless they amend and control their attitude, and once more overcome their lust with fear of God, they are to be numbered among the dead, whether they devote themselves to pleasures (hence the comment of the Apostle, 'She who devotes herself to pleasures is dead even while she lives'[83]) or to labours and fasting, for these are pointless without any correction of the heart, ministering to empty display rather than to improvement. [XXXIV]

To such as these I do not recommend great eagerness for humility, for their very pride is confused and blood-stained with the wound to their conscience. Again, I do not saddle with this great concern for devoted humility those who are drunkards or misers or who lie prostrate under any other kind of disease which brings damnation. Though they lay claim to bodily continence, their shameful behaviour is not in keeping with the title they bear. But perhaps they will even have the gall to flaunt themselves in these evil activities, not being content to have the punishment for them postponed. Nor am I concerned with those who seek to please, either with dress more elegant than the needs of their high calling demand, or with a bandeau conspicuous whether with protruding knots of hair or with veils so thin that the hair-nets lying below become visible.[84] These people are not yet to be instructed on

devil), Cyprian's *De habitu uirginum* 16, Jerome's *Epp*. 22 and 107. 5., and above all Ambrose's *De uirginibus* 1. 6. 28f., and other texts cited by Homes Dudden, *Saint Ambrose*, 153f., were familiar to Augustine. Ambrose attacks also attractive hair-styles (*De uirginibus* 71; *Exhort. uirg.* 64; *De inst. uirg.* 109). Augustine, *Ep.* 211. 10 (AD 423) uses virtually ths same phrase on hair as

his nondum de humilitate sed de ipsa castitate uel integritate pudicitiae danda praecepta sunt. Da mihi profitentem perpetuam continentiam atque his et huius modi omnibus carentem uitiis et maculis morum; huic superbiam timeo, huic tam magno bono ex elationis tumore formido. Quo magis inest unde sibi placeat, eo magis uereor ne sibi placendo illi displiceat qui superbis resistit, humilibus autem dat gratiam.[85]

[xxxv]   35. Certe praecipuum magisterium et uirginalis integritatis exemplum in ipso Christo contuendum est. Quid ergo amplius continentibus de humilitate praecipiam quam quod ille qui omnibus dicit: *Discite a me, quoniam mitis sum et humilis corde?*[86] Cum magnitudinem suam supra commemorasset, [et] id ipsum uolens ostendere quantus propter nos quantillus effectus est, *Confiteor* inquit *tibi, domine caeli et terrae, quoniam abscondisti haec a sapientibus et reuelasti ea paruulis. Ita, pater, quoniam sic placitum est coram te. Omnia mihi tradita sunt a patre meo, et nemo cognoscit filium nisi pater, et nemo cognoscit patrem nisi filius et cui uoluerit filius reuelare. Venite ad me omnes qui laboratis et onerati estis, et ego uos reficiam. Tollite iugum meum super uos, et discite a me quoniam mitis sum et humilis corde.*[87]

Ille cui omnia tradidit pater, et quem nemo cognoscit nisi pater, et qui patrem solus cognoscit et cui uoluerit reuelare, non dicit 'Discite a me mundum fabricare aut mortuos suscitare', sed *quia mitis sum et humilis corde.* O doctrinam salutarem! O magistrum dominumque mortalium, quibus mors poculo superbiae propinata atque transfusa est! Noluit docere quod ipse non esset, noluit iubere quod ipse non faceret. Video te, bone Iesu, oculis fidei quos aperuisti mihi, tamquam in contione generis humani clamantem ac dicentem *Venite ad me, et discite a me.* Quid, obsecro te, per quem facta sunt omnia fili dei, et idem qui factus es inter omnia fili hominis, quid ut discamus a te uenimus ad te? *Quoniam mitis sum* inquit *et humilis corde.* Hucine redacti sunt *omnes thesauri sapientiae et scientiae absconditi in te,*[88] ut hoc pro magno discamus a te, quoniam mitis es et

---

here: 'Let not the covering of your heads be so thin that the nets are visible under it.' The 'covering' refers to the white veil, which with the black overgarment was the habit of the consecrated virgin (Ambrose, *De uirginibus* 3. 1; Jerome, *Ep.* 147. 6).

[85] Cf. James 4: 6.   [86] Matt. 11: 29.   [87] Matt. 11: 25 ff.
[88] Col. 2: 3.

humility, but on chastity itself or on virgin purity. Give me one who proclaims lifelong continence, and who is free of these and all such vices and blemishes of behaviour. It is in one such as this that I fear pride, it is the great good which she possesses that makes me fearful of swollen conceit. The more a person is disposed to self-satisfaction, the greater is my fear that by being pleasing to herself she may displease him who resists the proud but grants grace to the humble.[85]

35. We must certainly observe in Christ himself the outstanding   [xxxv] teaching and the model of virginal purity. What more noble precept, then, can I enjoin on continent persons in the matter of humility than that which he addresses to all: 'Learn of me, for I am meek and humble of heart?'[86] After earlier recounting his greatness, in his desire to disclose the fact of that greatness and how small he had become for our sake, he said: 'I praise you, Lord of heaven and earth, because you have hidden these things from the wise, and have revealed them to little children. Yes, Father, for such was your gracious will. All things have been made known to me by my Father, and no one knows the Son except the Father, and no one knows the Father except the Son and anyone to whom the Son chooses to reveal him. Come to me, all you who labour and are burdened, and I will refresh you. Take my yoke upon you, and learn of me, for I am meek and humble of heart.'[87]

He to whom the Father assigned all things, and whom no one knows except the Father, and who alone, together with anyone to whom he has chosen to reveal him, knows the Father, does not say 'Learn from me how to create the world, or how to raise the dead', but 'for I am meek and humble of heart'. What salutary teaching! Hail, teacher and lord of mortal men, men for whom death was served up and poured out in the cup of pride! He refused to prescribe what he himself was not, he refused to command what he himself did not do. Good Jesus, I behold you with those eyes of faith which you opened for me; it is as if you cry out in the gathering of the human race, and say, 'Come to me, and learn from me.' I beg you, Son of God through whom all things were made, and Son of man too who were made among all else, what do we come to you to learn? 'For I am meek', he says, 'and humble of heart.' Is it in this that 'All the treasures of wisdom and knowledge hidden in you'[88] are concentrated, that we should learn from you as something great that you are meek and humble of heart? Is it so great a thing to be

humilis corde? Itane magnum est esse paruum ut nisi a te qui tam magnus es fieret, disci omnino non posset? Ita plane. Non enim aliter inuenitur requies animae nisi inquieto tumore digesto, quo magna sibi erat quando tibi sana non erat.

[XXXVI]   36. Audiant te et ueniant ad te, et mites atque humiles esse discant a te qui misericordiam et ueritatem tuam requirunt, tibi uiuendo, tibi non sibi; audiat hoc laborans et oneratus, qua sarcina premitur ut oculos ad caelum leuare non audeat, percutiens pectus ille peccator nec* propinquans de longinquo; audiat centurio non dignus cuius tectum subires; audiat Zacchaeus maior publicanorum quadruplo restituens lucra damnabilium peccatorum; audiat mulier in ciuitate peccatrix tanto lacrimosior pedibus tuis quanto fuerat alienior a uestigiis tuis; audiant meretrices et publicani, qui scribas et Pharisaeos praecedunt in regnum caelorum;[89] audiat omne genus aegrorum, cum quibus tibi pro crimine sunt obiecta conuiuia, uidelicet quasi a sanis qui medicum non quaerebant, cum tu non uenires uocare iustos sed peccatores in poenitentiam.[90] Hi omnes cum conuertuntur ad te facile mitescunt et humilantur coram te, memores iniquissimae uitae suae et indulgentissimae misericordiae tuae, quia *ubi abundauit peccatum, superabundauit gratia*.[91]

37. Sed respice agmina uirginum, puerorum puellarumque sanctarum; in ecclesia tua eruditum est hoc genus; illic tibi a maternis uberibus pullulauit, in nomen tuum ad loquendum linguam soluit, nomen tuum uelut lac infantiae suae suxit infusum. Non potest quisquam ex hoc numero dicere: *Qui prius fui blasphemus et persecutor et iniuriosus, sed misericordiam consecutus sum quia ignorans feci in incredulitate*;[92] immo, etiam quod non iussisti sed tantummodo uolentibus arripiendum proposuisti, dicens *Qui potest capere, capiat*, arripuerunt, uouerunt, et *propter regnum caelorum se ipsos* non quia minatus es sed quia hortatus es, *castrauerunt*.[93]

[XXXVII]   His inclama, hi te audiant, *quoniam mitis es et humilis corde*. Hi quanto magni sunt tanto humilent se in omnibus, ut coram te

---

[89] The tax-collector, Luke 18: 11 ff.; the centurion, Matt. 8: 5 ff.; Zacchaeus, Luke 19. 2 ff.; Mary Magdalen, Luke 7. 37 ff.; harlots and tax-collectors, Matt. 21. 31. The striking feature of this catalogue is that all have given evidence of humility, not pride; like the virgins exhorted by Augustine, they must beware of becoming arrogant in their humility.

[90] Matt. 9: 12 ff.   [91] Rom. 5: 20.

[92] 1 Tim. 1: 13, Paul's description of his former self.

[93] Matt. 19: 12.

---

* nec *scripsi*: et *codd.*, Zycha, Saint-Martin

small that it could not be learnt at all except from you who are so great? Such indeed is the case; for rest for the soul is found only by pricking that troublesome swelling which makes the soul great in its own sight but diseased in yours.

36. Those who seek your mercy and truth in living for you—for [XXXVI] you and not for themselves—must hearken to you and come to you, and learn from you to be meek and humble. That man must hearken who labours and is burdened, weighed down by such baggage that he does not presume to raise his eyes to heaven, that sinner who beats his breast and does not draw near from afar. The centurion must hearken who is not worthy that you should enter under his roof. Zacchaeus, chief of tax-collectors, as he restores fourfold the profits from sins which bring damnation, must hearken. The sinning woman in the city, who the further she had distanced herself from your steps the more she wept over your feet, must hearken. Harlots and tax-collectors who gain access to the kingdom of heaven before the scribes and Pharisees must hearken.[89] All classes of invalids must hearken, for you feasted with them and incurred reproaches thereby as though it were sinful; your accusers were evidently the healthy who had no need of a physician, for you came to call not the just but sinners to repentance.[90] When all these turn to you, they readily become meek and humble before you, being mindful of their utterly depraved lives and of your most forgiving mercy, for 'where sin abounded, grace abounded still more'.[91]

37. But direct your gaze upon the troops of virgins, saintly boys and girls. This group has been schooled in your Church. In it they grew up from their mothers' breasts for you; they first loosed their tongues in speech to utter your name; your name they sucked in like the milk imbibed in their childhood. None of this company can proclaim: 'Previously I was a blasphemer, a persecutor, one who inflicted harm, but I obtained mercy because I acted in the ignorance of unbelief.'[92] No, for they have embraced and vowed the life which you did not even enjoin but merely recommended should be undertaken by those who desired it, when you said: 'Let this be accepted by one who can'; and not through threats of yours but through your exhortations they have made themselves eunuchs for the sake of the kingdom of heaven.[93]

So cry aloud to them, and let them hear you saying that you [XXXVII] are meek and humble of heart. Let them humble themselves in all things in accord with their greatness, so that they may find favour in

inueniant gratiam. Iusti sunt; sed numquid sicut tu iustificans impium? Casti sunt; sed eos in peccatis matres eorum in uteris aluerunt. Sancti sunt; sed tu etiam sanctus sanctorum. Virgines sunt; sed nati etiam ex uirginibus non sunt. Et spiritu et carne integri sunt; sed uerbum caro factum non sunt. Et tamen discant non ab eis quibus peccata dimittis, sed a te ipso agno dei, *qui tollis peccata mundi, quoniam mitis es et humilis corde.*[94]

38. Non ego te, anima pia pudica, quae appetitum carnalem nec usque ad concessum coniugium relaxasti, quae decessurum corpus nec successori propagando indulsisti, quae fluitantia membra terrena in caeli consuetudinem suspendisti; non ego te ut discas humilitatem ad publicanos et peccatores mitto, qui tamen in regnum caelorum praecedunt superbos, non te ad hos mitto; indigni sunt enim qui ab immunditiae uoragine liberati sunt, ut ad eos imitandos mittatur illibata uirginitas; ad regem caeli te mitto, ad eum per quem creati sunt homines et qui creatus est inter homines propter homines; ad *speciosum forma prae filiis hominum*[95] et contemptum a filiis hominum prae* filiis hominum, ad eum qui dominans angelis immortalibus non dedignatus est seruire mortalibus. Eum certe humilem non iniquitas sed caritas fecit, *caritas quae non aemulatur, non inflatur, non quaerit quae sua sunt,* quia et *Christus non sibi placuit, sed sicut scriptum de illo est, opprobria exprobrantium tibi ceciderunt super me.*[96]

Vade, ueni ad illum, et disce *quoniam mitis est et humilis corde.* Non ibis ad eum qui oculos ad caelum leuare non audebat onere iniquitatis, sed ad eum qui de caelo descendit pondere caritatis; non ibis ad eam quae domini sui pedes lacrimis rigauit quaerens indulgentiam grauium peccatorum, sed ibis ad eum qui, cum daret indulgentiam omnium peccatorum, lauit pedes seruorum suorum. Noui dignitatem uirginitatis tuae; non tibi propono imitandum publicanum humiliter accusantem delicta sua, sed timeo tibi Pharisaeum superbe iactantem merita sua. Non dico 'Esto qualis illa de qua dictum est *Dimittuntur ei peccata multa, quoniam dilexit multum.*' Sed metuo ne, cum tibi modicum dimitti putas, modicum diligas.[97]

---

[94] John 1: 29; Matt. 11: 29.   [95] Ps. 44(45): 3.
[96] 1 Cor. 13: 4 f.; Rom. 15: 3, echoing Ps. 68(69): 10.
[97] For the examples of the tax-collector and Mary Magdalen see n. 89; on Mary Magdalen also Luke 7: 47.

---

* prae *scripsi:* pro *codd., Zycha, Saint-Martin*

your sight. They are just, but surely they do not make the sinner righteous, as you do? They are chaste, but their mothers nurtured them in their wombs in sins. They are holy, but you are more, the Holy of holies. They are virgins, but they are not also born of virgins. They are unsullied in both spirit and flesh, but they are not the Word made flesh. Yet they are to learn not from those whose sins you forgive, but from you yourself, the Lamb of God, 'You who take away the sins of the world', for you are meek and humble of heart.[94]

38. Devoted and chaste soul, you who have not indulged your carnal instinct even to embrace licit marriage, who have not given free rein to your mortal body even to beget a descendant, who have kept your transient earthly parts in abeyance to grow accustomed to life in heaven, I do not direct you to tax-collectors and sinners to learn humility, even though they gain entrance to the kingdom of heaven before the proud. I do not direct you to them, for those delivered from the abyss of uncleanness are unworthy objects of imitation for undefiled virginity. I direct you rather to the king of heaven, to him through whom men were created and who was himself created among men and for men, to him who was 'beauteous in form beyond the sons of men'[95] and was despised by the sons of men beyond the sons of men; to him who though he was lord over the immortal angels did not disdain to be a slave to mortals. What made him humble was certainly not inequality but charity, 'Charity which is not envious, which is not puffed up, which does not seek its own', for Christ though he was, 'he did not please himself, but as scripture says of him, "The insults of those who insult you have fallen on me." '[96]

Step forth, come to him, and learn that he is meek and humble of heart. You are not to go to the one who did not presume to raise his eyes to heaven because of the burden of his wickedness, but to him who came down from heaven because of the weight of his love. You are not to go to her who watered the feet of her lord with tears, seeking forgiveness for her previous sins, but to him who in granting pardon for all sins washed the feet of his servants. I acknowledge the high rank of your virginity; I do not set before you for your imitation the tax-collector humbly censuring his own faults, but I fear for the Pharisee in you proudly boasting of his merits. I do not say, 'Be like the woman of whom scripture states, "Many sins are forgiven her, because she has loved much." ' But I fear that in believing that you have little to be forgiven, you may love only a little.[97]

[XXXVIII]   39. Metuo, inquam, tibi uehementer ne, cum te agnum quocumque ierit secuturam esse gloriaris, eum prae tumore superbiae sequi per angusta non possis. Bonum tibi est, o anima uirginalis, ut sic, quomodo uirgo es, sic omnino seruans in corde quod renata es, seruans in carne quod nata es, concipias tamen a timore domini et parturias spiritum salutis. *Timor* quidem *non est in caritate, sed perfecta* sicut scriptum est *caritas foras mittit timorem*, sed timorem hominum, non dei, timorem temporalium malorum, non diuini in fine iudicii. *Noli altum sapere, sed time.*[98]

Ama dei bonitatem, time seueritatem; utrumque te superbam esse non sinit. Amando enim times ne amatum et amantem grauiter offendas. Nam quae grauior offensio quam ut superbia illi displiceas qui propter te superbis displicuit? Et ubi magis esse debet timor ille *castus permanens in saeculum saeculi* quam in te, quae non cogitas *quae sunt mundi, quomodo placeas coniugi*, sed *quae sunt domini, quomodo placeas domino?*[99] Ille alius timor non est in caritate; iste autem castus non recedit a caritate. Si non amas, time ne pereas; si amas, time ne displiceas. Illum timorem caritas foras mittit; cum isto intro currit. Dicit apostolus etiam Paulus: *Non enim accepimus spiritum seruitutis iterum in timore; sed accepimus spiritum adoptionis filiorum, in quo clamamus 'Abba, pater'.*[100] Illum eum timorem credo dicere qui datus erat in uetere testamento, ne amitterentur temporalia bona quae deus promiserat nondum sub gratia filiis, sed sub lege adhuc seruis.

Est etiam timor ignis aeterni, propter quem deuitandum deo seruire nondum est utique perfectae caritatis. Aliud est enim desiderium praemii, aliud formido supplicii. Aliae uoces sunt: *Quo abibo ab spiritu tuo? Et a facie tua quo fugiam?*[101] Et aliae uoces sunt: *Vnam petii a domino, hanc requiram, ut inhabitem in domo domini per omnes dies uitae meae, ut contempler delectationem domini et protegar ad* templum eius*; et *Ne auertas faciem tuam a me*; et *Desiderat et deficit anima mea in atria domini.*[102]

Illas uoces habuerit qui oculos leuare non audebat ad caelum, et quae rigabat lacrimis pedes ad impetrandam ueniam grauium peccatorum; has autem tu habeto quae sollicita es [circa]† ea quae sunt

[98] 1 John 4: 18; Rom. 11: 20.   [99] Ps. 18(19): 10; 1 Cor. 7: 32f.
[100] Rom. 8: 15.   [101] Ps. 138(139): 7.   [102] Ps. 26(27): 4; Ps. 26(27): 9; Ps. 83(84): 3.

* protegar ad *scripsi*: protegi *codd. plerique, Zycha*: protegar *cett.*
† circa *om. codd. plerique, Zycha*; cf. Hieronymus, *In Esaiam* 15.21: 'Eunuchi . . . qui sollicti sunt ea quae dei sunt.'

39. I am, I say, profoundly fearful that in boasting that [xxxviii]
you will follow the Lamb wherever he goes, you may be unable because
of swollen pride to follow him along narrow paths. The good which
you possess, virgin soul, is that virgin as you are and preserving totally
both your rebirth in heart and your birth as virgin in body, you yet
conceive from fear of the Lord and give birth to the spirit of salvation.
Truly 'There is no fear in love', but as scripture says, 'Perfect love casts
out fear.' But this is fear of men, not of God; it is the fear of transient ills,
not of the final judgement of God. 'Be not proud-minded, but fear.'[98]

Love God's goodness, but fear his sternness; neither allows you to
be proud. For in your love you fear that you may grievously offend
him who is loved and loves; for what greater offence can there be
than to displease by your pride him who for your sake displeased the
proud? And where ought 'that chaste fear that abides for ever' be
more in evidence than in you, who train your minds not on 'the
things of this world, how to please a husband', but on 'the things of
the Lord, how to please the Lord'?[99] That other fear has no place in
love, but this chaste fear does not part from love. If you do not love,
be fearful that you may perish; if you do love, be fearful that you may
displease. Love casts out that first fear; it courses with the second
within. The apostle Paul further says: 'For we did not receive the
spirit of slavery to fall back in fear, but we have received the spirit of
adoption as sons, in which we cry "Abba, father".'[100] I believe that
Paul speaks of the fear imposed in the Old Testament, the fear of
loss of the temporal goods which God had promised to those not yet
under grace as sons, but as slaves still under the Law.

Such fear is also fear of eternal fire; serving God to avoid this is
assuredly the mark of love which has not yet attained perfection, for
the desire for a reward is one thing, but fear of punishment another.
The words 'Where can I go from your spirit, and where can I flee
from your presence?'[101] are one thing, but these words are quite
another: 'One thing I have sought of the Lord, and this will I seek,
to live in the house of the Lord all the days of my life, to behold the
beauty of the Lord, and gain protection in his temple'; and again,
'Do not hide your face from me', and 'My soul longs and faints for
the courts of the Lord.'[102]

Those first words were to be uttered by the man who did not
presume to raise his eyes to heaven, and by the woman who watered
his feet with her tears to obtain pardon for her grievous sins. But
you must adopt those other words, for you are concerned with 'the

domini, ut sis sancta et corpore et spiritu.[103] Illis uocibus comitatur timor qui tormentum habet, quem perfecta caritas foras mittit; his autem uocibus comitatur timor domini castus permanens in saeculum saeculi. Et utrique generi dicendum est *Noli altum sapere, sed time,* ut homo nec de peccatorum suorum defensione nec de iustitiae praesumptione se extollat. Nam et ipse Paulus qui dixit *Non enim accepistis spiritum seruitutis iterum in timore,* tamen timore comite caritatis ait: *Cum timore et tremore multo fui ad uos,* et ea sententia quam commemoraui, ne aduersus fractos oleae ramos insertus superbiret oleaster, ipse usus est dicens: *Noli altum sapere, sed time;*[104] ipse omnia membra Christi generaliter admonens ait: *Cum timore et tremore uestram ipsorum salutem operamini; deus est enim qui operatur in uobis et uelle et operari pro bona uoluntate,* ne ad uetus testamentum uideatur pertinere quod scriptum est: *Seruite domino in timore, et exultate ei cum tremore.*[105]

[xxxix]   40. Et quae magis membra corporis sancti, quod est ecclesia, curare debent ut super ea requiescat spiritus sanctus quam uirginalem profitentia sanctitatem? Quomodo autem requiescit ubi non inuenit locum suum? Quid aliud quam cor humilatum quod impleat non unde resiliat, quod erigat non quod deprimat, cum apertissime dictum sit: *Super quem requiescet spiritus meus? Super humilem et quietum et trementem uerba mea?*[106] Iam iuste uiuis, iam pie uiuis, pudice, sancte, uirginali castitate uiuis; adhuc tamen hic uiuis et non humilaris audiendo *Numquid non temptatio est uita humana super terram?* Non te a praefidenti elatione reuerberat *Vae mundo ab scandalis?* Non contremescis ne deputeris in multis quorum *refrigescit caritas, quoniam abundat iniquitas?* Non percutis pectus quod audis *Quapropter qui se putat stare, caueat ne cadat?*[107] Inter haec diuina monita et humana pericula itane adhuc uirginibus sanctis humilitatem persuadere laboramus?

[xl]   41. An uero propter aliud credendum est permittere deum ut misceantur numero professionis uestrae multi et multae casurae et casuri, nisi ut his cadentibus timor uester augeatur quo superbia comprimatur? Quam sic odit deus ut contra hanc unam se tantum

---

[103] 1 Cor. 7: 34.
[104] Rom. 11: 20; Rom. 8: 15; 1 Cor. 2: 3; Rom. 11: 17, 20.
[105] Phil. 2: 12 f.; Ps. 2: 11.
[106] Isa. 66: 2, with slight variation from the Vulgate.
[107] Job 7: 1; Matt. 18: 7; Matt. 24: 12; 1 Cor. 10: 12.

things of the Lord, that you may be holy in both body and spirit'.[103]
Those first words have as their companion fear which tortures, and
which perfect love casts out; the companion of these other words is
the chaste fear of the Lord which endures for ever. To both types of
utterance our response must be: 'Be not proud-minded, but fear', to
ensure that man does not puff himself up either in defence of his sins
or in presumption of his righteousness. For the very Paul who said
'You did not receive the spirit of slavery to fall back in fear' none the
less also said, since fear is the companion of love, 'I was with you in
fear and much trembling.' He used also that expression which I
cited earlier, that the engrafted wild olive should not wax proud
over the broken branches of the olive, adding: 'Be not proud-
minded, but fear.'[104] In offering general counsel to all Christ's limbs,
he says: 'Work out your own salvation in fear and trembling, for it is
God who is at work in you, enabling you both to will and to work for
his good pleasure.' He said this so that the words of scripture, 'Serve
the Lord with fear, and rejoice in him with trembling',[105] should not
seem relevant merely to the Old Testament.

40. And which limbs of the holy body which is the Church [xxxix]
must ensure that the holy Spirit rests on them, more than those who
profess the sanctity of virginity? But how does he rest when he fails
to find his abode? What is his resting-place but the humble heart
which he invests and from which he does not recoil, which he exalts
and does not weigh down? For the words of scripture are crystal-
clear: 'Upon whom shall my spirit rest? Upon him who is humble
and at peace, who trembles at my words.'[106] Your life is already just
and devoted, chaste and holy, lived in virginal chastity; yet you are
still living here on earth, and you are not humbled when you hear, 'Is
not this life on earth a trial?' Do not the words 'Woe to the world
because of its stumbling-blocks!' repel you from overweening arrogance? Do you not tremble that you may be numbered among the
many to whom 'charity grows cold, since wickedness abounds'? Do
you not beat your breast at hearing 'Therefore let him who thinks he
stands beware lest he fall'?[107] Encompassed by these divine warnings and human perils, do we still find it difficult to persuade consecrated virgins to embrace humility?

41. What, are we to believe that God allows many men and [xl]
women who are sure to fall to intermingle with the ranks of your
profession for any reason other than that by their fall your fear may
be increased, and consequently your pride may be repressed? That

humilaret altissimus. Nisi forte reuera ideo minus timebis magisque inflaberis, ut modicum diligas eum qui te tantum dilexit ut traderet se ipsum pro te[108] quia modicum tibi dimisit, uiuenti uidelicet a pueritia religiose pudice, pia castitate, illibata uirginitate. Quasi uero non tu multo ardentius diligere debes eum qui flagitiosis ad se conuersis quaecumque dimisit, in ea te cadere non permisit! Aut uero ille Pharisaeus, qui propterea modicum diligebat quia modicum sibi dimitti existimabat,[109] ob aliud hoc errore caecabatur, nisi quia *ignorans dei iustitiam et suam quaerens constituere, iustitiae dei subiectus non erat?*[110]

Vos autem genus electum et in electis electius, uirginei chori sequentes agnum, etiam uos *gratia salui facti estis per fidem; et hoc non ex uobis sed dei donum est, non ex operibus ne forte quis extollatur. Ipsius enim sumus figmentum, creati in Christo Iesu in operibus bonis quae praeparauit deus, ut in illis ambulemus.*[111] Ergone hunc quanto eius donis ornatiores estis, tanto minus amabitis? Auerterit tam horrendam ipse dementiam!

Proinde quoniam uerum ueritas dixit quod ille, cui modicum dimittitur modicum diligit, uos ut ardentissime diligatis cui diligendo a coniugiorum nexibus liberi uacatis, deputate uobis tamquam omnino dimissum quicquid mali a uobis non est illo regente commissum. *Oculi* enim *uestri semper ad dominum, quoniam ipse euellet de laqueo pedes uestros*, et *Nisi dominus custodierit ciuitatem, in uanum uigilauit qui custodit.*[112] Et de ipsa continentia loquens apostolus ait: *Volo autem omnes homines esse sicut me ipsum; sed unus quisque proprium donum habet a deo, alius sic, alius autem sic.* Quis ergo donat ista? Quis *distribuit propria unicuique sicut uult*?[113] Nempe deus, apud quem non est iniquitas. Ac per hoc qua aequitate ille faciat alios sic, alios autem sic, homini nosse aut impossibile aut omnino difficile est; quin tamen aequitate faciat, dubitare fas non est. *Quid* itaque *habes quod non accepisti?*[114] Aut qua peruersitate minus diligis, a quo amplius accepisti?

[XLI]   42. Quapropter haec prima sit induendae humilitatis cogitatio, ne a se sibi putet esse dei uirgo quod talis est, ac non potius

---

[108] Cf. Gal. 2: 20.
[109] Cf. Luke 7: 47. This riposte of Jesus to Simon the Pharisee is repeatedly echoed in the exhortations to virgins that follow,
[110] Rom. 10: 3.   [111] Eph. 2: 8 ff.
[112] Ps. 24(25): 15; Ps. 126(127): 1.
[113] 1 Cor. 7: 7; 12: 11.   [114] 1 Cor. 4: 7.

pride God so hates that from his great height he humbled himself so
much to oppose it. Or perhaps you will in fact fear less and pride
yourself the more, so as to love but a little him who loved you so
much that he surrendered his life for you,[108] having little to pardon
you for, since doubtless you have lived from childhood scrupulously,
chastely, with devoted purity and inviolate virginity! As though in
fact you should not love all the more zealously him who did not
allow you to fall into whatever sins he forgave in the wrongdoers
who turned to him! Or was that Pharisee, who loved but little
because he thought that but little was forgiven him,[109] blinded by
this error for any reason other than this—that 'in his ignorance of
the justice of God and his desire to establish his own, he did not subject himself to God's justice'?[110]

But you, a chosen race, especially chosen among the chosen, virgin choirs who follow the Lamb, you too 'have been saved by grace
through faith, and this not of yourselves but by the gift of God; not by
your own works, lest anyone boast. For we are his handiwork, created
in Christ Jesus for good works which God prepared beforehand to be
our way of life'[111] So will you love him less, the more you are adorned
by his gifts? May he himself avert such unspeakable madness!

So since Truth has uttered the truth that he to whom little is forgiven loves but little, to ensure that you most zealously love him
whom you are free to love since you are not imprisoned by the bonds
of marriage, you must regard yourselves as wholly forgiven for any
sins which through his guidance you have failed to commit. For 'Your
eyes are ever on the Lord, for he will pluck your feet from the snare',
and 'Unless the Lord guards the city, in vain has he who guards it kept
watch'.[112] And in speaking of continence itself, the Apostle says: 'I
would have all to be like myself, but each has his gift from God, one
in this way, and another in that.' So who bestows these gifts? Who
'allots to each man his own, according to his will'?[113] Surely God, in
whom there is no injustice. As for the fairness with which in dispens-
ing this he treats some persons in one way and others in another, this
is either impossible or extremely difficult for men to grasp, but that he
does it with fairness it is irreligious to doubt. Hence 'What have you
that you have not received?'[114] Or by what disordered thinking do
you love less him from whom you have received more?

42. So this should be your first motive for donning the mantle [XLI]
of humility, that God's virgin should not think that such a status has
been conferred on her by herself rather than that this best of gifts

hoc donum optimum desuper descendere a patre luminum, *apud quem non est transmutatio nec momenti obumbratio.*[115] Ita enim non putabit modicum sibi esse dimissum, ut modicum diligat et *ignorans dei iusti- tiam ac suam uolens constituere*[116] iustitiae dei non subiciatur. In quo uitio erat Simon ille, quem superauit mulier cui dimissa sunt pec- cata multa quoniam dilexit multum.

Sed cautius et uerius cogitabit omnia peccata sic habenda tamquam dimittantur, a quibus deus custodit ne committantur. Testes sunt uoces piarum deprecationum in scripturis sanctis, quibus ostenditur ea ipsa quae praecipiuntur a deo non fieri nisi dante atque adiuuante qui praecepit. Mendaciter enim petuntur si ea non adiuuante eius gratia facere possemus. Quid tam generaliter maximeque praecipitur quam oboedientia qua custodiuntur man- data dei? Et tamen hanc inuenimus optari. *Tu* inquit *praecepisti man- data tua custodiri nimis*; deinde sequitur *Vtinam dirigantur uiae meae ad custodiendas iustificationes tuas; tunc non confundar dum inspicio in omnia mandata tua.*[117] Quod deum praecepisse supra posuit, hoc ut a se impleretur optauit.

Hoc fit utique ne peccetur; quod si peccatum fuerit, praecipitur ut paeniteat, ne defensione et excusatione peccati pereat superbi- endo qui fecit, dum non uult paenitendo perire quod fecit. Etiam hoc a deo petitur, ut intellegatur non fieri nisi eo praestante a quo petitur. *Pone,* inquit *domine, custodiam ori meo et ostium continentiae circum labia mea. Non declines cor meum in uerba mala ad excusandum excusationes in peccatis cum hominibus operantibus iniquitatem.*[118] Si ergo et oboedientia, qua eius mandata seruamus, et paenitentia, qua peccata nostra non excusamus sed accusamus, optatur et petitur, manifestum est quia, cum fit, illo dante habetur, illo adiuuante completur. Apertius etiam dicitur propter oboedientiam, *A domino gressus hominis diriguntur, et uiam eius uolet;*[119] et de paenitentia dicit apostolus *Ne forte det illis deus paenitentiam.*[120]

43. De ipsa etiam continentia nonne apertissime dictum est: *Et cum scirem quia nemo esse potest continens nisi deus det, et hoc ipsum erat sapientiae scire, cuius esset hoc donum?*[121]

[115] James 1: 17.   [116] Rom. 10: 3.
[117] Ps. 118(119): 4 ff.   [118] Ps. 140(141). 3 f.
[119] Ps. 36(37): 23.   [120] 2 Tim. 2: 25.
[121] Wis. 8: 21.

'comes down from the Father of lights, with whom there is no variation or shadow of change'.[115] For with such thoughts she will not believe that little has been forgiven her to cause her to love but little, and 'in her ignorance of the justice of God and her desire to establish her own',[116] she does not submit herself to God's justice. This was the fault of Simon; the woman whose many sins were forgiven because she loved much rose superior to him.

But her thinking will be more circumspect and true if all sins which God protects us from committing are regarded as forgiven. The words of devoted entreaties in the holy scriptures witness to this. They reveal that those very injunctions given by God are carried out only by the gift and help of him who enjoined them. Those entreaties are insincerely uttered, should we be able to achieve them without the aid of his grace. What injunction is so universal and important as the command to obedience by which God's instructions are observed? Yet we find that this is prayed for. 'You', says the Psalmist, 'have commanded that your precepts be most diligently kept', and what comes next is 'O, that my ways be directed to observe your justifications! Then I shall not be confounded while I gaze on all your commandments.'[117] He prayed that he would fulfil what he earlier set down as God's command.

This is clearly performed so that no sin may be committed. But if sin has been committed, repentance is enjoined, so that the perpetrator should not perish through pride by defending and excusing his sin while showing reluctance to see his deed effaced by repentance. We further beg God for an understanding that this occurs only by the gift of him from whom we beg it. 'O Lord,' says the Psalmist, 'set a watch on my mouth, and a door of restraint on my lips. Let not my heart relapse into evil words to make excuses for committing sins with men who work iniquity.'[118] If therefore both the obedience by which we keep his commands, and the repentance by which we accuse and not excuse our sins, are both desired and requested, plainly when this occurs it is obtained by his gift, and fulfilled by his help. Scripture also speaks more clearly of obedience: 'By the Lord are the steps of a man directed, and he shall will his way.'[119] And on repentance the Apostle says: 'In case the Lord grant them repentance.'[120]

43. On the subject of continence itself, has scripture not also declared most clearly: 'And as I know that no one can be continent save by God's gift, and it was the mark of wisdom to know whose this gift was'?[121]

[XLII]   Sed forte continentia donum dei est, sapientiam uero sibi ipse
homo praestat, qua illud donum non suum sed dei esse cognoscat.
Immo, *Dominus sapientes facit caecos*, et *Testimonium dei fidele, sapientiam
praestat paruulis*, et *Si quis indiget sapientia, postulet a deo, qui dat omnibus
affluenter et non improperat, et dabitur ei.*[122] Sapientes autem esse uirgines
decet ne lampades eorum exstinguantur. Quomodo sapientes, nisi
non alta sapientes sed humilibus consentientes?[123] Dixit enim homini ipsa
Sapientia: *Ecce pietas est sapientia.*[124] Si ergo nihil habes quod non
accepisti, *noli altum sapere, sed time,*[125] et noli modicum diligere, quasi
a quo tibi modicum dimissum est, sed potius multum dilige, a quo
tibi multum tributum est. Si enim diligit cui donatum est ne red-
deret, quanto magis debet diligere cui donatum est ut haberet?
Nam et quisquis ab initio pudicus permanet, ab illo regitur; et
quisquis ex impudico pudicus fit, ab illo corrigitur; et quisquis
usque in finem impudicus est, ab illo deseritur. Hoc autem ille
occulto iudicio facere potest, iniquo non potest. Et fortasse ideo
latet ut plus timeatur et minus superbiatur.

[XLIII]   44. Deinde iam sciens homo gratia dei se esse quod est,
non incidat in alium superbiae laqueum, ut de ipsa dei gratia se
extollendo spernat ceteros. Quo uitio alius ille Pharisaeus et de
bonis quae habebat deo gratias agebat et tamen se super publicanum peccata confitentem extollebat. Quid igitur faciat uirgo,
quid cogitet ne se extollat super eos uel eas quae hoc tam magno
dono carent? Neque enim simulare debet humilitatem, sed
exhibere; nam simulatio humilitatis maior superbia est. Ideo scriptura uolens ostendere ueracem humilitatem esse oportere, cum
dixisset *Quanto magnus es, tanto humila te in omnibus*, mox quoque subdidit *Et coram dei inuenies gratiam*,[126] utique ubi se fallaciter humilare
non posset.

[XLIV]   45. Proinde quid dicemus? Estne aliquid quod uirgo dei
ueraciter cogitet, unde se fideli mulieri, non tantum uiduae uerum
etiam coniugatae, praeferre non audeat? Non ego reprobam dico;
nam quis nesciat oboedientem mulierem inoboedienti uirgini
praeponendam? Sed cum ambae sunt oboedientes praeceptis dei,

[122] Ps. 145(146): 8; Ps. 18(19): 8; James 1: 5.
[123] Cf. Matt. 25: 4 ff.; Rom. 12: 16.
[124] Job 28: 28.
[125] Cf. 1 Cor. 4: 7; Rom. 11: 20.
[126] Ecclus. 3: 20.

But perhaps continence is a gift of God but man bestows [XLII]
wisdom on himself, the wisdom to realise that the gift is bestowed by
God and not by himself? Not so; 'The Lord makes the blind wise',
and 'The witness of the Lord is faithful; he affords wisdom to little
ones', and 'If anyone is wanting in wisdom, let him ask God for it,
for he gives abundantly to all, and does not upbraid, and it will be
given to him'.[122] It is fitting for virgins to be wise so that their lamps
may not be snuffed out. How will they become wise but 'by not
manifesting haughty wisdom, and agreeing with the humble'?[123]
Wisdom itself has said to man: 'Behold, religious observance is wisdom.'[124] So 'if you have nothing which you have not received', 'do
not be proud-minded, but fear',[125] and do not love but little, as
though he has pardoned you but little, but rather love him much, for
much has been bestowed on you by him. For if one who has been
excused payment of debts shows love, how much more ought he to
love who has been given possessions to keep? For the person who
remains chaste from the outset is governed by him; whoever
becomes chaste after being unchaste is corrected by him; and whoever remains unchaste to the end is abandoned by him. He can
accomplish this by a judgement hidden from us, but not by an
unjust judgement; and perhaps it lurks unseen so that it may instill
more fear and less pride.

44. Next, once a man knows that he is what he is by God's [XLIII]
grace, he must not fall into another snare of pride so that in raising
himself by God's grace, he despises all others. This was the fault by
which the other of the two, the Pharisee, both thanked God for the
blessings which he possessed, and yet at the same time preened himself above the tax-collector who was confessing his sins. So what
should a virgin do or think, to avoid raising herself above men or
women who lack that great gift of hers? She must certainly not feign
humility, but demonstrate it, for pretence of humility is a greater
form of pride. This is why scripture, wishing to demonstrate that
humility must be genuine, after stating 'The greater you are, the
more you must humble yourself in all things', immediately after-
wards added 'and you will obtain favour before God',[126] for especially before him a person could not feign humility.

45. So what are we to say? Is there any consideration which [XLIV]
a virgin of God may truthfully entertain which causes her not to
presume to rank herself above a woman of faith—not merely a
widow, but also a married woman? I do not refer here to the

itane trepidabit sanctam uirginitatem etiam castis nuptiis et continentiam praeferre conubio, fructum centenum praeire triceno?[127]
Immo uero non dubitet hanc rem illi praeponere. Haec tamen uel
haec uirgo oboediens et deum timens illi uel illi mulieri oboedienti
et deum timenti se anteferre non audeat; alioquin non erit humilis,
et *Deus superbis resistit.*[128] Quid ergo cogitabit? Occulta scilicet dona
dei, quae nonnisi interrogatio temptationis etiam in semet ipso
unicuique declarat. Vt enim cetera taceam, unde scit uirgo, quamuis *sollicita quae sunt domini, quomodo placeat domino,*[129] ne forte propter
aliquam sibi incognitam mentis infirmitatem nondum sit matura
martyrio, illo uero mulier cui se praeferre gestiebat iam possit
bibere calicem dominicae humilitatis, quem prius bibendum discipulis amatoribus sublimitatis opposuit?[130] Vnde, inquam, scit ne
forte ipsa nondum sit Thecla, iam sit illa Crispina?[131]

[XLV]   Certe nisi adsit temptatio, nulla doni huius fit demonstratio.

46. Hoc autem tam magnum est ut eum fructum centenum
quidam intellegant. Perhibet enim praeclarissimum testimonium
ecclesiastica auctoritas, in qua fidelibus notum est quo loco martyres et quo defunctae sancti-moniales ad altaris sacramenta
recitentur.[132] Sed quid significet fecunditatis illa diuersitas, uiderint
qui haec melius quam nos intellegunt; siue uirginalis uita in centeno
fructu sit, in sexageno uidualis, in triceno autem coniugalis; siue
centena fertilitas martyrio potius imputetur, sexagena continentiae,
tricena conubio; siue uirginitas accedente martyrio centenum fructum impleat, sola uero in sexageno sit, coniugati autem tricenum

---

[127] See below [XLV] 46 and n.   [128] James 4: 6.
[129] 1 Cor. 7: 32.   [130] Cf. Matt. 20: 20 ff.
[131] *The Acts of Paul and Thecla*, a continuation of the 2nd-cent. apocryphal *Acts of St Paul* first
mentioned by Tertullian at *De baptismo* 17, is a Christian romance which grows out of
Acts 13: 51 ff., Paul's preaching at Iconium. Thecla is captivated, and renounces her proposed
marriage with the leading citizen of the town to live a life of chaste virginity. After condemnation to the arena and miraculous survival, she returns to Iconium to preach the gospel, and
dies peacefully there. For a full account see Tomas Hägg, *The Novel in Antiquity* (Berkeley,
1983), 154 ff. Thecla later blossoms into a full-blown historical figure in the Greek Fathers,
and thereafter in the West in Ambrose, *De uirginibus* 2. 19 f., *Ep.* 63. 34 (one of the two ancient
basilicas at Milan bore her name). Augustine regards her as the protomartyress who is the
counterpart to Stephen. Until her recent demotion she had a feast-day in the calendar of the
Western Church (23 Sept.). Crispina, an African noblewoman, was one of Augustine's hero-
ines. She was probably a native of his city Thagaste (*Thagarensis* in Anastasius, *Acta S. Crispinae*
(*PL* 129. 787): may be a corruption of *Tagastensis*). She suffered martyrdom under Diocletian
at Theveste (Tebessa) in 304. Augustine describes how she was beheaded at *Enarr. in
Ps.* 120. 13, part of a sermon delivered on her anniversary (see also *Enarr. in Ps.* 137. 3).

unworthy virgin, for who could be unaware that an obedient lay-woman is to be ranked above a disobedient virgin? But when both are obedient to God's commands, will the virgin then be fearful of promoting sacred virginity above marriage however chaste, and continence above the married state, so that fruit a hundredfold ranks above that which is thirtyfold?[127] Indeed not; she should not hesitate to put the first before the second. But the individual virgin who is obedient and fears God should not presume to raise herself above one laywoman or another who is obedient and fears God. Otherwise she will not be humble, and 'God resists the proud'.[128] So what will her attitude be? She will surely reflect on God's hidden gifts, which only the questions raised at a time of trial clarify for an individual in her own mind. To say nothing of other factors, how does a virgin, however concerned for 'the things of the Lord, how she may please the Lord',[129] realize that perhaps because of some mental weakness unknown to her, she may not yet be ripe for mar-tyrdom, whereas the woman above whom she sought to rank herself can already drink of the cup of the Lord's humility, which he set before his disciples to be drunk first when they were enamoured of high position?[130] How, I ask, does she know that perhaps she is not a Thecla yet, and that the other is already a Crispina?[131] At any rate, no proof of this gift is forthcoming unless a time of trial looms.

46. But this gift of martyrdom is so great that some regard [XLV] it as the fruit a hundredfold, for the authority of the Church pro-vides the clearest witness. Through it the faithful are made aware of the order in which martyrs and nuns who have died are cited dur-ing sacrifices at the altar.[132] But let those who understand these mat-ters better than we ourselves attend to the significance of this variation in fruitfulness; whether the virgin's life represents fruit a hundredfold, the widow's life sixtyfold, and married life thirtyfold. Or alternatively, whether fruitfulness a hundredfold is to be assigned rather to martyrdom, the sixtyfold to continence, and the thirtyfold to marriage; or again, whether virginity and martyrdom combined make up the hundredfold, while virginity alone occupies the sixtyfold, and married people who possess the thirtyfold

---

[132] The practice of commemorating the dead in the eucharistic liturgy according to the nature of their calling was already established before Augustine's time; see Cyprian, *Ep.* 1 (with reference to *sacerdotes* and *ministri*). It is clear from other evidence that martyrs were commemorated before consecrated virgins; see, e.g. Augustine, *Serm.* 273. 7: 'in recitatione . . . loco meliore recitantur.'

ferentes ad sexagenum perueniant si martyres fuerint;[133] siue quod probabilius mihi uidetur, quoniam diuinae gratiae multa sunt munera et est aliud alio maius ac melius (unde dicit apostolus *Imitamini autem dona meliora*)[134] intellegendum est plura esse quam ut in tres differentias distribui possint.

Primum, ne continentiam uidualem aut in nullo fructu constituamus, aut ad coniugalis pudicitiae meritum deponamus aut uirginali gloriae coaequemus,[135] aut coronam martyrii uel in habitu animi, etiamsi desit temptationis examen, uel in ipsa passionis experientia constitutam, cuilibet illarum trium castitati sine ullo incremento fertilitatis accedere existimemus. Deinde ubi ponimus quod multi ac multae ita custodiunt continentiam uirginalem, ut tamen non faciant quae dominus ait: *Si uis esse perfectus, uade, uende omnia quae habes et da pauperibus, et habebis thesaurum in caelo; et ueni, sequere me*, nec audeant eorum cohabitationi sociari in quibus nemo dicit aliquid proprium, sed sunt eis omnia communia,[136] nihilne putamus fructificationis accedere uirginibus dei, cum hoc faciunt? Aut sine ullo fructu esse uirgines dei, etiamsi hoc non faciant?

[XLVI]   Multa ergo sunt dona, et aliis alia clariora ac superiora singulis singula, et aliquando alter fructuosus est donis paucioribus sed potioribus, alter inferioribus sed pluribus. Et quemadmodum inter se uel coaequentur uel distinguantur in accipiendis aeternis honoribus, quis hominum audeat iudicare? Dum tamen constet et multa esse ista diuersa et non ad praesens tempus, sed in aeternum prodesse meliora. Sed dominum tres arbitror uoluisse

---

[133] See *De bono coniugali* [XVIII] 22 and n. 83. The Greek Fathers (John Chrysostom, *Serm.* 45; Gregory Nazianzen, *Serm.* 28) were already interpreting the yields in the parable of the Sower (Matt. 13: 4ff; Mark 4: 3ff.; Luke 8: 4ff.) as symbolic of the contrasting merits of different kinds of saintly lives. Jerome (*In Matt.* 13, *Contra Iou.* 1) applied the yields of a hundredfold, sixtyfold, and thirtyfold to the merits of consecrated virgins, chaste widows, and married women respectively. Augustine earlier (*Quaestiones euangeliorum* 1. 9, AD 397) followed the lead of Cyprian, *De habitu uirginum* 21, in applying the three yields in descending order to martyrs, virgins, and married spouses. For a more detailed survey see J. Saint-Martin, *Oeuvres de Saint Augustin*, iii (Paris, 1949), 458 f.

[134] 1 Cor. 12: 31.

[135] In a society in which girls married at about fourteen, and the average life-expectancy of men was relatively low, it was natural for young widows to contemplate remarriage. The increasing promotion of continence by the Greek Fathers as the ideal form of Christian life led to widespread discouragement of second and later marriages. The more positive spokesmen (Clement of Alexandria, Origen, John Chrysostom) do not condemn them, but counsel chaste widowhood as the better course; others are more stringent. Athenagoras regards second marriages as 'decent adultery'; Basil demands a year's penitence for a second marriage. Ambrose in the West advises: 'Non prohibemus, sed non probamus'; Jerome claims 'Aliud

advance to the sixtyfold if they become martyrs.[133] Or what seems
to me more likely, since the gifts of divine grace are many, and one is
greater and better than another (hence those words of the Apostle,
'Strive for the greater gifts'),[134] we are to realize that there are more
gifts than can be allocated to these different categories.

In the first place, we must not assess a widow's continence as
bearing no fruit, or relegate it to the merits of married chastity, or
equate it with the glory of the virgin.[135] Or again, we must not
regard the crown of martyrdom, whether established in mental disposition (though proof by trial is wanting) or in actual experience of
suffering, as gaining no increase in fruitfulness when joined to any
of these three modes of chastity. Second, many men and many
women maintain virginal chastity but without fulfilling those words
of the Lord: 'If you will be perfect, go, sell all you have, and give to
the poor, and you will have treasure in heaven; and come, follow
me.' Moreover, they do not venture to join a community of those
amongst whom no one claims anything as his own, but who possess
all things in common.[136] When we take account of this, do we
believe that no fruitfulness is imparted to God's virgins when they
do the Lord's bidding? Or do we believe that even if they do not,
God's virgins are left fruitless?

So there are many gifts, some more glorious and outstanding [XLVI]
than others, and each person has his own. Sometimes one person is
fruitful in fewer but worthier gifts, and another in lesser but more
numerous ones. Which person among us would presume to pass
judgement on how the gifts are to be ranked equal to each other or
differently from each other in gaining distinctions in eternity? That
is, so long as it is clear that these diverse gifts are many, and the better ones profit us not at the present time but for eternity. But I
believe that the Lord wished to specify three different levels of
fruitfulness and left the rest to our understanding; indeed, one of the

est uoluntas dei, aliud indulgentia'. Augustine later (AD 414) devotes his *De bono uiduitatis* to the
question, and takes a similar line to that of Ambrose; he does not condemn second marriages,
but he urges on the widow Juliana the preferable good of widowhood, which in merit he
ranks above chaste marriage though below consecrated virginity. For the texts, see L. Godefroy, *DTC* 9. 2. 2045 ff.

[136] Matt. 19: 21; cf. Acts 2: 44, 4: 32. Augustine distinguishes between women who continued to live in their own residences and those who joined the convents which he had established. Both at Rome under Jerome's inspiration and at Milan in Ambrose's day life in community was not the norm, and Augustine here seems implicitly critical of the comfortable
life-style of those who lived a life of consecrated virginity in private.

fructificationis commemorare differentias, ceteras intellegentibus reliquisse. Nam et alius euangelista solum commemorauit centuplum. Numquid ideo putandus est alia duo uel improbasse uel ignorasse, ac non potius intellegenda reliquisse?[137]

47. Sed ut dicere coeperam, siue centenus fructus sit deo deuota uirginitas siue alio aliquo modo, uel quem commemorauimus uel quem non commemorauimus, sit illa fertilitatis intellegenda distantia, nemo tamen, quantum puto, ausus fuerit uirginitatem praeferre martyrio, ac nemo dubitauerit hoc donum occultum esse si examinatrix desit temptatio.

[XLVII]   Habet itaque uirgo quod cogitet quod ei prosit ad seruandam humilitatem, ne uiolet illam quae supereminet donis omnibus caritatem, sine qua utique quaecumque alia uel pauca uel plura uel magna uel parua habuerit, nihil est; habet, inquam, quod cogitet ut non infletur, non aemuletur, ita se scilicet bonum uirginale coniugali bono multo amplius et melius profiteri, ut tamen nesciat utrum illa uel illa coniugata iam pati pro Christo possit, adhuc uero ipsa non possit, et in hoc ei parcatur quia infirmitas eius temptatione non interrogatur. *Fidelis* enim *deus*, ait apostolus, *qui non uos permittat temptari super id quod potestis, sed faciat cum temptatione etiam exitum ut possitis sustinere.*[138]

Fortassis ergo illi uel illae* coniugalis uitae retinentes in suo genere laudabilem modum iam possint contra inimicum ad iniquitatem cogentem etiam laniatu uiscerum et effusione sanguinis dimicare; illi autem uel illae* a pueritia continentes seque castrantes propter regnum caelorum, nondum tamen ualeant talia uel pro iustitia uel pro ipsa pudicitia sustinere. Aliud est enim pro ueritate ac proposito sancto non consentire suadenti atque blandienti, aliud non cedere etiam torquenti atque ferienti. Latent ista in facultatibus et uiribus animorum, temptata panduntur, experientia propalantur. Vt ergo quisque non infletur ex eo quod se peruidet posse, humiliter cogitet quod ignorat aliquid praestantius se fortasse non posse, aliquos autem qui illud quo sibi gloriose notus est nec habent nec profitentur, hoc quod ipse non potest posse. Ita seruabitur non

---

[137] With reference to Luke 8: 8.
[138] 1 Cor. 10: 13.

---

* illi uel illae *codd. deteriores, Saint-Martin*: illi uel illi *cett., Zycha*

evangelists cited only the hundredfold. We are surely not on that account to imagine either that he disapproved of the other two or was unaware of them, rather than that he left them to be understood?[137]

47. But as I had begun to say, whether the virginity dedicated to God counts as fruit a hundredfold, or whether the difference in fruitfulness is to be understood in any other way such as I have mentioned or omitted, in my opinion no one will presume to rank virginity above martyrdom, and no one will doubt that martyrdom is a gift that lies hidden, should there be no testing trial.

A virgin therefore has a point of reference to aid her to maintain humility and to prevent her from doing violence to chastity, which transcends all gifts and without which—whatever her other gifts, few or more numerous, great or small—she is clearly nothing. As I say, she has a point of reference enabling her not to be puffed up or envious; namely, to claim that virginity is a good much greater and better than the good of marriage, but with the rider that she does not know whether a particular married woman can already suffer for Christ while she herself cannot, and that she is spared this knowledge because her weakness is not put into question by trial. 'For God is faithful', says the Apostle, 'for he does not allow you to be tried beyond your strength, but with the testing he will also provide a way out so that you may be able to endure it.'[138]   [XLVII]

So perhaps individual men or women who continue in a mode of married life praiseworthy of its kind could already come to grips with an enemy who sought to constrain them, even by disembowelling and shedding their blood, to act wickedly, whereas individual men or women who have remained continent from childhood and have made themselves eunuchs for the sake of the kingdom of heaven would not yet be able to endure such treatment in defence of either justice or chastity itself. For it is one thing not to be complaisant in defence of truth and holy vocation when someone seeks to persuade and to flatter, but another to refuse to yield if he also turns to the rack and the sword. Responses such as this lie hidden in the resources and strengths of our minds, but they emerge when put to the test and are exposed by trial. Accordingly so that each of us should not be puffed up by what he realizes he can do, he should humbly reflect on his being unaware of something more outstanding that he perhaps cannot do, and that some persons who neither have nor claim to have what for him is his proud boast, can

fallaci sed ueraci humilitate; *Honore mutuo praeuenientes* et *alter alterum existimantes superiorem sibi.*[139]

[XLVIII]   48. Quid iam dicam de ipsa cautela et uigilantia non peccandi? *Quis gloriabitur castum se habere cor? Aut quis gloriabitur mundum se esse a peccato?*[140] Integra est quidem ab utero matris sancta uirginitas; sed *Nemo* inquit *mundus in conspectu tuo, nec infans cuius est unius diei uita super terram.*[141] Seruatur et in fide inuiolata quaedam castitas uirginalis, qua ecclesia uni uiro uirgo casta coaptatur;[142] sed ille unus uir non tantum fideles mente et corpore uirgines, sed omnes omnino Christianos ab spiritalibus usque ad carnales, ab apostolis usque ad ultimos paenitentes tamquam *a summis caelorum usque ad terminos eorum*[143] docuit orare, et in ipsa oratione dicere admonuit: *Dimitte nobis debita nostra, sicut et nos dimittimus debitoribus nostris,*[144] ubi per hoc quod petimus quid etiam nos esse meminerimus ostendit. Neque enim pro eis debitis quae totius praeteritae uitae in baptismo per eius pacem nobis dimissa esse confidimus, nos praecepit orare dicentes *Dimitte nobis debita nostra, sicut et nos dimittimus debitoribus nostris*; alioquin hanc orationem catechumeni potius usque ad baptismum orare deberent. Cum uero eam baptizati orant praepositi et plebes, pastores et greges, satis ostenditur in hac uita quae tota temptatio est neminem se tamquam ab omnibus peccatis immunem debere gloriari.

[XLIX]   49. Proinde etiam uirgines dei irreprehensibiles quidem sequuntur agnum quocumque ierit, et peccatorum purgatione perfecta et uirginitate seruata, quae non rediret amissa; sed quia eadem ipsa Apocalypsis, ubi tales tali reuelati sunt, etiam hinc eos laudat quod in ore eorum non sit inuentum mendacium,[145] meminerint etiam in hoc esse ueraces ne se audeant dicere non habere peccatum. Idem quippe Iohannes qui illud uidit hoc dixit: *Si dixerimus quia peccatum non habemus, nos ipsos decipimus, et ueritas in nobis non est. Quodsi confessi fuerimus delicta nostra, fidelis est et iustus, ut dimittat nobis peccata nostra et purget nos ab omni iniquitate. Quodsi dixerimus quoniam non peccauimus, mendacem faciemus eum, et uerbum eius non erit in nobis.*[146] Hoc certe non

---

[139] Rom. 12: 10; Phil. 2: 3.

[140] Prov. 20: 9, perhaps paraphrased here rather than a variant text.

[141] Job 25: 4. The citation differs considerably from the Vulgate text; it appears to lend greater force to the doctrine of original sin.

[142] 2 Cor. 11: 2.   [143] Matt. 24: 31.   [144] Matt. 6: 12.

[145] Cf. Apoc. 14: 4 f.; 'a revelation of like to like' because the apostle John as virgin (cf. *De bono coniugali*, n. 96) addresses virgins.

[146] 1 John 1: 8 ff.

do what he himself cannot. In this way he will be protected by a true and not a feigned humility. 'Each outdoing the other in showing honour', and 'Each regarding the other as better than himself'.[139]

48. What am I now to say about being circumspect and watchful against sinning? 'Who will boast that he has a chaste heart? Or who will boast that he is pure from sin?'[140] True, holy virginity is undefiled from the mother's womb, but 'No one', says scripture, 'is pure in your sight, not even a child who has lived a single day upon the earth.'[141] A kind of virginal chastity is preserved inviolate also in the realm of faith, in which the Church is joined as a chaste virgin to one husband.[142] But that one husband schooled in prayer not only virgins faithful in mind and body, but also all Christians without exception, both spiritual and carnal, from the apostles down to the meanest penitents, as 'from the heights of heaven to its furthest bounds'.[143] In that prayer he instructed us to say 'Forgive us our debts, as we too forgive our debtors'.[144] In those words he shows us that by what we ask for we are to remember also what we are. When we say 'Forgive us our debts, as we too forgive our debtors', he did not bid us pray with regard to those debts which were contracted through the whole of our past lives, and which we trust have been forgiven us in baptism through his peace. Otherwise this would be a prayer rather for catechumens up to the time of their baptism to utter. But since it is a a prayer expressed by the baptized, both by rulers and by the common folk, by shepherds and their flocks, it is made sufficiently clear that in this life, all of which is a trial, no one should boast as though he were subject to no sins. [XLVIII

49. So even God's virgins who are blameless do indeed follow the Lamb wherever he goes, but after they have attained cleansing of their sins and have maintained that virginity which once lost could not be regained. But because that very Apocalypse, which was a revelation of like to like, praises them also because no lie was found in their mouths,[145] they must remember to be truthful as well in not presuming to claim that they are free from sin. For the same John who had that vision said this: 'If we say that we have no sin, we deceive ourselves, and the truth is not in us. But if we confess our faults, he is faithful and just in forgiving all our sins and cleansing us of all our wickedness. But if we say that we have not sinned, we shall make him a liar, and his word will not be in us.'[146] This is [XLIX]

illis aut illis, sed Christianis omnibus dicitur, ubi et uirgines se debent agnoscere. Sic enim erunt sine mendacio, quales in Apocalypsi apparuerunt. Ac per hoc quamdiu nondum est in caelesti sublimitate perfectio, inuituperabiles facit in humilitate confessio.

50. Sed rursus, ne per occasionem huius sententiae quisquam cum mortifera securitate peccaret, seque trahendum permitteret tamquam mox delendis facili confessione peccatis, continuo subiecit: *Filioli mei, haec scripsi uobis ut non peccetis, et si quis peccauerit, aduocatum habemus ad patrem Iesum Christum iustum; et ipse propitiator est peccatorum nostrorum.*[147] Nemo itaque a peccato tamquam rediturus abscedat, nec se huius modi quasi societatis pacto cum iniquitate constringat, ut eam confiteri quam cauere delectet.

[L]   Sed quoniam etiam satagentibus uigilantibusque ne peccent, subrepunt quodam modo ex humana fragilitate peccata, quamuis parua quamuis pauca, non tamen nulla, eadem ipsa fiunt magna et grauia, si eis superbia incrementum et pondus adiecerit; a sacerdote autem quem habemus in caelis, si pia humilitate perimantur, tota felicitate* purgantur.[148]

51. Sed non contendo cum eis qui adserunt hominem posse in hac uita sine ullo peccato uiuere.[149] Non contendo, non contradico. Fortassis enim ex nostra miseria magnos metimur, et comparantes nosmet ipsos nobismet ipsis[150] non intellegimus. Vnum scio, quod isti magni, quales non sumus, quales nondum experti sumus, quanto magni sunt tanto humilant se in omnibus ut coram deo inueniant gratiam. Quamlibet enim magni sint, *Non est seruus maior domino suo, uel discipulus magistro suo.* Et utique ille est dominus qui dicit *Omnia mihi tradita sunt a patre meo,* et ille est magister qui dicit *Venite ad me omnes qui laboratis, et discite a me.* Et tamen quid discimus? *Quoniam mitis sum* inquit *et humilis corde.*[151]

[LI]   52. Hic dicet aliquis: 'Non est hoc iam de uirginitate, sed de humilitate scribere.' Quasi uero quaecumque uirginitas ac non illa

---

[147] 1 John 2: 1 f.   [148] Cf. Hebr. 4: 14 f.

[149] It seems clear that this is a reference to the early stages of the Pelagian movement, which was emerging at Rome from about 394. See Peter Brown, 'Pelagius and his Supporters', *JRS* 19 (1968), 93 ff. (= *Religion and Society in the Age of Saint Augustine*, 183 ff.). One of the heresies with which the Pelagians were later charged was that even before Christ's coming there were individuals who lived wholly sinless lives. Augustine at this time listened respectfully to Pelagian arguments; see Brown, *Augustine of Hippo*, 345 ff.

[150] Cf. 2 Cor. 10: 12.   [151] Ecclus. 3: 20; John 13: 16; Matt. 11: 27 ff.

---

* felicitate *CP, Zycha*: facilitate *K, Saint-Martin*

surely addressed not to one group or another, but to all Christians, amongst whom virgins too must recognize themselves. In that way they will be free from lying, as depicted in the Apocalypse. And by this means, for so long as they do not yet attain perfection in the heights of heaven, their humble confession renders them without blame.

50. But again, he sought to ensure that no one would exploit that statement to sin through fatal reassurance, and to allow himself to be lured into the belief that his sins were soon to be expunged by ready confession, so he immediately added: 'My dear children, I have written these things to you so that you may not sin; and if anyone does sin, we have as advocate with the Father, Jesus Christ the righteous one, and he is the one who seeks indulgence for our sins.'[147] So no one must abandon sins with the intention of returning to them, nor make a compact of alliance, as it were, with wickedness to take pleasure in confessing sins rather than eschewing them.

But even when people try hard and keep watch against sinning, [L] sins somehow creep up on us out of our human weakness; though small and few, they are none the less of some account, and they become great and grievous if pride lends them increase and weight. But if cancelled out by devoted humility, they are wholly and happily effaced by the Priest whom we possess in heaven.[148]

51. But I do not argue with those who claim that a person can live in this life without committing any sin.[149] I do not dispute or gainsay it. For perhaps we measure the great by our own wretchedness, and in comparing ourselves with ourselves[150] we fail to understand. One thing I do know is that these great men, the like of whom we are not and the like of whom we have as yet not encountered, humble themselves the more as they are greater in order to find favour in God's eyes. For however great they are, 'No servant is greater than his lord, and no disciple is greater than his master'. And assuredly he is Lord who says, 'All things have been entrusted to me by my Father', and he is master who says, 'Come to me, all you who labour, and learn from me.' Yet what is it that we learn? 'That I am meek', he says, 'and humble of heart.'[151]

52. At this point someone will say: 'This is no longer a treatise [LI] on virginity, but on humility'—as if it were any kind of virginity which we have undertaken to proclaim, and not that which God approves! The greatness of this good as I envisage it is matched by

quae secundum deum est a nobis praedicanda suscepta est! Quod
bonum quanto magnum uideo, tanto ei, ne pereat, in futurum†
superbiam pertimesco. Non ergo custodit bonum uirginale nisi
deus ipse qui dedit, et *deus caritas est.*[152] Custos ergo uirginitatis caritas; locus autem huius custodis humilitas. Ibi quippe habitat qui
dixit super humilem et quietum et trementem uerba sua requi-
escere spiritum suum.[153]

Quid itaque alienum feci si bonum quod laudaui uolens tutius
custodiri curaui etiam locum praeparare custodi? Fidenter enim
dico nec mihi ne irascantur timeo, quos ut mecum sibi timeant sol-
licitus moneo. Facilius sequuntur agnum, etsi non quocumque ierit,
certe quousque potuerint, coniugati humiles quam superbientes
uirgines. Quomodo enim sequitur ad quem non uult accedere? Aut
quomodo accedit, ad quem non uenit ut discat *Quoniam mitis est et
humilis corde?* Illos proinde sequentes agnus quocumque ierit ducit, in
quibus prius ipse ubi caput inclinet inuenerit. Nam et quidam superbus et dolosus hoc ei dixerat: *Domine, sequar te quocumque ieris.* Cui
respondit: *Vulpes foueas habent et uolatilia caeli nidos; filius autem hominis
non habet ubi caput suum inclinet.*[154] Arguebat nomine uulpium astutam
dolositatem, et nomine uolucrum uentosam elationem, in quo ubi
requiesceret piam non inueniebat humilitatem. Ac per hoc
nusquam omnino secutus est dominum qui se promiserat non usque
ad quemdam provectum, sed omnino quocumque ierit secuturum.

[LII]   53. Quapropter hoc agite, uirgines dei, hoc agite; sequimini
agnum quocumque ierit, sed prius ad eum quem sequamini uenite,
et discite *quoniam mitis est et humilis corde.* Humiliter ad humilem uenite si amatis, et ne discedatis ab illo ne cadatis. Qui enim timet ab illo
discedere, rogat et dicit: *Non mihi ueniat pes superbiae.*[155] Pergite uiam
sublimitatis pede humilitatis. Ipse exaltat humiliter sequentes quem
descendere non piguit ad iacentes. Dona eius illi seruanda commit-
tite, fortitudinem uestram ad illum custodite.[156] Quidquid mali ipso
custodiente non committitis tamquam remissum ab illo deputate,
ne modicum uobis existimantes dimissum, modicum diligatis,[157]

---

[152] 1 John 4: 8.   [153] Cf. Isa. 66: 2.
[154] Matt. 8: 19 f. 'That arrogant and crafty fellow' is Augustine's gloss on 'a certain scribe'
in the Matthew text. The interpretation of 'foxes' and 'birds' echoes that in his *Quaest XVI in
Matt. V* (CCSL 44B, 121): the birds represent 'inanem iactantiam', the foxes 'the feigned obedience of a disciple'.
[155] Ps. 35(36): 12.   [156] Cf. Ps. 58(59): 10.   [157] Cf. Luke 7: 47 and n. 109 above.

---

† in futurum *C, Zycha*: furem *PK, Saint-Martin*

my apprehension of the pride which may in future cause it to be lost. So no one protects this good of virginity but God himself, who bestowed it, and 'God is love'.[152] So love is the guardian of virginity, and the residence of this guardian is in humility; for in that place dwells he who said that his spirit rests on the humble and peaceable person who trembles at his words.[153]

So what have I done which is foreign to my theme, if in desiring that the good which I have praised be more securely guarded, I have taken care also to prepare a place for its guardian? I say this with confidence, and without fear that those whom I anxiously warn to share my fear may be angry with me. Married persons who are humble more easily follow the Lamb—not wherever he goes but at any rate as far as they can—than virgins who are arrogant. For how can a person follow him without wishing to draw near him? Or how does a person draw near him without coming to learn that he is meek and humble of heart? So the followers whom the Lamb leads wherever he goes are those in whom first he finds a place to lay his head. There was that arrogant and crafty fellow who had said to Jesus: 'Lord, I will follow you wherever you go.' Jesus answered him: 'Foxes have their holes, and the birds of the air have their nests, but the Son of man has nowhere to lay his head.'[154] By speaking of 'foxes' he was reproving crafty guile, and by 'birds' windy arrogance; in these he found no devoted humility wherein to rest. In this sense the man who had promised to follow the Lord not to some further point but wherever he possibly went followed him nowhere at all.

53. So this is what you must do, virgins of God; this is what [LII] you must do. Follow the Lamb wherever he goes, but first come to him whom you are to follow, and learn that he is meek and humble of heart. Approach the humble One humbly, if you love him, and do not part from him lest you fall; for the person who fears to part from him utters this plea: 'Let not pride impress its foot upon me!'[155] Advance on the path to the heights, but with the foot of humility. He who was not ashamed to descend to the prostrate exalts those who follow him with humility. Entrust his gifts to him for safe-keeping; keep your strength in safety close to him.[156] Any evil which you refrain from committing under his protection, regard as forgiven by him; otherwise, through believing that little has been forgiven you, you may love only a little,[157] and with disastrous boasting you may despise tax-collectors as they beat their breasts. When your powers

et tundentes pectora publicanos ruinosa iactantia contemnatis. De
uiribus uestris expertis cauete ne, quia ferre aliquid potuistis,
inflemini; de inexpertis autem orate ne supra quam potestis ferre
temptemini. Existimate aliquos in occulto superiores, quibus estis in
manifesto meliores.¹⁵⁸ Cum aliorum bona forte ignota uobis
benigne creduntur a uobis, uestra uobis nota non comparatione
minuuntur, sed dilectione firmantur; et quae forte adhuc desunt,
tanto dantur facilius quanto desiderantur humilius.

Perseuerantes in numero uestro praebeant uobis exemplum;
cadentes autem augeant timorem uestrum. Illud amate ut imitem-
ini, hoc lugete ne inflemini. Iustitiam uestram nolite statuere, deo
uos iustificanti subdite. Veniam peccatis donate alienis, orate pro
uestris; futura uigilando uitate, praeterita confitendo delete.¹⁵⁹

[LIII] 54. Ecce iam tales estis ut professae atque seruatae uirginitati
ceteris etiam moribus congruatis. Ecce iam non solum homicidiis,
sacrificiis diabolicis et abominationibus, furtis rapinis fraudibus
periuriis ebriositatibus omnique luxuria et auaritia, simulationibus
aemulationibus impietatibus crudelitatibus abstinetis, uerum etiam
illa quae leuiora uel sunt uel putantur non inueniuntur nec oriuntur
in uobis; non improbus uultus, non uagi oculi, non infrenis lingua,
non petulans risus, non scurrilis iocus, non indecens habitus, non
tumidus aut fluxus incessus; iam non redditis *malum pro malo, nec
maledictum pro maledicto*;¹⁶⁰ iam postremo illam mensuram dilectionis
impletis, ut ponatis animas pro fratribus uestris.¹⁶¹ Ecce iam tales
estis quia et tales esse debetis. Haec addita uirginitati angelicam
uitam hominibus, et caeli mores exhibent terris. Sed quanto magni
estis, quicumque ita magni estis, tanto *humilate uos in omnibus, ut
coram deo inueniatis gratiam*, ne superbis resistat, ne se exaltantes
humilet, ne inflatos per angusta non traiciat;¹⁶² quamquam super-
flua sit sollicitudo ne ubi feruet caritas desit humilitas.

¹⁵⁸ Cf. Ambrose, *De officiis* 3: 28.

¹⁵⁹ In view of Augustine's glowing account of the virgins' conduct in the next section, it is
clear that he does not refer here to the rite of public penance traditionally demanded for the
three major sins of unchastity, idolatry, and homicide. Ambrose (*De spiritu sancto* 3. 18) indicates the practice at Milan of supplication to God before the altar in the presence of the community, followed by a declaration in the name of the Trinity that sins were forgiven.
Presumably a similar procedure was followed at Hippo. See in general O. D. Watkins, *A History of Penance* (London, 1920), esp. 433ff.

¹⁶⁰ Cf. 1 Pet. 3: 9.

have been put to the test, be chary of becoming puffed up because you have been able to show some endurance; as for those which have not been tested, pray that you may not be tried more than you can bear. Regard some as your betters inwardly, though outwardly you are better.[158] When the good qualities of others which happen to be unknown to you are generously acknowledged by you, those of your own which are known to you are not diminished by comparison, but are enhanced by love. As for those which as yet you happen to lack, they are ascribed to you the more readily as you desire them more humbly. Those of your company who remain steadfast must be your model; those who fall must increase your fear. Love the first example to imitate it; lament over the second, to avoid arrogance. Do not vaunt your righteousness, but submit to the God who makes you righteous. Grant pardon to the sins of others, and pray for your own; avoid sins in future by vigilance, and expunge those of the past by confessing them.[159]

54. Now, as you see, your character is such that the rest of [LIII] your manners are in keeping with the virginity which you have professed and maintained. Why, now you not merely refrain from murders, sacrifices to demons and such loathsome practices, thefts, plunderings, deceits, jealousies, impious activities, cruelties; why, even the faults which are minor or are considered so are not found in you nor arise in you: shameless countenances, roaming eyes, unbridled tongues, wanton laughter, licentious joking, immodest clothing, a haughty or dissolute tread. You do not now render 'evil for evil, nor curse for curse'.[160] And finally, you already fulfil that noble criterion of love in laying down your lives for your brethren.[161] Why, you are already like this because it is your duty to be like this. This enhancement to your virginity demonstrates the life of angels to men, and the ways of heaven to the regions of earth. But as for those of you now great, your humility in all things must correspond with your greatness so that you may find favour in God's eyes; thus he may not resist your pride, nor humble you for raising yourselves high, nor debar you in your arrogance from passing through the narrows.[162] But it is idle to worry that humility may be lacking where there is glowing love.

---

[161] Cf. 1 John 3: 16. Augustine presumably refers here to 'the sporadic brutalities of an extreme wing of the Donatist Church, the Circumcellions' (Brown, *Augustine of Hippo*, 229, with further bibliography; see also the contributions of W. H. C. Frend on p. 440 there.)

[162] Cf. Ecclus. 3: 20; James 4: 6; 1 Pet. 5: 5; Luke 18: 14; Matt. 7: 14.

144 DE SANCTA VIRGINITATE

[LIV]   55. Si ergo nuptias contempsistis filiorum hominum, ex quibus gigneretis filios hominum, toto corde amate *speciosum forma prae filiis hominum;*[163] uacat uobis, liberum est cor a coniugalibus uinculis. Inspicite pulchritudinem amatoris uestri; cogitate aequalem patri, subditum et matri; etiam in caelis dominantem et in terris seruientem; creantem omnia, creatum inter omnia. Illud ipsum quod in eo derident superbi inspicite quam pulchrum sit; internis luminibus inspicite uulnera pendentis, cicatrices resurgentis, sanguinem morientis, pretium credentis, commercium redimentis.

[LV]   Haec quanti ualeant cogitate. Haec in statera caritatis appendite, et quidquid amoris in nuptias uestras impendendum habebatis, illi rependite.

56. Bene, quod interiorem uestram pulchritudinem quaerit, ubi uobis dedit potestatem filios dei fieri.[164] Non quaerit a uobis pulchram carnem, sed pulchros mores quibus refrenatis et carnem. Non est cui de uobis quisquam mentiatur et faciat saeuire zelantem. Videte cum quanta securitate ametis, cui displicere falsis suspicionibus non timetis. Vir et uxor amant se quoniam uident se, et quod non uident timent in se; nec certi gaudent ex eo quod in manifesto est, dum in occulto suspicantur plerumque quod non est. Vos in isto, quem oculis non uidetis et fide conspicitis nec habetis uerum quod reprehendatis nec eum metuitis ne de falso forsitan offendatis. Si ergo magnum amorem coniugibus deberetis, eum propter quem coniuges habere noluistis quantum amare debetis! Toto uobis figatur in corde, qui pro uobis est fixus in cruce; totum teneat in animo uestro quidquid noluistis occupari conubio. Parum uobis amare non licet, propter quem non amastis et quod liceret. Sic amantibus mitem et humilem corde nullam uobis superbiam pertimesco.

[LVI]   57. Pro modulo itaque nostro et de sanctitate qua sanctimoniales proprie dicimini,[165] et de humilitate qua conseruatur quidquid magnum dicimini, satis locuti sumus. Dignius autem illi tres pueri, quibus refrigerium in igne praebebat, quem corde feruentissimo

---

[163] Cf. Ps. 44(45): 3.
[164] Cf. John 1: 12.
[165] *sanctimonialis* is a word adopted by Christian writers from Classical usage. *sanctimonia* (moral purity) appears more than once in Cicero, and Tacitus speaks of a 'priscae sanctimoniae uirgo' and a 'femina sanctimonia insignis' (*Annals* 3. 69, 12. 6). In Christian Latin *sanctimonialis* rapidly gains the technical sense of consecrated virgin, as here and in *Retract.* 2. xxii. 1; *monialis* alone becomes frequent in Medieval Latin for nun.

55. If therefore you have come to despise marriages with the sons [LIV] of men, to beget from them the sons of men, you must love whole-heartedly him who is beauteous in form beyond the sons of men.[163] You are at liberty, and your heart is free from the bonds of marriage. Gaze on the beauty of your lover; contemplate him as equal to the Father and also subject to his mother; as one who while still lord in the heavens became a servant on earth; as one who both created all things and was created among all things. Observe the beauty of that very feature in him which is mocked by the proud: gaze with the mind's eye on his wounds as he hangs on the cross, on his scars as he rises again, on his blood as he dies, on the ransom for the believer, on the transaction made by the Redeemer.

Consider how much these things are worth. Weigh them in the [LV] scale of affection, and whatever love you had available to be devoted to your marriages, repay to him.

56. It is good that it is your inner beauty that he seeks, for it is there that he has given you the power to become children of God.[164] He does not demand of you a handsome body, but handsome manners by which you discipline the body as well. He is not one to whom anyone can lie about you and cause him to fly into a jealous rage. See how very assured is your love for him, for you are not afraid to displease him with ungrounded suspicions. A husband and wife love each other because they look upon each other, and they fear in each other what they do not see. Their joy in what they see is not assured as long as they inwardly suspect what for the most part does not exist. You do not look on your lover with your eyes, but you discern him by faith; you find no true grounds for rebuking him, and you have no fear of possibly offending him with false charges. So if you would owe great love to partners in marriage, how much ought you to love the one for whose sake you declined to take a partner in marriage! He must be impacted upon your whole heart, as he was nailed for you on the cross; he must possess in your mind all that you refused to have usurped by marriage. You cannot have too little love for him for whose sake you did not indulge even in licit love. If you love in this way him who is meek and humble of heart, I have no fear of any pride in you.

57. So in our modest way we have discoursed sufficiently on [LVI] both the holiness which gives you the distinctive title of 'holy nuns',[165] and the humility by which such claim to greatness as is accorded you is preserved. But those three celebrated children, on

146 DE SANCTA VIRGINITATE

diligebant, uos de hoc opusculo nostro uerborum quidem numero longe breuius, sed pondere auctoritatis multo grandius,[166] in hymno quo ab eis deus honoratur, admoneant. Nam sanctitati humilitatem in dei laudatoribus coniungentes apertissime docuerunt, ut tanto quisque caueat ne superbia decipiatur quanto sanctius aliquid profertur. Proinde uos quoque laudate eum, qui uobis praestat ut in ardore medio saeculi huius quamuis coniugio non copulemini non tamen uramini,[167] et orantes etiam pro nobis: *Benedicite, sancti et humiles corde, dominum; hymnum dicite et superexaltate eum in saecula.*[168]

---

[166] Dan. 3: 20 ff.; see n. 70 above. 'The Song of the Three Holy Children' (Dan. 3: 52–90) is one of three additions to the *Book of Daniel* which are assigned to the Apocrypha of the OT; they are later Greek writings which found their way into the Septuagint.

[167] Cf. 1 Cor. 7: 9. The play on the literal and metaphorical senses of 'burning' provides an apt theme for the peroration of the treatise.

[168] Dan. 3: 87, a verse nicely chosen for its emphasis on humility.

whom the One they loved with glowing hearts bestowed cool refreshment in the fire, more worthily advise you on the subject of this modest work of ours; in that hymn in which God is praised by them, they speak much more briefly in count of words but much more impressively in weight of authority.[166] For by joining humility to holiness in their praises of God, they taught most clearly that each and all should beware the more of being beguiled by pride the more a measure of holiness is displayed. So you too must praise him, for though you dwell in the midst of the heat of this world, and though you are not joined in marriage, he ensures that you do not burn.[167] Praise him as on our behalf you too make that prayer: 'You who are holy and humble of heart, bless the Lord, sing a hymn, and exalt him above all for ever.'[168]

APPENDIX 1
Retractationes 2. 22 (AD 426–7)

De bono coniugali liber unus

1. Iouiniani haeresis[1] sacrarum uirginum meritum aequando pudicitiae coniugali tantum ualuit in urbe Roma ut nonnullas etiam sanctimoniales de quarum pudicitia suspicio nulla praecesserat deiecisse in nuptias diceretur, hoc maxime argumento cum eas urgeret dicens: 'Tu ergo melior quam Sara, melior quam Susanna siue Anna?, et ceteras commemorando testimonio sanctae scripturae commendatissimas feminas, quibus se illae meliores uel etiam pares cogitare non possent. Hoc modo etiam uirorum sanctorum sanctum caelibatum commemoratione patrum coniugatorum et comparatione frangebat. Huic monstro sancta ecclesia quae ibi est fidelissime ac fortissime restitit. Remanserant autem istae disputationes eius in quorumdam sermunculis ac susurris quas palam suadere nullus audebat.[2] Sed etiam occultis uenenis repentibus facultate quam donabat dominus occurrendum fuit, maxime quoniam iactabatur Iouiniano responderi non potuisse ⟨cum laude⟩* sed cum uituperatione nuptiarum. Propter hoc librum edidi cuius inscriptio est *De bono coniugali*, ubi de propagatione filiorum prius quam homines mortem peccando mererentur, quoniam concubitus mortalium corporum res uidetur, quaestio magna dilata est; sed in aliis postea litteris nostris satis quantum arbitror explicatur.[3]

2. Dixi etiam quodam loco: 'Quod enim est cibus ad salutem hominis, hoc est concubitus ad salutem generis; et utrumque non est sine delectatione carnali, quae tamen modificata et temperantia refrenante in usum naturalem redacta, libido esse non potest.'[4] Quod ideo dictum est quoniam libido non est bonus et rectus usus libidinis.† Sicut enim malum est male uti bonis, ita bonum est bene uti malis; de qua re alias, maxime contra nouos haereticos Pelagianos,[5] diligentius disputaui. De Abraham quod dixi, ex hac oboedientia pater ille Abraham, qui sine uxore non

---

[1] See Introd., p. xix f.

[2] Since Jovinian's views had been condemned by a synod at Rome as early as 393, and heavily criticized by Jerome's *In Iouinianum* within a year, the traditional dating of *De bono coniugali* in AD 401 (so H. I. Marrou and A. M. La Bonnardière, *S. Augustin et l'augustinisme*, Paris, 1955, 183) has been challenged by M.-F. Berrouard, *Aug. Lex.* i. 658–66, who proposes an earlier date of *c*.397. But Augustine indicates here that he is responding not merely to Jovinian and Jerome, but also to the continuing influence of Jovinian's views, as a result of which many nuns and priests have married. This time-lag from 394 could well have extended to 401.

[3] Augustine returns repeatedly to the theme of the role of the sexual act in Eden before the Fall, to argue that it was then controlled by the will and could therefore have begotten offspring. The works to which he refers include *De nuptiis et concupiscentia*, *Contra Iulianum*, and *De ciuitate Dei*.

[4] *De bono coniugali* [XVI] 18.

APPENDIX 1
Reconsiderations 2. 22 (AD 426–7)

A single book On The Good of Marriage

1. The heresy of Jovinian,[1] in equating the merit of consecrated virgins with conjugal chastity, gained such wide currency in the city of Rome that it was said that quite a number of nuns whose chastity had earlier been under no suspicion had withdrawn into marriage. When pressure was applied to them, the argument chiefly cited was 'So are you better than Sara, or better than Susanna or Anna?', with mention made of the other women highly praised by the testimony of holy scripture, in comparison with whom the nuns could not consider themselves better or even equal. In this way he also undermined the holy celibacy of holy men by reference to and comparison with the Fathers who were married. The holy Church at Rome most faithfully and most resolutely opposed this outrage, but those arguments had survived in petty discussions and whisperings, though no one dared to urged them openly.[2] Though these poisonous claims of Jovinian creeping in were below the surface, they had to be confronted with such abilities as the Lord granted, most of all because it was being commonly claimed that a response to Jovinian had been possible only by denigration rather than praise of marriage. For this reason I published the book entitled *The Good of Marriage*, in which the important question concerning the begetting of children before mankind incurred death by sinning— for intercourse seems to be an activity of mortal bodies—was postponed; but in my view it is sufficiently explained later in other books of mine.[3]

2. In one passage I further stated: 'As food is for the health of the individual, so is sexual intercourse for the health of the race; and each is not without its physical pleasure, but if restrained and confined to natural use by the controlling reins of temperance, it cannot be lust.'[4] The idea was expressed in this way because the good and right application of bodily craving is not lust; but just as the evil application of good things is evil, so the good application of evil things is good. I have argued this with greater rigour elsewhere, especially against the Pelagians, a new band of heretics.[5] My comment on Abraham, 'By virtue of this obedience the patriarch Abraham, not without a wife, was ready to dispense with his only son and

---

[5] He refers in particular to *De nuptiis et concupiscentia* (AD 419), which he summarizes in the *Retractationes* (2. 53) as follows: 'We indeed maintain that marriage is a good, and that it must not be supposed that the concupiscence of the flesh . . . is a fault of marriage. Conjugal chastity makes good use of the evil of concupiscence by the procreation of children.'

---

* cum laude *add. edd.*

† libidinis *codd. antiquiores*: libidinis naturalis *plerique recentiores*

fuit, esse sine unico filio et a se occiso paratus fuit, non satis approbo.[6] Magis enim filium, si esset occisus, resuscitatione sibi mox fuisse reddendum credidisse credendus est, sicut in epistula legitur quod est ad Hebraeos.[7] Hic liber sic incipit: 'Quoniam unusquisque homo humani generis pars est'.

2.23 *De sancta uirginitate liber unus*

Posteaquam scripsi *De bono coniugali*, exspectabatur ut scriberem de sancta uirginitate, nec distuli; atque id dei munus et quam magnum et quanta humilitate custodiendum esset, uno sicut potui uolumine ostendi. Hic liber sic incipit: 'Librum de bono coniugali nuper edidimus'.

[6] *De bono coniugali* [XXIII] 31.   [7] Hebr. 11: 17.

to kill him with his own hand', does not sufficiently satisfy me.[6] It is better to ascribe to him the belief that if his son had been killed, he would soon have been restored to him by resuscitation, as we read in *The Letter to the Hebrews*.[7] This book begins: 'Since every individual belongs to the human race . . .'

2.23 *A single book On Holy Virginity*

After I composed *The Good of Marriage*, it was anticipated that I would write *On Holy Virginity*, and I did not postpone it, and in a single book to the best of my ability I pointed out that this was a gift of God, how important it was, and with what great humility it was to be maintained. This book begins: 'I recently issued a book on the good of marriage . . .'

APPENDIX 2
Variant Citations of Scripture from the Vulgate

		Augustine: *De bono coniugali*	*Vulgate*
2	Gen. 1: 28	implete	replete
		dominamini eius	subiicit eam
	Ps. 137: 3	multiplicabis me in anima	multiplicabis in anima
		mea in uirtutem	mea uirtutem
	1 Thess. 4: 17	nos uiuentes qui reliqui	nos qui uiuimus, qui
		sumus simul cum illis	relinquimur, simul
		rapiemur in nubibus in	rapiemur cum illis in
		obuiam Christo	nubibus obuiam Christo
4	1 Cor. 4: 7	non habet potestatem	sui corporis potestatem
6		corporis sui . . . non habet	non habet . . . sui
		potestatem corporis sui	corporis potestatem non
		(also §32)	habet
	Matt. 5: 32	excepta causa	causa excepta
8	Hebr. 13: 4	honorabiles nuptiae	honorabile connubium
	Eph. 5: 12	etiam	et
	1 Cor. 13: 8	cadet	excidit
	Luke 10: 39	ad pedem domini et audiens	secus pedes domini
			audiebat
10	1 Cor. 7: 7	uellem omnes esse	uolo enim omnes uos esse
	1 Cor. 7: 29 ff.	hoc autem . . . tamquam non	hoc itaque . . . tamquam
		ementes . . . uolo . . . cogitat ea	non possidentes . . . uolo
		quae sunt domini, quomodo	autem . . . sollicitus est
		placeat domino. Qui autem	quae domini sunt,
		matrimonio iunctus est, cogi-	quomodo placeat deo.
		tat quomodo placeat uxori. Et	Qui autem cum uxore est,
		diuisa est mulier innupta et	sollicitus est quomodo
		uirgo; quae innupta est sol-	placeat uxori, et diuisus
		licita est ea quae . . . sollicita	est. Et mulier innupta et
		est quae sunt mundi (also	uirgo cogitat quae . . .
		De sancta uirginitate 22)	cogitat quae sunt mundi
	1 Cor. 7:9	se non (also 19, 25)	non se
11	1 Cor. 7: 36	nubat (also 21, 25)	si nubat
	1 Cor. 7: 28	peccat	peccauit

12	1 Cor. 7: 19	nescitis quia corpora uestra templum in uobis est spiritus sancti	an nescitis quoniam membra uestra templa sunt spiritus sancti qui in uobis est
13	1 Cor. 7: 14	in uxore . . . in fratre	per mulierem fidelem . . . per uirum fidelem
14	1 Tim. 2: 9f.	ornando se . . . non et margaritis et ueste, per bonam conuersationem	ornantes se est non . . . aut margarita uel ueste . . . per opera bona
	1 Pet. 3: 1ff.	mulieres obaudientes maritis suis . . . sine loquela lucrifieri possint, uidentes timorem et castam conuersationem uestram; ut sint non quae a foris ornantur capillorum crispationibus aut circumdatae auro aut ueste decora, sed ille absconditus cordis uestri homo in illa perpetuitate . . . qui et apud dominum locuples est. Nam sic quaedam sanctae mulieres,, quae in domino sperabant, . . . obsequentes uiris suis, quomodo Sara obaudiebat Abrahae, dominum illum uocans, cuius factae estis filiae . . . non timentes ullum uanum timorem. Viri simili ratione concordes et caste uiuentes cum uxoribus uestris, et tamquam uasi infirmiori et subiecto tribuite honorem quasi coheredibus gratiae, et uidete ne impediantur orationes uestrae	et mulieres subditae sint uiris suis . . . sine uerbo lucrifiant, considerantes in timore castam conuersationem uestram. Quarum non sit extrinsecus capillatura, aut circumdatio auri, aut indumenti uestimentorum cultus, sed qui absconditus est cordis homo in incorruptibilitate . . . qui est in conspectu domini locuples. Sic enim aliquando et sanctae mulieres sperantes in domino . . . subiectae propriis uiris, sicut Sara obaudiebat Abrahae, dominum eum uocans, cuius estis filiae . . . non pertimentes ullam perturbationem. Viri similiter cohabitantes secundum scientiam, quasi infirmiori uasculo mulieri impertientes honorem tamquam et coheredibus gratiae, ut non impediantur orationes uestrae
15	1 Thess. 4: 5	non in morbo desiderii, sicut gentes	non in passione desiderii sicut et gentes
21	1 Cor. 4: 5	cum reuelauerit occulta tenebrarum et manifestauerit	qui et illuminabit abscondita tenebrarum et

		cogitationes cordis, ut tunc laus sit	manifestabit consilia cordium, et tunc laus erit
26	Matt. 11: 19	non manducans . . . et dixerunt . . . et dixerunt: Ecce uorax et uinaria, amicus publicanorum et peccatorum	neque manducans . . . et dicunt . . . et dicunt: Ecce homo uorax et potator uini, publicanorum et peccatorum amicus
31	Apoc. 14: 4	se non conturbauerunt	non sunt coinquinati
35	Eccles. 3: 20	tanto humila te (also *De sancta uirginitate §§* 31, 33, 44)	humilia te

De sancta uirginitate

3	Matt. 12: 48 ff.	aut qui sunt . . . Extendens manum super discipulos suos ait: Hi sunt fratres mei; et quicumque . . . patris mei, ipse mihi frater et mater et soror est (but at §5 as Vulgate)	et qui sunt . . . Et extendens manum in discipulos suos dixit: Ecce mater mea et fratres mei; quicumque enim . . . patris mei qui in caelis est, ipse meus frater et soror et mater est
7	Gal. 5: 6	per dilectionem	per caritatem
13–14	1 Cor. 7: 25 f.	ut fidelis essem propter praesentem necessitatem, quia (also §§ 18, 21)	ut sim fidelis . . . propter instantem necessitatem, quoniam
14	1 Cor. 15: 41	differt in gloria (also §26)	differt in claritate
	1 Cor 7: 26	Bonum est ergo	quoniam bonum est
15	1 Cor. 7: 27	Ne quaesieris . . . ne quaesieris . . . non peccat (also §19)	noli quaerere . . . noli quaerere . . . non peccauit
	1 Cor. 7: 10	His autem qui sunt in coniugio	Iis autem qui matrimonio iuncti sunt
17	1 Cor. 7: 38	qui dat nuptum . . . et qui non dat nuptum (also §21)	et qui matrimonio iungit uirginem suam . . . et qui non iungit
	1 Cor. 7: 40	secundum meam sententiam . . . et ego	secundum meum consilium . . . quod et ego
18	1 Cor. 7: 39	quamdiu	quanto tempore
20	Dan. 13: 23	in conspectu dei	in conspectu domini

23	Matt. 19: 10 f.	si talis est causa . . . uerbum hoc. Sunt enim spadones qui ita nati sunt; sunt autem alii qui ab hominibus facti sunt; et sunt spadones	si ita est causa . . . uerbum istud sed quibus datum est. Sunt enim eunuchi qui de matris utero sic nati sunt; et sunt eunuchi qui facti sunt ab hominibus; et sunt eunuchi . . .
25	Isa. 56: 5	et in muro meo locum nomi-natum, meliorem multo quam filiorum atque fil-iarum. nomen aeternum . . . nec unquam deerit (also §30)	et in muris meis locum et nomen melius a filiis et filiabus. nomen sem-piternum . . . quod non peribit
26	1 Cor. 15: 41	gloria . . . gloria	claritas . . . claritas . . . claritas
	1 Cor. 12: 18	singulum quodque . . . prout	unumquidque . . . sicut
27	Ps. 95: 1	uniuersa terra	omnis terra
28	2 Cor. 8: 9	pauper	egenus
	Matt. 11: 29	quoniam (also §35)	quia
	Luke 23: 34	ignosce . . . quia nesciunt	dimitte . . . non enim sciunt
31	Phil. 2: 7 f.	in similitudine . . . humilauit	in similitudinem . . . humiliauit
32	Ps. 137: 6	excelsa autem . . . cognoscit	et alta . . . respicit
	Matt. 15: 27	ita . . . nam et canes	etiam . . . nam et catelli
	Luke 18: 10 ff.	tibi ego . . . ceteri homines, iniusti raptores, sicut et publicanus iste . . . quae-cumque possideo. Publi-canus autem de longinquo stabat, nec . . . audebat . . . Amen dico uobis, descendit . . . de templo publicanus magis quam ille Pharisaeus. Quoniam is qui	ego tibi . . . ceteri hominum, raptores iniusti, uelut etiam hic publicanus . . . quae possideo. Et publicanus, a longe . . . stans, nolebat . . . Dico uobis, descendit hic . . . in domum suam . . . ab illo. Quia omnis qui
	Matt. 18: 3	nisi fueritis sicut puer iste	nisi conuersi fueritis et efficiamini sicut paruuli
34	1 Tim. 5: 13, 11	uerum etiam curiosae et uerbosae . . . iuniores . . . euita. cum enim in deliciis egerint . . . quoniam	sed et uerbosae et curiosae . . . Adulescen-tiores . . . deuita. Cum enim luxuriatae fuerint . . . quia
	1 Tim. 5: 6	in deliciis agit	in deliciis est

35	Matt. 11: 29 ff.	domine . . . quaniam . . . a sapientibus . . . placitum est coram te . . . cognoscit filium, et nemo cognoscit patrem . . . uos reficiam . . . quoniam	pater, domine, . . . quia . . . a sapientibus et prudentibus . . . fuit placitum ante te . . . nouit filium, neque patrem quis nouit . . . reficiam uos . . . quia
36	Rom. 5: 20	peccatum	delictum
37	1 Tim. 1: 13	iniuriosus . . . misericordiam	contumeliosus . . . misericordiam dei
38	Rom. 15: 3	sed sicut scriptum de illo est, opprobria exprobrantium	sed sicut scriptum est, improperia improperantium
	Luke 7: 47	dimittuntur	remittuntur
39	Ps. 18: 10	castus	sanctus
	Ps. 138: 7	quo abibo ab . . . et a facie tua quo	quo ibo a . . . et quo a facie tua
	Ps. 26: 4	per omnes dies . . . ut contempler delectationem . . . et protegar ad (?)	omnibus diebus . . . ut uideam uoluptatem . . . et uisitem
	Ps. 83: 3	desiderat	concupiscit
	Phil. 2: 12	cum timore . . . et operari	cum metu . . . et perficere
	Isa. 66: 2	Super quem requiescet spiritus meus? Super humilem et quietum et trementem uerba mea?	Ad quem autem respiciam nisi ad pauperculum et contritum spiritu et trementem uerba mea?
40	Job 7: 1	numquid non temptatio est uita humana	militia est uita hominis
	1 Cor. 10: 12	qui se putat stare, caueat ne cadat	qui se existimat stare, uideat ne cadat
41	Rom. 10: 3	constituere (also §42)	statuere
	Eph. 2: 8 ff.	salui facti estis . . . ne forte quis extollatur . . . figmentum	estis saluati . . . ut ne quis glorietur . . . factura
	Ps. 126: 1	Nisi dominus custodierit ciuitatem, in uanum uigilauit qui custodit	Nisi dominus aedificauerit domum, in uanum laborauerunt qui aedificant eam
	1 Cor. 7: 7	omnes homines . . . alius sic, alius autem sic	omnes uos . . . alius quidem sic, alius uero sic
42	James 1: 17	momenti	uicissitudinis
	Ps. 118: 4	praecepisti . . . dum inspicio in omnia mandata tua	mandasti . . . cum perspexero in omnibus mandatis tuis

	Ps. 140: 3 f.	continentiae circum . . . in uerba mala	circumstantiae . . . in uerba malitiae
	Ps. 36: 23	a domino	apud dominum
	2 Tim. 2: 25	ne forte det illis deus	nequando deus det illis
43	Wis. 8: 21	Et cum scirem quia nemo esse potest continens	Et ut sciui quoniam aliter non possem esse continens
	Ps. 145: 8	sapientes facit	illuminat
	Ps. 18: 8	dei . . . praestat	domini . . . praestans
	Job 28: 28	Ecce pietas	timor domini
46	1 Cor. 12: 31	imitamini . . . dona	aemulamini carismata
47	1 Cor. 10: 13	non uos permittat . . . cum temptatione etiam exitum	non patietur uos . . . etiam cum tentatione prouentum
	Rom. 12: 10	mutuo	inuicem
	Phil. 2: 3	alter alterum existimantes superiorem sibi	superiores sibi inuicem arbitrantes
48	Job. 25: 4	Nemo mundus in conspectu tuo, nec infans cuius est unius diei uita super terram	Numquid iustificari potest homo comparatus deo, aut apparere mundus natus de muliere
49	1 John 1: 8 ff.	quia . . . nos ipsos . . . quodsi confessi fuerimus delicta nostra, . . . ut dimittat . . . et purget . . . si dixerimus . . . non erit	quoniam . . . ipsi nos . . . si confiteamur peccata nostra . . . et remittat . . . et emundet . . . quodsi dixerimus . . . non est
50	1 John 2: 1 f.	haec scripsi . . . ad patrem . . . et ipse propitiator est peccatorum nostrorum	haec scribo . . . apud patrem . . . et ipsa est propitiatio pro peccatis nostris
51	John 13: 16	uel discipulus magistro suo	neque apostolus maior est eo qui misit illum
52	Matt. 8: 19	domine . . . uolatilia . . . ubi caput suum inclinet	magister . . . uolucres . . . ubi caput reclinet
52	Dan. 3: 87	dominum; hymnum dicite	domino; laudate

APPENDIX 3
Divergences from Zycha's CSEL Text

This Edition		*Zycha*
De bono coniugali		
3	uoluptati	uoluptatis
5	uelle	uel
6	praecepit	praecipit
7	hac	ex hac
21	cogitationes	occulta
27	impudentem	imprudentem
33	illi	illis
35	qui	quia
De sancta uirginitate		
7	utraeque	utraque
26	iis . . . iis	his . . . his
27	quae	quia
30	si quid	quidquid
34	conscientia	concupiscentia
35	cognoscit . . . cognoscit	agnoscit . . . agnoscit
36	nec	et
38	prae	pro
39	protegar ad	protegi
47	illi uel illae	illi uel illi

INDEX OF BIBLICAL PASSAGES CITED

GENERAL INDEX